Praise for

The THOUGHT LEADERSHIP HANDBOOK

"If you want to be taken seriously as a thought leader, *read this book*."

MEL ROBBINS, *New York Times* bestselling author; host of *The Mel Robbins Podcast*

"If you're an expert eager to share your insights with a wider audience, buy this book, use it, and watch your influence grow! Bill Sherman, Peter Winick, and Naren Aryal have been guiding leadership experts for decades. Their book is the most comprehensive, practical, and inspiring resource I've seen on sharing your message with the world."

KEN BLANCHARD, coauthor, *The One Minute Manager* and *The Secret: What Great Leaders Know and Do*

"Many books celebrate ideas; far fewer show how to steward them responsibly into the world. *The Thought Leadership Handbook* stands out for the clarity, rigor, and real-world wisdom it brings to scaling meaningful ideas while honoring their integrity. It is an exceptional and timely guide for anyone serious about moving ideas from insight to enterprise, and from aspiration to lasting impact and meaningful contribution."

STEPHEN M. R. COVEY, *New York Times* and #1 *Wall Street Journal* bestselling author, *The Speed of Trust* and *Trust and Inspire*

"You don't need more followers. You need more impact. I've seen brilliant minds stall out because they never built systems to spread their ideas. This book hands you the tools to build reach, relevance, and revenue without wasting time."

KEITH FERRAZZI, founder, chairman, and CEO, Ferrazzi Greenlight; *New York Times* bestselling author, *Never Eat Alone*, *Who's Got Your Back*, and *Never Lead Alone*

"Every thought leader asks two questions: Are my ideas good enough? How can I create more impact? *The Thought Leadership Handbook* gives you the frameworks and tools you need to answer both. Sherman, Winick, and Aryal show you how to strengthen your ideas and multiply your reach."

DEANNA MULLIGAN, CEO, Ceres Life Insurance; former president, CEO, and board chair, Guardian Life Insurance of America

"It's never been harder to be heard as a thought leader. This book gives you the tools to find your audience and scale your impact."

MICHAEL BUNGAY STANIER, author, *The Coaching Habit*

"This book makes it clear why Bill, Peter, and Naren are already trusted by so many thought leaders. They've seen what actually works and distilled those lessons into practical, actionable steps. The result is a durable framework for meaningful success. This book is essential!"

DR. MARSHALL GOLDSMITH, Thinkers50 #1 Executive Coach and *New York Times* bestselling author of *The Earned Life, Triggers,* and *What Got You Here Won't Get You There*

"The most important ideas are those that outlast us. I've seen this framework take shape through real leadership moments—where choosing what to say, and when, truly matters. This book offers leaders a disciplined, experience-grounded approach to elevating ideas with intention, focusing on impact over attention and building influence that endures."

JANET FOUTTY, former chair, Deloitte US; former CEO, Deloitte Consulting

"This excellent treatise on thought leadership triggers a reflection regarding a quote from a former mentor of mine, Stephen R. Covey: 'To learn and not to do, is really not to learn. To know and not to do, is really not to know.' In their thorough work on thought leadership, Winick, Sherman, and Aryal embrace this mindset fully. All the thought leaders they profile ultimately migrate from thinking, to learning, to practicing, to doing. I commend their work to all aspiring leaders."

DOUGLAS R. CONANT, retired president and CEO, Campbell Soup Company; retired chair, Avon Products; founder and CEO, ConantLeadership

"If you have a powerful idea and a passion to stand out, you're on the doorstep of thought leadership. Now the hard work begins. *The Thought Leadership Handbook* is your essential guide to what it actually takes to succeed—and profit."

JOSH BERNOFF, bestselling author; creator, Bernoff.com and the Virtual Book Coach

"I loved this insight from *The Thought Leadership Handbook*: Your best ideas should be able to travel without you. Peter Winick and Bill Sherman spent eight years interviewing over 700 thought leaders about what actually works. If you're an expert who wants to learn thought leadership, this book is your must-have resource."

CHARLENE LI, *New York Times* bestselling coauthor, *Winning with AI: The 90-Day Blueprint for Success*

"*The Thought Leadership Handbook* treats sharing your expertise as a distinct skill set you can develop, separate from your domain knowledge. The book acknowledges that being brilliant at your work doesn't automatically make you brilliant at sharing that knowledge. You can learn thought leadership skills. This book shows you how."

CHIP CONLEY, *New York Times* bestselling author; hospitality entrepreneur

"I wish I'd had a copy of *The Thought Leadership Handbook* when I first stumbled into thought leadership. In this gem of a book, you'll hear the behind-the-scenes stories of great leaders—how they started out and what they learned along the way. More importantly, Sherman, Winick, and Aryal have done the hard work of finding the patterns, creating frameworks, and building the tools you need for your journey. This book deserves a permanent place on your bookshelf. You will read it again and again!"

CHESTER ELTON, executive coach; bestselling author, *The Carrot Principle* and *Leading with Gratitude*

"Most people have ideas. Very few know how to turn them into influence. *The Thought Leadership Handbook* bridges that gap with clarity, credibility, and hard-earned insight from the front lines of thought leadership. It's one of the most practical and grounded guides I've seen for anyone serious about amplifying their ideas."

WALDO WALDMAN, author, *New York Times* bestseller, *Never Fly Solo* and *Commit, Commit!*

"*The Thought Leadership Handbook* works on two levels. Sherman, Winick, and Aryal give you immediately useful guidance for building your thought leadership practice. They also address why this work matters. Sharing what you know serves others even when your knowledge is incomplete. That deeper purpose kept me engaged while the practical advice helped me take action. Whether you want tactics or meaning, this book delivers both."

CLAUDE SILVER, chief heart officer, VaynerX

"Many CEOs have an interest or a need to be viewed as a thought leader in their industry or beyond. And all effective CEOs must be seen as a thought leader within their company and by key stakeholders, including the board of directors and private equity partners. Similarly, many private equity partners (or up-and-comers) have a desire or need to establish themselves as thought leaders in order to win deals and advance careers. This rarely just happens. *The Thought Leadership Handbook* provides essential and effective methods to help CEOs and PE professionals accomplish this personal positioning so essential to their career success—in the current job, the next job, and the legacy career. I highly recommend it!"

DAVE GOLDBERG, former PE CEO; current PE independent board member

"True thought leadership is not about being loud. It's about being useful. This book understands that distinction. It treats thought leadership as an act of service, grounded in learning, clarity, and contribution—not ego or self-promotion. The ideas here are practical, thoughtful, and designed to help people think better, lead more intentionally, and share what they've learned in ways that genuinely help others. During my leadership at WD-40 Company, I learned that trust is built by leaders who teach what they know, admit what they're still learning, and invite others on that journey. This book reflects that same belief. If you see thought leadership as a responsibility rather than a title, you'll find this work both credible and valuable."

GARRY RIDGE, chairman emeritus, WD-40 Company; *USA Today* bestselling author, *Any Dumb Ass Can Do It*

"Do you have a big, bold idea that is worthy to share, but you aren't sure how to get that idea out into the world? Then this book is for you! *The Thought Leadership Handbook* shares a proven road map for creating, building, and executing the right strategy to elevate and spread your big idea. This practical how-to manual highlights best practices to target the right audience, craft the ideal message, and scale your ideas to maximize your influence and impact. This gem by Sherman, Winick, and Aryal is a must-have for anyone in thought leadership!"

KELLY BRESLIN WRIGHT, founder and CEO of Culture Driven Sales; former EVP Sales, Tableau Software; former president and COO, Gong

"*The Thought Leadership Handbook* is a valuable resource for anyone committed to building a sustainable thought leadership path. Sherman, Winick, and Aryal distill decades of experience into practical guidance that helps you strengthen your voice, expand your platform, and navigate the realities of sharing ideas in an imperfect world. The insights are actionable, and the underlying message is compelling: your expertise can create impact when you learn how to use it effectively."

JAYSHREE SETH, 3M chief science advocate; Thinkers50 2025 Radar member; author, *The Heart of Science* book trilogy

"In a world where ideas increasingly float about using shallow memes in social media and minimal online projection, Sherman, Winick, and Aryal take the understanding of idea promotion and expansion to a new level. *The Thought Leadership Handbook* shows how to manage brilliant thinking in ways that go far beyond traditional marketing. It's a remarkable publication that not only helps those of us who are thought leaders but also contributes significantly to people's understanding and appreciation of important ideas. *The Thought Leadership Handbook* is extraordinarily unique. Readers will have read nothing like it, and they will be taken to a modern level of understanding of how original thoughts develop, grow, and are shared."

BRIGADIER GENERAL TOM KOLDITZ, PHD, leader; author; Thinkers50 Coaching Legend

"*The Thought Leadership Handbook* isn't just another business book; it's the field guide for anyone who wants their ideas to actually matter. Drawing on decades of real-world experience with hundreds of top thinkers, the authors reveal why expertise alone isn't enough and how you can turn your insights into lasting impact. Whether you're a CEO, consultant, or accidental expert, you'll find practical frameworks, candid real-world stories, and a healthy dose of contrarian advice to help you escape the 'thought leadership trap' and build influence that outlasts your calendar. Prepare to challenge your assumptions, sharpen your strategy, and finally bring your ideas to life."

CRAIG JOSEPH, MD, chief medical officer, Nordic Consulting; coauthor, *Designing for Health*

"The journey to thought leadership is a winding road without a singular road map. In this book, the authors provide a breakdown of the critical components that take many years to learn. I enjoyed the frank commentary on the triumphs, failures, and hard-earned lessons—from the personal accounts of the thought leaders who have ideas to make a difference in the world. Highly recommend this wonderful contribution!"

JANE HYUN, global leadership strategist; coach; author, *Breaking the Bamboo Ceiling* and *Leadership Toolkit for Asians*; coauthor, *Flex: The New Playbook for Managing Across Differences*

"From case studies of success to actionable tool kit for success, *The Thought Leadership Handbook* brings together the essentials every thought leader should know but might not have articulated yet. For authors and would-be thought leaders looking to expand their impact, this book focuses on the why behind the work and empowers you with a road map to achieving the type of impact you aspire to make."

SANYIN SIANG, Duke University professor; CEO advisor; Thinkers50 Coaching Hall of Fame

"Thought leadership has become a noisy arena of hot takes, superfluous models, and recycled jargon. Fortunately, Sherman, Winick, and Aryal have delivered an excellent antidote with *The Thought Leadership Handbook*, which restores rigor with a practical system for shaping a core idea and building the assets that make it travel, stick, and scale."

DAN PONTEFRACT, leadership strategist; award-winning author, *The Future of Work Is Grey*

"Rich with practical guidance, *The Thought Leadership Handbook* shows how to build ideas that create real value today and a legacy that lasts. It's a smart, grounded resource for anyone serious about turning expertise into meaningful, sustained impact."

JOSEPH MICHELLI, *New York Times* #1 bestselling author of thirteen books, including *All Business Is Personal* and *The New Gold Standard*

"The missing manual for building thought leadership like a practice—not a persona."

DAVID BURKUS, bestselling author, *Best Team Ever*

"*The Thought Leadership Handbook* gives experts a clear path to turn their ideas into forward motion. With candid stories and practical tools, it helps you build a thoughtful, sustainable practice around your best thinking. Highly recommend!"

ALISA COHN, author, *From Start-up to Grown-up*

"Why force the wrong approach when you can choose what actually fits your needs? I have had the privilege to work directly with Bill and Peter. Their deep well of expertise is now the gold in your hands. Enjoy and thrive!"

FREDDIE RAVEL, keynote maestro; founder, Life in Tune®

"This book pushed me to revisit the principles of Self-Reliant Leadership®—doing the inner work, owning the hard truths, and showing up with purpose. If you're willing to be stretched, this book won't let you hide from your potential."

JAN RUTHERFORD, founder, Self-Reliant Leadership, LLC

"True thought leadership isn't about visibility—it's about stewardship. *The Thought Leadership Handbook* captures that distinction beautifully. Sherman, Winick, and Aryal combine rare empirical depth with moral clarity, showing how serious ideas are shaped, tested, and carried responsibly into the world."

JEFF DEGRAFF, author, The Art of Change

"If you've got an idea that matters, *The Thought Leadership Handbook* shows you how to build a business around it. Clear, practical, and rooted in experience. This is the guide every expert needs."

JOHN JANTSCH, author, Duct Tape Marketing

"This book had me at hello. It flowed like a word symphony. Full of actionable 'I can do this today' insights and real-life stories that illustrate every point and offer proof of concept. Read it and reap."

SAM HORN, founder, The Force for Good Project

"Thought leadership is one of the most misunderstood ideas in modern business. Too often it's treated as personal branding with better lighting or expertise amplified through louder social media channels. *The Thought Leadership Handbook* cuts through that confusion. Bill Sherman, Peter Winick, and Naren Aryal reveal what actually sustains a life built around the business of ideas and thinking—the doubt, the discipline, the responsibility, and the long game. Having spent decades building, testing, and monetizing thought leadership across media, publishing, consulting, and platforms, I have enormous respect for work that treats ideas not as content but as a business model that demands rigor, generosity, and patience. This book does exactly that and then some. It doesn't romanticize visibility or promise scale without cost. Instead, it offers an honest look at what it takes to move from knowing things to shaping thinking, from delivering insights to creating enduring value. This isn't a book about building an audience quickly. It's a book about earning relevance over time. For experts who believe ideas matter and who want to build a sustainable career around them, *The Thought Leadership Handbook* provides clarity and a practical path forward. Such a great read."

MITCH JOEL, cofounder, ThinkersOne; author, Six Pixels of Separation and CTRL ALT Delete

"Entrepreneurship is about taking good ideas to scale. That requires skill, systems, and processes as you grow. *The Thought Leadership Handbook* shows entrepreneurs how to attract attention for your idea—among employees, clients, and investors—so that you can grow your business. Thought leadership gives you a lasting competitive advantage. Good ideas, when packaged well, can create impact that lasts for decades."

MICHAEL CAITO, CEO, MAP Consulting; cofounder, Restaurants on the Run; former Global Chair, Entrepreneurs' Organization

"Most leaders I work with don't lack insight. They lack focus and a clear path forward. That's why *The Thought Leadership Handbook* resonated with me. It treats ideas the same way we treat businesses at EOS: define them, strengthen them, and deploy them with purpose. This book helps leaders turn hard-earned experience into thinking that actually moves people and organizations forward."

MARK O'DONNELL, visionary, CEO, EOS Worldwide

"Thought leadership doesn't happen by accident and it doesn't come from chasing visibility alone. *The Thought Leadership Handbook* gives authors and experts a clear, practical framework for turning ideas into influence. Sherman, Winick, and Aryal demystify what it really takes to build credibility, clarity, and momentum around your thinking. This is an essential resource for anyone who wants their ideas to travel further—and matter more."

SANDY POIRIER SMITH, CEO, Smith Publicity

"Marketing icon Seth Godin famously said, 'The difference between amateurs and professionals is that professionals get up every day, clear about the difference they want to make in the world, and go about doing it.' *The Thought Leadership Handbook* is a complete road map to take you from just having a point of view to being a professional. Sherman, Winick, and Aryal's deep expertise and vast experience guiding thought leaders will help anyone turn their passion for making a difference into a practical, authentic, and effective business strategy."

NATE REGIER, founder and CEO, Next Element Consulting

"*The Thought Leadership Handbook* is a rigorous, research-driven book that will become the definitive source on thought leadership. Sherman, Winick, and Aryal move past inspiration to show how ideas are built, scaled, and made to last. If you want your thinking to create real, durable impact, this is essential reading. I can't recommend it enough!"

TAAVO GODTFREDSEN, coauthor, bestselling The 5x CEO; cofounder, AdvantageCEO

"*The Thought Leadership Handbook* begins in darkness, a situation that many who ply their trade as consultants and coaches will know well. What do I do next? How do I do next? And will anyone really care what I do next? Fortunately, this handbook has answers that will enable those with something to say and do navigate the challenging waters of channeling what you have to offer into provocative and compelling services that clients will clamor for. This book is more than a guide; it is a companion that anyone who is in the business of helping clients reach their potential will want to have on their bookshelves."

JOHN BALDONI, Thinkers360 Top Thinker; author, fifteen books and three collections of poetry

"*The Thought Leadership Handbook* is for anyone who thinks the hardest part of writing a book is writing it. Spoiler alert—the hardest part is getting it in front of the people who can benefit from it. Sherman, Winick, and Aryal are the experts in not just how to do that but in all the ways that those of us who traffic in ideas can best share them with the world. *The Thought Leadership Handbook* is both a road map and a gift for anyone who knows they have something important to say and share but haven't yet figured out how to get it out there."

SCOTT EBLIN, globally recognized executive coach; bestselling author, *The Next Level*

"*The Thought Leadership Handbook* is the clearest, most practical playbook I've seen for anyone serious about building influence in today's crowded marketplace. After twenty-five-plus years working alongside some of the country's top thought leaders, I consider this book mandatory reading for anyone who wants to grow their brand with intention, impact, and credibility."

MICHELLE JOYCE, founder, president, Michelle Joyce Speakers

"*The Thought Leadership Handbook* captures what most experts never understand about thought leadership: great ideas are not enough. You need a clear strategy that turns those ideas into lasting influence. Sherman, Winick, and Aryal show how to shape, scale, and share your best thinking so it reaches the right people and creates real impact. This book delivers clarity that every expert needs."

STEPHEN M. SHAPIRO, author, *Invisible Solutions* and *Pivotal*; creator of Personality Poker®

"Thought leadership isn't about being louder. It's about being worth listening to. In *The Thought Leadership Handbook*, Bill, Peter, and Naren cut through the noise to show what real thought leadership looks like, rooted in clarity, responsibility, and service. This book will help you see patterns you can't see alone, understand why your ideas matter, and recognize the duty that comes with sharing them. Because influence isn't something you take. It's something people give you when they feel understood."

CHRIS VOSS, former FBI lead hostage negotiator, *New York Times* bestselling author, *Never Split the Difference*

"As founder and CEO of Jenkins Group, I've seen firsthand how many of our clients benefit from Peter's exceptional thought leadership expertise. This book captures that same clarity, practicality, and vision. *The Thought Leadership Handbook* is a must-read for anyone committed to developing and scaling their ideas."

JERRY JENKINS, founder and CEO, Jenkins Group, Inc.

"How do you make your ideas heard in the marketplace? *The Thought Leadership Handbook* gives you the answer. Sherman, Winick, and Aryal provide proven systems for sharpening what you say and expanding who hears it. Your ideas deserve this level of clarity."

DR. NICK MORGAN, president, Public Words, Inc., speaker, and author, forthcoming The Embodied Voice

"In a world where information can be cheap and unreliable, *The Thought Leadership Handbook* pushes back and asks: What does it take to truly be a leader of thought? Rich in case studies, frameworks, and tools, this book guides readers on a journey to uncover and activate their thought leadership—and impact the world with their ideas."

STACY ENNIS, bestselling author; book strategist; CEO, Creatively

"*The Thought Leadership Handbook* distills years of practice, research, and lived experience into a guide that is both deeply practical and surprisingly energizing. Bill, Peter, and Naren surface the patterns that actually move ideas forward and give experts a clear path for building influence without burnout. Their frameworks make the work feel doable, and their stories remind you why the work matters in the first place. This is the rare book that meets you where you are and shows you how to take the next leap."

KENNETH GILLETT, founder and principal, Target Marketing Digital

"Bursting with insights from today's most respected thought leaders, *The Thought Leadership Handbook* is a practical guide to succeeding at the most influential field of our time. But it is so much more. It's an invigorating read that will inspire anyone to lead a life of ideas and to recognize why it matters."

MARK FORTIER, founder, Fortier Public Relations

"After launching hundreds of business books, I can say this with certainty: Extraordinary impact begins with extraordinary ideas. *The Thought Leadership Handbook* reveals how you can shape, clarify, and strengthen your big ideas before they ever reach the marketplace. A must-read for anyone who wants their book to truly matter in today's congested markets."

CAROLYN MONACO, book launch strategist, Monaco Associates

"If you want better ideas and greater impact, you need *The Thought Leadership Handbook*."

DAN JANAL, executive ghostwriter, author, *Write Your Book in a Flash!*

"A book is an important tool in a thought leader's career, but so many ideas cross my desk that are underdeveloped, untested, or unprepared for the realities of publishing successfully. That's why I'm so glad *The Thought Leadership Handbook* weaves book publishing into the bigger journey of doing meaningful work as a thought leader. This is essential reading for every speaker or entrepreneur who's ready to get their ideas on the printed page and create real impact in the world through their work."

RICHELLE FREDSON, publishing consultant; creative development coach; host, *Bound + Determined* Podcast

"I have long said that Peter Winick and his team wrote the book on thought leadership strategy, and now, along with publishing expert Naren Aryal, they have actually done it. Infused with invaluable insights gained from two decades of partnering with some of the top experts in the world, this handbook will help countless executives, consultants, and advocates parlay their authority and credibility in career-changing and life-changing ways."

DAN GERSTEIN, CEO, Gotham Ghostwriters

"As someone who has supported thought leaders and helped experts bring their work to life for years, I'm genuinely grateful this book exists. *The Thought Leadership Handbook* brings clarity to a space that often feels crowded with buzzwords and confusion. It creates a shared language and helps you understand where you are, what drives you, and where your energy is best applied. It's so powerful that I now strongly encourage it as essential reading for anyone serious about getting their expertise into the world with intention and impact."

PARCHELLE OSUMARÉ, executive producer, Osumaré Learning

"*The Thought Leadership Handbook* is the rare guide that makes thought leadership feel less like improvisation and more like a disciplined practice. With a clear vocabulary, smart frameworks, and deeply human insights drawn from hundreds of real journeys, this handbook helps you clarify your voice, choose your strategy, and scale ideas that matter."

MARK THOMPSON, CEO coach, *New York Times* bestselling author

"Thought leadership runs on opinionated, well-spoken, and above all competent individuals sharing their ideas, so it's puzzled me why so many capable leaders fall flat when they explain their thoughts to the world. Reading *The Thought Leadership Handbook*, I finally figured it out: No one's explained the industry like this before. Peter, Bill, and Naren have written something essential that every new thought leader needs to read. If you're looking to up your game as a thought leader, this is the book you need."

JOSH LINKNER, five-time tech entrepreneur; *New York Times* bestselling author; venture capitalist

"Most professionals don't struggle with ideas. They struggle with alignment, trust, and follow-through. That's why *The Thought Leadership Handbook* resonated with me so strongly. It treats thought leadership the way I treat negotiation: as a discipline of empathy, structure, and responsibility. If you want your ideas to land, last, and lead others forward, this book offers a road map for success."

JONATHAN B. SMITH, bestselling author, *Fight Less, Win More*

"Having worked with Bill Sherman and Peter Winick, I've seen firsthand how deeply they understand the thought leadership business. This book captures that expertise in practical frameworks accessible to all."

EDUARDO BRICEÑO, author, *The Performance Paradox*

"In *The Thought Leadership Handbook*, Bill, Peter, and Naren show you how ideas grow legs, find their voice, and actually make an impact. They blend hard-won wisdom, behind-the-scenes stories, and practical tools into a road map for anyone ready to move from 'someday' to 'let's go.' If you've been carrying a message, a book, or a big idea around in your head for years, this is your nudge—and your playbook."

JACQUELYN LANE, author, *Becoming Coachable*; president, cofounder, 100 Coaches Agency; Forbes 30 Under 30

"How do you succeed as a thought leader? Speakers who have already made it can tell you what worked for them, give insight into their process, and show a little of the magic that helped them get where they are. But that journey is as individual as their ideas: it isn't guaranteed to work for everyone. *The Thought Leadership Handbook* is different. Naren, Peter, and Bill have helped shape and platform hundreds of thought leaders over the years. They've dissected the common elements it takes for every thought leader to reach success, and presented them in a cutting, incisive book. Excellent work!"

STUART CRAINER and DES DEARLOVE, founders, Thinkers50

"Most thought leaders, I suspect, are focused almost entirely on fleshing out their models, their insights, their framing of a key theme. Rarely do they turn their focus on their own category, that of thought leadership. That's what this book does. It reframes the reframers. It offers a meta-view of the 'business' of thought leadership. It shows people who have become known for unique perspectives that their situation is not unique at all. There are patterns they share with other creators of uniqueness. I had more ah-ha's per page than with any other book I've read in years."

CHARLES H. GREEN, coauthor, *The Trusted Advisor* and *The Trusted Advisor Fieldbook*; author, *Trust-Based Selling*; founder, Trusted Advisor Associates

The THOUGHT LEADERSHIP HANDBOOK

How the Experts Elevate Their Big Ideas—and How You Can Too

Bill Sherman
Peter Winick
Naren Aryal

Foreword by Lisa Bodell

amplifypublishinggroup.com **thoughtleadershipleverage.com**

The Thought Leadership Handbook:
How the Experts Elevate Their Big Ideas—and How You Can Too

For more information, please contact:
Amplify Publishing, an imprint of Amplify Publishing Group
620 Herndon Parkway, Suite 100
Herndon, VA 20170
info@amplifypublishing.com

Library of Congress Control Number: 2025925223

CPSIA Code: PRV0226A

ISBN-13: 979-8-89138-532-0

Printed in the United States

IDEAS CANNOT SPEAK FOR THEMSELVES.

YOU CAN.

Contents

Section Four: The Tools to Act

Foreword

Thought leadership and the title "thought leader" are relatively recent phenomena. When I started working in the early 1990s, we certainly read authors, admired experts, and attended events with speakers, but no one ever pointed to someone onstage or behind a book jacket and said, "Wow, they're an amazing thought leader!" The term just wasn't part of the broader cultural vocabulary.

People shared ideas because they had lived them, tested them, practiced them, and earned them—not because they aspired to a title. In fact, the phrase *thought leader* only entered the lexicon in 1994, when Joel Kurtzman, then editor in chief of *Strategy & Business*, described it as someone "recognized by peers, customers and industry experts" for their original ideas and deep understanding of their field. It was meant to signal substance and clarity, not a job title.

Today, though, the world is bombarded with people offering opinions, frameworks, content, podcasts, advice, and social media commentary. Ideas are everywhere. But the volume of ideas does not guarantee their value. In fact, it often does the opposite. We now scroll through digital environments overloaded with untested hypotheses, unearned certainty, and noise masquerading as meaning. It raises two urgent questions: **What is wisdom worth sharing, and what insights aren't worth our time?**

This book provides a much-needed answer. It argues not only that thought leadership must be more rigorously defined, but that it must be undertaken with intention, responsibility, and a sense of duty. It challenges the way we've allowed the term to drift into the culture without guardrails, standards, or meaningful expectations. And perhaps most importantly, it restores a truth that has always existed underneath the buzzword: Thought leadership, when done well, isn't about elevating oneself but about elevating others.

That's why I was drawn to what Peter, Bill, and Naren have created here. Their work is both practical and philosophical. It acknowledges that wisdom, thinking, and ideas are meant to be shared, and it makes a compelling argument that we have an obligation (a duty, even) to do so. They demonstrate how knowledge, generously offered, can strengthen not only individuals but entire systems. They push back against the instinct to gatekeep learning or hide insights behind jargon, ego, or fear. As humans, we grow because others before us chose to share what they discovered: through their stories, mistakes, breakthroughs, and most importantly, their lived experience.

My own journey into publishing, speaking, and thought leadership as a practice was never part of a master plan.

All that changed when I was approached by some senior leaders who had experienced me facilitating my Kill the Company exercise at their corporate off-site. It's a provocative technique where teams pretend to be their top competitor and ruthlessly attempt to put themselves out of business. The experience was transformative and cathartic for the leaders. How often do you get permission to boldly say what isn't working at work?

Afterward, one of the leaders commented, "You should put all of this into a book so more people can learn how to do it." I immediately had an allergic reaction to the suggestion: *Are you serious? No.* And I had a long list of reasons why not: *Who would want to hear from me? How would I fill a whole book? Who would read it?* And the biggest reason: *Book writing is for people with egos. They do it for themselves. I'm not that person.*

But the encouragement persisted. And I reluctantly agreed. What followed was two years of excessive caffeine, late nights, and more fetal-position moments than I'd like to admit. I asked myself constantly whether any of it mattered. At one point, I said to my publisher, "Are these ideas unique enough? Why hear from me?" My agent responded with something that stayed with me: "You have original ideas. Don't you feel people could learn from them?"

That response shifted something in me. When my first book was published, everything changed. More people connected with the ideas. They shared their stories of how it helped them, and I was relieved. I realized that thought leadership, at its best, is not a self-centered act; it's a form of service. Because by doing this work you don't just offer ideas or wisdom; you make people feel part of something bigger, and more importantly, you can make them feel that they are not alone in what they are experiencing.

It was only when I began sharing my own experiences more vulnerably—how hard it was to be a leader, how building a business takes time, how much I questioned myself, how often things didn't go as planned, what worked and what didn't—that people began to reciprocate. And suddenly, I wasn't alone. I discovered that many people felt the same way I did: the thrill and exhaustion of running a business, the disappointment when an idea fell flat, the tension of navigating a field without a road map, the challenge of balancing creation with delivery, and the universal desire to matter, to contribute, to leave something meaningful behind.

Those moments of exchange made me realize that thought leadership, in its truest form, isn't just about transferring ideas; it's about creating connection. When we share honestly, we help others, and we help ourselves. There's clarity and healing in saying, "This is what I've learned," especially when it invites someone else to say, "Me too."

What this book makes abundantly clear is that sharing ideas should not be done on a whim. It should not be driven by the desire for visibility or status. It should not be entered into arrogantly or self-servingly. True thought leadership requires clarity of purpose and humility, knowing not everyone will agree with what you say. It asks you to examine what you have to offer, why it matters, and who will care. It asks you to consider whether your ideas illuminate and elevate or simply create more noise without added value.

What I appreciate most is that this book doesn't glorify the spotlight; instead, it asks hard questions:

- What do you have to say that is truly worth someone else's attention?
- How will your idea make someone else's world better?

- Why should anyone follow you—not because you are loud, but because you are useful?
- And how do you ensure your ideas outlive your presence?

For me, these questions sit at the heart of why I do this work. I wanted to share my ideas not because I needed to be heard, but because I hoped people might think differently, question assumptions more boldly, navigate their challenges with greater clarity, and feel empowered to transform their circumstances. Ideas are among the most powerful tools we have for doing exactly that.

So as you read this book, I invite you to not think of thought leadership as a title to claim but as a practice to embody. Let it remind you that your voice, used responsibly, can create real impact. And let it reinforce that the world does not need more noise; it needs more clarity. It needs leaders who think deeply, speak honestly, and share generously. It needs you, not as a performer of thought leadership, but as a steward of it.

Because the purpose of having ideas is not to keep them. It is to elevate others. This book will show you how.

—LISA BODELL, CEO, FutureThink

SECTION ONE

ELEMENTS & EQUATIONS

! ✓ V→ %

I P Co Mkt

Chapter 1

Illuminating the Darkness

Eduardo Briceño woke at 12:35 a.m. to darkness. Not just the expected darkness of his Santa Fe bedroom but the unsettling darkness of a dead house. No digital clock glow. No ambient hum of electronics. Eduardo flipped the light switch. Nothing.

Power outage. Complete neighborhood blackout.

In ninety-five minutes, he was scheduled to deliver a keynote to senior partners at Boston Consulting Group (BCG) who were scattered across multiple continents.

The session had been planned for months, with customized content, practice runs, and coordination across time zones. BCG's learning and development team had requested that Eduardo share his research on the Performance Paradox—how to learn while performing at the highest levels.

Now, sitting in absolute darkness, Eduardo faced his own framework. He had to both perform at a high level and learn new ways to deliver a virtual presentation. No electricity meant no computer, no lighting setup, and no reliable internet. Santa Fe's coffee shops close long before 1:00 a.m. He had ninety-five minutes to solve the problem.

How did Eduardo get here? Venezuelan born and then Ivy League educated, Eduardo had climbed the traditional ladders of finance and tech investing. He'd worked on Wall Street as a successful investment banker. Then, he'd shifted into venture capital and worked on Sand Hill Road in Silicon Valley.

But the outward signals of success came at a cost. He internalized the pressure. His body carried constant tension, and then his hands began to hurt. A little and then a whole lot. Everyday tasks—such as brushing his teeth, typing, and driving—all triggered severe pain.

Eduardo met people who lived with the same condition. Some used their hands for just ten minutes a day. That possible future was real, and it scared him.

During his illness, Eduardo had time to think. He reflected on his current work and the value he created. Silicon Valley startups would attract investors whether he was involved in the deals or not. The money would continue to flow. What impact was he making through his work? He couldn't say. And he needed a better answer.

Eduardo's recovery required him to embrace both physical therapy and a different mindset. He applied to Stanford for a master's degree. There, he met Carol Dweck, the renowned psychologist whose research on Growth Mindset was revolutionizing how people thought about learning and development.

Dweck needed someone with business experience. Someone who could help her translate her academic insights into organizational practice. Eduardo became her mentee, and it grew into a thriving partnership. Dweck would continue her academic research on Growth Mindset. She would write and speak about her ideas. Meanwhile, Eduardo would bring Growth Mindset to schools and corporations.

People wanted to hear about Dweck's Growth Mindset. She was invited to deliver a TEDx Talk in Manhattan Beach, but she couldn't make the date work.

Eduardo had a realization: *We can't let that opportunity go by without one of us there.*

Eduardo was an introvert with zero public speaking experience. He could easily have told himself, *I can't do it*, but his Growth Mindset told him, *I can learn.*

So, Eduardo made an offer: "I could work hard and do a TEDx Talk. Potentially, it could reach a lot of people." Dweck agreed and promised her support. Over the next six weeks, Eduardo prepared obsessively. He wrote and rewrote his script, he videotaped himself repeatedly, he practiced delivery with Dweck in her office, and he sought feedback.

When Eduardo walked onto the TEDx stage, he avoided eye contact with the audience entirely. He focused on the back wall and the stage lights. But he was prepared with stories, data, and a powerful call to action. The ten-minute talk went viral—eventually reaching over 5.3 million views—and suddenly Eduardo found himself in demand as a speaker, sharing stages around the world.

Eduardo's success opened doors he had never imagined. Organizations didn't just want to implement Growth Mindset—they wanted Eduardo personally to guide their transformations. He began developing his own frameworks, building on Dweck's foundation and extending into new territory.

The Performance Paradox emerged from his observations: Most people and most organizations undermine their learning when they focus exclusively on performing; the most effective approach requires doing both.

Eduardo became a client of Thought Leadership Leverage. We helped him with his thought leadership strategy, and then we represented him as he sold his ideas into enterprise.

At the end of every conversation, Eduardo would ask, "How can I improve?" He asked it on client calls and on calls with us and the team. We joked that it was his *Que sais-je?*—his "What do I know?"

But we knew Eduardo was serious. Eduardo always wanted to learn and get better. Each interaction offered him a chance to refine his ideas, to understand how they landed differently with different groups, and to discover new applications he hadn't considered.

This continuous learning mindset had brought him to the current moment in Santa Fe's darkness.

Eduardo looked outside. The entire neighborhood was dark. Even if someone had power and WiFi, it would be too dark for BCG partners to see him presenting. He could try presenting from his car using its interior lighting, but that would create an awkward video setup, and he wasn't sure he could park close enough to anyone's WiFi signal.

Then he had an idea. A slightly insane idea that made him smile even in the stress of the moment.

He went to his garage and began setting up what he would later call his "impromptu desk"—a folding table positioned in his driveway. He and his wife had two cars. If he lined them up just right, their headlights could illuminate a makeshift stage. His phone could serve as an internet hotspot for the laptop. The external battery pack would keep everything powered.

I decided that was my best bet, and I went for it.

The clock was ticking. No time to rehearse. He had to learn on the fly whether his phone would hold an internet connection, whether the audio would work, whether the lighting would be sufficient. He adjusted the car positions and tested camera angles.

Eduardo was living his Performance Paradox framework in real time. The safe, practiced approach he had rehearsed with BCG wasn't possible. He leaped into the Learning Zone even while performing. The BCG partners in the session would learn the framework and witness a real-world, unscripted example.

At 1:40 a.m. Mountain time, Eduardo stood in his driveway, illuminated by two sets of headlights, and delivered his keynote on the Performance Paradox to BCG partners in multiple time zones.

The session succeeded beyond expectations. Participants engaged actively, asked thoughtful questions, and gave it excellent reviews. The story spread within BCG, becoming part of its organizational lore about adaptability and creative problem-solving.

That night, Eduardo had literally made light in the darkness—both for himself and for hundreds of executives around the world eager to learn how to balance performance with growth. But he'd also done something more fundamental: He had embodied what the psychologist Carl Jung once observed about human existence: "As far as we can discern, the sole purpose of human existence is to kindle a light in the darkness of mere being."

What This Book Is, and How We Know This

The Thought Leadership Handbook distills over two decades of direct observation, documentation, and pattern recognition across the thought leadership landscape.

On its surface, *The Thought Leadership Handbook* is exactly what its subtitle promises: a practical guide for experts who want to elevate their big ideas. If you're here to improve your thought leadership practice, you'll find frameworks for evaluating your ideas, strategies for building sustainable impact, and insights about how to move from personal effort to systematic influence. You'll discover why some ideas thrive while others languish, how to escape the trap of being the bottleneck in your own success, and what distinguishes truly influential thought leaders from mere experts.

This book has three authors—Bill Sherman, Peter Winick, and Naren Aryal—who together have served the North American and global business thought leadership market for a combined sixty years.

Peter Winick and Bill Sherman have spent twenty years building Thought Leadership Leverage, working directly with hundreds of thought leaders to codify, productize, and scale their ideas. We've been inside the intellectual attics of some of the world's most influential business thinkers, organizing half-formed insights into coherent frameworks and turning individual expertise into systematic impact. Our clients have included sitting and retired Fortune 500 C-level executives, authors who have sold fifty thousand to over one million books, academics at the world's most respected business schools, Hall of Fame speakers, Nobel Prize candidates, and people very early in their thought leadership journey.

Since 2018, we've hosted the *Leveraging Thought Leadership* podcast, conducting over seven hundred in-depth interviews with practicing thought leaders. We didn't ask the guests about their expertise and insights. Instead, we created space to have a metaconversation about thought leadership. How did they get into thought leadership? What were their raw struggles, breakthrough moments, and candid reflections?

We were honored when our guests became deeply vulnerable. They shared their deeper aspirations, fears, regrets, and insights. Each interview peeled back the curtain on how thought leadership had worked for them.

Naren Aryal brings a different but crucial perspective as CEO of Amplify Publishing Group. He and his team have guided hundreds of authors in the thought leadership and business world through the complex journey from idea to published book, observing firsthand which approaches create lasting impact and which fade quickly. His experience provides insight into how ideas move from manuscript to market influence.

Peter and Bill's clients and Naren's authors vary widely in their ideas, methods, and audiences, but their purpose—to create impact that benefits others—leads them to us.

Together, our three perspectives create something unprecedented: an empirical foundation for understanding thought leadership as a discipline and a practice in this time and place.

The frameworks in this book aren't abstract theoretical constructs. They're patterns that emerged from analyzing real experiences of real practitioners over decades.

When we say certain approaches work while others fail, we're drawing on case studies from hundreds of clients and interview subjects. When we identify common traps thought leaders fall into, it's because we've seen them repeatedly across different industries, personality types, and organizational contexts. When we describe the emotional journey of building ideas into movements, it's because people trusted us with their most vulnerable stories about the costs they paid and the joys they experienced.

This approach distinguishes *The Thought Leadership Handbook* from both academic research and guru pronouncements. We're not prescribing what should work. We're documenting what does work in this time and place, across a wide spectrum of thought leadership practice.

Most of the stories in this book were drawn from episodes of the *Leveraging Thought Leadership* podcast. If someone's story intrigues you, we encourage you to listen to their episode. However, not all stories in this book come from the podcast. Some come from follow-up interviews with guests. Others come from our consulting and publishing clients. During the review process, many thought leaders provided additional context, clarifications, and examples. Some people also contributed new stories specifically for this book.

How We Organized This Book

This book is organized into four parts:

Section 1 establishes the foundations: how people enter into thought leadership and why they struggle without a strategy; how to evaluate whether you're practicing it as a Hobbyist, a Practice Owner, or a Business Builder. You'll learn the Four Elements that every piece of thought leadership must contain, and you'll discover the Impact Equation that determines whether ideas will create lasting change.

Section 2 introduces the Five Avatars and explores each in depth. These aren't just categories—they're reasons people take on the fundamental challenge of thought leadership.

Section 3 offers our candid perspectives on the fields of thought leadership and publishing. What are they today? What must they become? And most importantly, how can you thrive within them?

Section 4 provides tools and frameworks for overcoming common obstacles and accelerating your impact. The tools we have selected for this book are common across the Five Avatars. They're based on questions we have heard from people like you: "What should I consider in publishing a book? How do I find my core idea? How do I increase velocity for these ideas?"

There are three ways to read this book. The first two are relatively obvious, and we invite you to choose your own adventure.

> **LINEAR:** You can read this book from cover to cover. Frameworks and stories build on each other.
>
> **AS A HANDBOOK:** If you're primarily interested in practical frameworks and strategies, read section 1 (chapters 1 to 5) to understand the foundations of thought leadership; skim chapter 6 on the Five Avatars to identify your type, and then jump directly to your relevant avatar chapter (chapters 6 to 11). After that, read section 3 for a vision for thought leadership and publishing (chapters 12 to 14). Then, refer to section 4 to find tools and resources.

If you read the book in either of these ways, you'll encounter stories of transformation, challenge, and occasional triumph. You'll meet people who've built global businesses on single insights, who've walked away from lucrative careers to chase uncertain visions, and who've faced mortality while ensuring their ideas would survive them. These people all have a specific, meaningful insight they have chosen to share with the world.

If you're curious about the deeper currents, linger with these stories. Notice how each chapter operates on multiple levels. Pay attention to the moments of vulnerability, uncertainty, and profound commitment that define thought leadership work.

But there's a third, less obvious way to read this book. If you've been practicing thought leadership for more than a few years, it's our recommended approach to the book. And it requires explanation.

A Call for Change

In early 2026, we prereleased chapter 12 online. We could have simply released chapter 1, but that felt wrong. We wanted to spark a much-needed conversation within the field of thought leadership.

If you feel experienced with the basics of thought leadership, finish this chapter. Then go straight to chapter 12 before reading the rest of the book.

Chapter 12 is a manifesto, a confession, and a formal defense—*apologia*—of the field of thought leadership. We examine what has held thought leadership back as a field; we identify our involvement in those errors; we argue why thought leadership must evolve to meet the challenges of the twenty-first century; and we provide a challenge and call to action to thought leadership practitioners, the field's critics, and our community as a whole.

If you already read chapter 12 online and said, "OK, that's interesting," welcome and thank you. Maybe you agreed excitedly and want to learn more, or you bought this book because you want to debate us. Fantastic. We can't wait to talk.

Thought Leadership: Why?

Liz Wiseman, author of the bestselling *Multipliers* and a member of the prestigious Thinkers50 list, once shared an insight that pierces to the heart of what thought leadership actually demands: "Every day has to be amazing."

As someone who's delivered hundreds of keynotes worldwide, Liz knows that when you stand in front of an audience—whether it's in person or via video to a distributed global team—people aren't just receiving your content. They're placing their trust in your ideas. They're investing their most precious resource—time—in what you have to share. You don't get to have a bad day.

This responsibility shapes how thought leaders live and work. Liz learned this not just as a speaker but in her previous role as head of Oracle University, where she regularly hired renowned thinkers like C. K. Prahalad, Clay Christensen, and Rosabeth Moss Kanter to speak to Oracle's senior leadership. She remembers the fear in sponsors' eyes during those first critical minutes: "What if the speaker says something stupid? What if people don't play along? What if this falls flat?"

This terror would later drive Liz when she left Oracle and launched her own thought leadership initiative. She knew she could not let her ideas arrive in an organization without the systems ready to support them.

Consider what this means in practice. Lisa Bodell, author and expert on simplification, innovation, and bold change, regularly flies from New York to deliver keynotes around the globe. On one recent trip, she flew to Greece, spent exactly twelve hours on the ground delivering her presentation, and then immediately flew to Florida for her next speaking engagement. Twelve hours in Greece. Just long enough to kindle light in darkness for one group of strangers before racing to illuminate ideas for another. That type of travel schedule isn't sustainable. And so Lisa became a thought leadership Business Builder. She describes the work of herself and her team: "You need things that will scale and work together as a journey. We thought it through carefully." They built a system of services, a training model, and an on-demand business for resellers.

Lisa has achieved what many thought leaders aspire to. She makes money in her sleep. The business's cash flow funds its own innovation and productization.

But most importantly, Lisa says, "I always want to be able to weather the storm. 'Cause that's what I grew up with. I was taught how to weather the storm." For Lisa, the storm is more than business cycles or a weak quarter. It's managing your own internal chaos so that you can build a business and create impact.

To understand thought leadership, we must look beyond the polished exterior of thought leadership success. Behind every bestselling business book, every viral TED Talk, and every framework that reshapes how organizations operate, there are human beings making both business decisions and profound sacrifices to keep important ideas alive in the world.

These thought leadership practitioners explore fundamental questions about how we can live, work, and create meaning in our limited time on earth. They're asking themselves, *What do I believe so deeply that I'm willing to repeat it to strangers on multiple continents? What insights matter enough that I'll spend years researching, refining, and advocating for them?*

Eduardo setting up headlights in his driveway tells a story about crisis management and innovative problem-solving. It's also a story about someone who believes so completely in the value of learning while performing that he'll literally illuminate that idea in the darkness.

After the event, Eduardo received emails from attendees sharing how they'd implemented Performance Paradox thinking in their own organizations. One partner described restructuring their team meetings to include learning components even during high-pressure projects. Another had changed how they approached client work, building reflection and adjustment into their methodologies. That's the potential impact we can make with ideas.

If you have practiced thought leadership for a while, you may have nodded along as you read about Eduardo's power outage, Lisa's brutal travel schedule, and Liz's careful focus on the sponsor's worry in the front row of the audience. You may have even thought to yourself, *I've done something like that!*

But why? What's the spark that sustains someone (such as you) to do this work? This book explores how incredibly motivated and accomplished humans create meaning through their ideas, all the while grappling with questions of mortality, legacy, and purpose. Questions that have occupied thoughtful humans since before the first cities and written language.

When people choose a life of ideas, it transforms them. For some, it's a sudden epiphany with a sharp line distinction between before and after. For others, the idea and the individual enter a form of symbiosis. The thought leader carries the idea around the world. They speak for it. In return, the idea generates revenue and offers a sense of purpose. Among many of the thought leaders we spoke with, many conflated the idea with their sense of self: "It's in my DNA." "It's who I am." "I cannot see myself ever fully retiring, because this work is me."

We do not claim their answers are universal answers. But we see recurring patterns in the meaning that the thought leadership practitioners found through their work.

What This Book Offers You

In these pages, you'll discover why we see thought leadership as simultaneously one of the most rewarding and most demanding paths a knowledge worker can choose. You'll learn why some people seem to stumble into it while others deliberately pursue it. You'll understand why the journey often feels lonely—and why community matters so much.

You'll see through the experiences of successful practitioners that thought leadership isn't just about having smart ideas. You must take responsibility for those ideas in the world. You must build systems that create impact even when you're not in the room. You must accept that your highest purpose might require you to repeat the same essential message at the "101 level" for decades. Telling the same stories. Drawing the same images on a whiteboard. Searching for new ways to kindle familiar light for different audiences.

Most importantly, you'll understand why this work matters—and why it brings such deep satisfaction to those who embrace it fully. Eduardo checking his email weeks after his midnight presentation, reading about BCG teams implementing the Performance Paradox. Liz hearing that organizations still use *Multipliers* concepts years after her initial engagement. These moments of lasting connection between ideas and application justify every sacrifice the work demands.

In a world increasingly driven by data and AI automation, the need for human insight, interpretation, and meaning making has never been greater. Thought leaders serve as bridges between complex realities and practical application, between academic research and organizational implementation, between what is and what could be.

Whether you're just discovering that others are interested in hearing about your ideas or you're a seasoned practitioner looking to create lasting legacy, this book will meet you where you are and help you navigate what comes next.

The darkness is real. The technical failures, the impossible travel schedules, the weight of others' expectations—these are genuine challenges faced by anyone who chooses to make their ideas public.

But so is the light. Every breakthrough in organizational effectiveness, every framework that helps people lead better lives, every concept that reshapes how we think about working together—these changes begin with individuals willing to set up headlights in the darkness and share what they've learned.

Eduardo's middle-of-the-night keynote succeeded because he solved a technical problem and also because he embodied the principle he was teaching. In a world that often demands choosing between learning and performing, he showed that the most powerful moments come when we do both simultaneously. We leap into the unknown while maintaining our commitment to serving others.

The journey begins with a single recognition: You have ideas worth sharing. What happens next—and how you navigate the profound challenges and opportunities of thought leadership—is what the rest of this book explores.

Thought leadership is the arena where everyday ideas can become action, where individual insights shape collective understanding, and where ordinary people choose the extraordinary path of making their thinking public.

It's harder than it looks. It's more rewarding than most people understand. And yet, if you're willing to set up headlights in your driveway when everything else fails, it might just be the most meaningful work you ever do.

Chapter 2

The Uncomfortable Mirror

The *Inc.* magazine article wasn't supposed to be a big thing for Keith Ferrazzi. In 2003, it really shouldn't have been. He'd written pieces for *Harvard Business Review* since 1992; he'd appeared in *CIO* magazine; he'd been on the cover of *Brand Week*.

Keith learned from the writer that *Inc.* had commissioned a roundup article focused on successful people. Rather than respond immediately, Keith asked the writer for twenty-four hours.

That night, Keith reflected on his own success: CMO of Deloitte and CMO of Starwood Hotels. He made a list of ten reasons that he thought he was successful. He never used the word *networking* in the list or in the interview with the writer the next day. Keith was one of many people interviewed, so he figured he might appear in a paragraph or two. *A good media hit, but nothing life changing*, he thought.

But that's not the story *Inc.* published. The writer received Keith's list and refocused the article on his tips. The article, "The 10 Secrets of a Master Networker," caught fire. People read with unexpected interest. The world started to label Keith Ferrazzi as a leading voice on networking. People wanted more about networking from him. He got inquiries for keynote speeches and workshops. He got a book offer.

This cascade of events shocked Keith: "I was disgusted by the idea that I was now the 'networking' guy."

Keith had always planned to write a book, just never one about networking. His expertise lay in enterprise transformation and team coaching, making his discomfort acute: "I never actually considered myself a networking thought leader."

This misalignment was particularly striking given Keith's background: Yale undergraduate, Harvard Business School MBA, and former Fortune 500 CMO. If anyone could strategically align thought leadership with business interests, it should have been him. He understood brand building at the highest level. He'd overseen the launch of the W Hotel brand. The brand portfolio included premier brands like St. Regis.

Keith had shaped how markets perceived a brand, but now he was watching the market shape *his* brand, and he was struggling to regain control. He accepted the book offer, because he wanted to shift the conversation away from networking to topics he cared more deeply about. "I wrote the book because I wanted to tell the story my way. Not Keith Ferrazzi the networker. Instead, I wanted to tell a story about meaningful relationships, authenticity, vulnerability, and being of generous service."

Never Eat Alone launched as a bestseller, and then it continued to sell and sell. It has now sold over a million copies and become one of the bestselling business books of the last half century. Yet, Keith felt increasingly distant from his authentic interests. In fact, as Keith would later admit, "I hated the networking brand." Yet that's the topic the world wanted him to share.

Soon after *Never Eat Alone*'s explosive success, Keith assembled a team to help him crack the code on turning his intuitive relationship building into teachable, scalable frameworks. The team included two of us: Peter Winick and Bill Sherman. That's how we met. Peter, an entrepreneur who had led the turnaround of a training business in Australia, would build and lead Keith's speaking and training business for three years. Bill Sherman, a partner in a custom training and development company, took on the challenge of codifying the book's content into training workshops and scalable resources.

Neither of us were thought leadership strategists at the time. We were businesspeople. We read a lot of business books. And we were facing our first serious foray into the discipline of thought leadership. And we were wrestling with an incredibly hard business strategy problem.

We met in a converted bungalow in Los Angeles, which served as the West Coast office of Ferrazzi Greenlight. While the main house buzzed with people focused on executive team transformation, the *Never Eat Alone* team (focused on the speaking and training business) would gather in the backyard in a converted garage. We gathered in the early morning around a large conference table surrounded by stacks of folders, printouts, and endless presentation decks. Meetings would last all day and often into the evening.

Keith ran those meetings like the former Deloitte partner he was, encouraging high-octane intellectual debate. We faced a crucial problem: We had no empirical evidence or data. We were trying to create frameworks and training from a sample size of one: Keith himself. And we were doing so after the book had been published and after people had fallen in love with the concepts in *Never Eat Alone*.

The central challenge was inside Keith himself. He was trying to reverse engineer his own natural relationship-building ability—something he did as intuitively as breathing. How do you systematize genuine curiosity about people? How do you teach someone to care about others' success?

Our attempts produced various relationship pyramids—sometimes five levels, sometimes six, or even seven. The names of the levels changed from session to session. The day before a client event, Keith completely revised his relationship pyramid during our tabletop walk-through. We raced to Kinko's and manually updated workbooks until midnight.

The absurdity peaked during a speaking engagement for Ernst & Young's LGBT group in Manhattan. Keith and Peter had booked flights too close to the event and got delayed in Buffalo, and suddenly Keith called Bill—at the time a youthful-looking thirtysomething with a long ponytail, barely out of graduate school—asking Bill to speak on his behalf.

Bill had been in the back of the room for plenty of Keith's keynotes. He knew the basic beats, but he couldn't claim to be someone who'd grown up dirt poor in Pittsburgh and through a combination of opportunity and effort had risen to become the youngest partner at Deloitte, CMO of Starwood, and a bestselling author.

Bill stood in an Ernst & Young event space, high above Times Square, trying to replicate Keith's magic and explain the relationship-building concepts that we were still desperately trying to systematize ourselves. The audience had come to see a rock star. They didn't get even a cover band. They got the roadie. The talk was a disaster, exactly as you would expect.

Looking back, the real problem wasn't the frameworks and tools we helped Keith create. The problem was strategic misalignment at the deepest level. Keith's heart was in his consulting work. He loved working with Fortune 500 brands. He wanted to help executive team members support each others' growth and not let each other fail. That was the core of the business he wanted to build. But he had written a wildly successful networking book, and the world had latched on to him as "the networking guy."

Keith had signed a two-book deal with his publisher. And the publisher wanted him to write *Never Eat Alone 2*. However, he felt the tension between the work the world knew him for and the work he wanted to do. Keith and the Greenlight Institute conducted research and many interviews. The second book, *Who's Got Your Back?*, Keith recalls, "was trying to thread the needle between two different concepts: relationship building and high-performing teams, and as a book, it fell flat." It wasn't the book that the market wanted.

Peter and Bill both left Ferrazzi Greenlight around that time. We had spent years bouncing between the W Hotel on Lexington Avenue in Manhattan and Ferrazzi Greenlight's West Coast headquarters in an LA bungalow. We went our separate ways, but each of us carried hard-won lessons about the gap between thought leadership success and strategic coherence that would shape our careers for decades.

Twenty years after *Never Eat Alone*'s release, Keith would make a startling admission: "I don't think I ever really, back in the day, latched on to this asset that I had—this massively successful book—and made it congruent with my core business."

His retrospective honesty understates the profound challenge he faced. He wasn't just misaligned strategically; he was challenged by his own success. Each time he delivered "networking" thought leadership, Keith had commercial success. But the work also pulled him away from his authentic interests.

It took him years to reconcile that he had two distinct businesses. The Greenlight Institute continued research into the dynamics of executive teams: small groups that elevate each other and refuse to let each other fail. His book *Never Lead Alone* built on the heritage of *Who's Got Your Back?*; it allowed Keith to speak to the challenges of executive teams, and he built a successful business, Ferrazzi Greenlight, around that work. Keith later launched Beyond Connections, which draws on the heritage of *Never Eat Alone* in a cohort-based learning community.

"I have found my way, but it took twenty years to do that. They're two very different businesses. And what's been successful is recognizing that."

The Expert's Paradox

Keith's story illustrates something unsettling we've learned after two decades of working with thought leaders: Even sophisticated practitioners struggle with strategic alignment. Keith had every advantage. Few could match his brand expertise, thought leadership experience, and media savvy. If someone with Keith's advantages struggled this much, what about the rest of us?

Very smart, successful people can build careers on their expert knowledge. They are the authority in the room. They get paid for what they know. People call them thought leaders. But ask them to explain how thought leadership works, and they provide some combination of tips, anecdotes, and personal insights. That's better than nothing, but it's not enough.

Expertise in a specific field and expertise in thought leadership are two separate skill sets. You can have world-class knowledge in your field of expertise and still not know how thought leadership works as a business. Without a strategy, you're busy traveling and practicing thought leadership. And yet, you lack the map and the compass you need to reach your goals.

Thought leadership is not part of the standard business school curriculum. Yes, there are plenty of thought leadership consultants. But each of them uses their own language and frameworks. There's not an established body of knowledge or even common language in the field. Some thought leaders take a "learn as they go" mindset. Others seek mentors in the author, speaker, or consulting communities. We've had hundreds of thought leaders engage Thought Leadership Leverage as consultants. And we spend a surprising amount of our strategy session providing "thought leadership 101."

We find we cannot talk coherently with our clients about strategy until we share a common language about thought leadership and discuss how the field works. Once the baseline is established, we can help our clients define their goals and craft a custom thought leadership strategy.

The Courage to Begin Again

Michael Bungay Stanier, whose *The Coaching Habit* has sold over a million copies, poses the question that haunts every serious thought leader: "If you're a thought leader, you eventually ask yourself: what matters more. Somebody loving you or your ideas changing the world? And then you ask yourself, what will I say 'no' to so I can say 'yes' to having more impact?"

This question cuts to the heart of why strategic assessment feels so threatening. We must confront the gap between what we say we want (impact) and what we actually do (whatever feels good or comes naturally).

Dr. Nick Morgan is a thought leader's thought leader who focuses on communication theory and has spent a career as a teacher and speaking coach. When you listen to him speak, he has the gravitas befitting his CV. He's a former fellow at the Center for Public Leadership at Harvard's Kennedy School of Government. His books—including *Working the Room*, *Power Cues*, and *Trust Me*—sit on our bookshelves within arm's reach. We love talking to Nick. We assumed that speaking came naturally to him. Quite the opposite.

In childhood, a life-threatening brain injury put Nick in a coma. When he awoke, he had lost the ability to read people's affect (their intent). "I couldn't tell what they were thinking, or feeling. Their mouths moved, and words came out, but without a sense of intent behind them, they didn't make much sense to me."

Nick developed his expertise in nonverbal communication so that he could understand other people. Then, he was asked to share his knowledge through teaching. "The biggest concern I initially had was a lot of impostor syndrome. What the heck do I know about teaching? What do I know about curricula and all that?"

Nick had coached Fortune 50 CEOs on high-stakes communication, yet he felt imposter syndrome when entering a new domain within his own field of expertise. Even as an expert in nonverbal communication, he needed to learn how to become a teacher. He had the courage to begin again, and he embraced that even when he knew some things, he didn't know everything.

Nick's self-awareness allowed him to evade a trap that catches many thought leaders. The surface problem is strategic. People practice thought leadership without systematic thinking about what they're doing. But the deeper challenge is psychological.

You can be an expert in your field and also a novice at thought leadership. To practice thought leadership well requires something most successful people find difficult: embracing "beginner's mind" in the work of thought leadership while your clients see you as an expert. If you show too much uncertainty, clients will wonder if you really have expertise. If you convince yourself that you're an expert in thought leadership without study, you will crash into avoidable obstacles and then wonder why things didn't work out the way you wanted.

We encourage you to examine your thought leadership with the same rigor you'd apply to any skill you want to learn or improve.

Your thought leadership requires strategic clarity, intentional distribution, and systematic execution of ideas that align with your authentic voice and actual goals.

The assessment below transforms these topics into questions you can answer and then act on. By examining where you are, what you want, and what shapes your practice, you'll discover whether your current approach aligns with your deepest intentions.

Your Thought Leadership Assessment

Before you can practice thought leadership strategically, you must honestly conduct self-reflection in three areas:

1. **Your current state:** Where you actually stand in your thought leadership journey—not just what you're doing but how it's working and how you feel about it.
2. **Your goals:** What are you actually trying to achieve through thought leadership? Not what you think you should want but what genuinely matters to you. And why.
3. **Your context:** What constraints and opportunities shape your practice? What are you willing to do, not do, or give up?

These sound like simple questions. They're not. When we guide clients through our strategy process, we consistently see the same pattern: The more accomplished the expert, the harder these questions become. Answering them honestly requires confronting the gap between their actual actions and what strategic thought leadership demands.

It may feel awkward to step back and ask these questions. You've been polishing ideas and trying to reach wider audiences. Isn't that enough?

No. You can't manage what you can't measure. Additionally, in our experience a lot of thought leaders track the wrong things. They stay incredibly busy, and yet they fail to create the impact they desire.

Your Current State: Where You Are

Where Are You on Your Journey?

People often answer this question by telling us about their current project—a book, a research paper, an impressive consulting engagement.

Stop. You don't need to impress anyone with your answer. Instead, be candid and tell yourself the truth. Here are some answers we've heard over the years:

- “I just increased my fee. I’m still amazed that people pay me to do this.”
- “I’m fighting burnout. Too much travel.”
- “I’m on the emotional high of my first book.”
- “I’m still fighting impostor syndrome.”
- “Cash flow is good, but the margins are awful.”
- “I thought the business would be bigger by now.”

Where are you really? Not where you wish you were, not where others think you are, but where you actually stand in your thought leadership practice.

How Do You Currently Practice Thought Leadership?

Many thought leaders describe their practice by their primary delivery method—author, keynote speaker, consultant, researcher, facilitator.

That’s the surface level. Go deeper. How do you actually do thought leadership work? Is your creation and deployment pipeline structured or chaotic? Focused or scattered? Do you spend more time creating ideas or delivering them? What’s your relationship with your own content? What does your sales pipeline look like?

How Do You Feel About Your Thought Leadership Work?

This question often surprises people. They get so wrapped up in doing the work that they never pause to assess their emotional relationship with it.

Some answer emotionally: “Excited.” “Curious.” “Still uncertain about my content.” Others respond pragmatically: “I get referrals.” “I like seeing people ‘get it’ and take ownership of the ideas.”

Your responses reveal important truths about alignment and sustainability.

How Do You Feel About the Impact You’ve Made So Far?

Do you see clear evidence of impact? Or do you wonder if you’ve made any real difference at all?

There are many ways to create impact through thought leadership, from changing individual lives through coaching to reshaping global organizations.

The question is whether your current impact aligns with your intentions.

Michael Bungay Stanier captures the emotional reality: "I have bigger ambitions for the impact I want to have in this world. I want to infect a billion people with the possibility virus." His assessment of his current impact versus his desired impact drives every strategic decision.

What's Your Immediate Next Step?

How do you choose your next actions? Are choices based on impulse? Client requests? Or do you have a clear strategy that guides what you say yes and no to? Unless you honestly examine your content, deployment, and reach—both where you are and where you want to be—you can't create a strategy for growth.

Your Goals: What You Want

Let's examine your goals and challenges more deeply. What do you want to achieve through thought leadership? Is it internal satisfaction, external rewards, or both? We divide thought leadership goals into three categories:

Your Intrinsic Goals

Intrinsic goals align with your passions, curiosity, and desire for experiences. Examples include the following:

- "I want to push myself out of my comfort zone."
- "There's a better way to think about [my topic], and I wake up excited to share it."
- "When I get emails from people saying my ideas sparked something in them, it makes my week."

Intrinsic motivators come from within. They sustain you through the inevitable challenges of thought leadership work.

Your Extrinsic Goals

Extrinsic goals connect to external outcomes and recognition:

- Speaking at specific events
- Achieving certain revenue targets
- Building wealth through sharing ideas
- Advancing your career
- Making a specific level of income per year

You can achieve both intrinsic and extrinsic goals simultaneously, but the strategies differ significantly.

Your Exit Goals

Your exit goals include your timeline, your transition out of thought leadership, and your financial goals or necessities. Every thought leader eventually steps away from their ideas. These factors should not be deferred until the last moment. They should shape your entire strategy and the actions you take each day:

- How long do you want to actively carry these ideas?
- Do you see yourself retiring? If so, when, and what would that look like for you?
- Do you want to retire from thought leadership work entirely? When?
- Do you want to sell your business? Would you be willing to sell a part of it? To whom? For how much?

Your Context: You and Your Reality

Your personal context is crucial for strategic alignment. Whenever Peter and Bill start working with a new client, we do far more than read their work and ask about their business goals. We take time to get to know them as a person. Understanding a thought leader's inner passions, top priorities, preferences, values, beliefs, and history is every bit as important as a deep analysis of their intellectual property.

We've talked to thought leaders who have preferences like the following:

- "I like three-day weekends; never book me for a client event on a Friday."

- "I'll do anything you want, but I hate being on video. I won't make videos."
- "I never want to work for companies in the _____ industry."

We had to respect these preferences when we created that practitioner's thought leadership strategy. What was important to them had to be reflected in what they did *and* how they did it.

Personal context includes health issues, family needs, personal traumas, and so much more. This context shapes how they engage with their audiences, impacts how they structure their days, and determines which projects they pursue.

Be honest with yourself. Document your own context with specificity. Only then can you build your thought leadership practice in a way that serves you.

In the table below, we offer a small sample of the deeply personal insights that thought leaders have shared about themselves and their context over the years:

PERSONAL CONTEXT	YOUR PRIORITIES	YOUR BUSINESS PREFERENCES
• I have acute stage fright. • I do not want to create videos. • I do not enjoy writing. My brain works differently than most (e.g., ADHD, dyslexia, dyscalculia). • My thought leadership work is informed by my identity as part of a nondominant cultural group or community.	• I want to generate income through my ideas. • Thought leadership is part of my job at work. • I want to use thought leadership to grow my existing business.	• I don't want to work with companies in _____ industry. • I don't want to spend more than _____ days on the road per month. • I do not want to have employees. • I don't like managing other people. • I want to do less coaching. • I hate selling and marketing.
YOUR HOMELIFE	**YOUR FINANCIAL REALITIES**	**YOUR WORK LIFE**
• I am the primary earner in my family. • I am a caregiver for a spouse or other family member. • I am going through a divorce. • I have young kids and want to spend time with them.	• I am living paycheck to paycheck. • I am financially secure and have a reserve. • I inherited generational wealth.	• Thought leadership is not my day job. • I do my thought leadership work in my evenings and weekends. • Thought leadership is part of my job at the place I work. • Thought leadership is my full-time job.

Sometimes these thought leadership contexts close paths that others choose. Your contexts can also create opportunities unavailable to others. Whatever your context, integrate it into your strategy. So, what's *your* thought leadership context?

Moving Forward with Clarity

Once you've completed this assessment, you'll have a clear understanding of what you're trying to achieve, what constraints you face, and how thought leadership fits into your larger professional and personal goals.

This clarity isn't the end of the journey. It's the beginning of a strategic thought leadership practice.

As Michael Bungay Stanier discovered, "I've always been driven mostly by the legacy piece, and that's been a helpful frame. It's helped me step away from being CEO of Box of Crayons."

His self-reflection revealed that his deepest goals weren't about continuing to run a business—they were about creating lasting impact. His clarity allowed him to make strategic decisions that seemed counterintuitive but were aligned with his authentic priorities.

Complete the assessment of your current state, your goals, and your context. Then, sit with whatever discomfort that assessment creates. You may realize that your past or planned actions do not align with these priorities. Or you may see just a need for small tweaks. Your assessment is the first step toward practicing thought leadership strategically.

In the next chapter, we'll explore the three fundamentally different ways people approach thought leadership—as Hobby, Practice Owner, or Business Builder—and why understanding this distinction is key to identifying your strengths, predicting future challenges, and developing successful strategies.

Chapter 3

Hobby, Practice, or Business?

Just seventy-five days before his retirement, Doug Conant launched his first business book, *Touchpoints*. These two milestone dates were incredibly, intentionally close.

Doug was ready to retire from his role as CEO of the Campbell Soup Company. He had led one of the most successful corporate turnarounds in Fortune 500 history. And yet, as he explained to his longtime executive assistant, Diana Hansen, "I'm not ready to step away from the craft of leadership."

Doug had practiced thought leadership for years as Campbell's CEO. He personally taught leadership courses to seventy-five of the company's high-potential leaders over six years. He had done similar work prior to Campbell's in his stint as president of Nabisco Food Company.

Campbell's board never asked Doug to teach leadership courses. His time spent teaching wouldn't be visible in the next quarter's financial statements. He could have easily skipped sessions. When we asked Doug why he ran these leadership sessions, he explained:

> *My leadership work at Campbell was very purpose-driven and core to my transformation efforts. At the heart of it, I just didn't believe we could transform the company unless we seriously leaned into the notion of transforming our corporate leadership. And, rightfully or wrongfully, I just didn't believe anyone could do that better than me, with my deep understanding of the challenges in front of us. I could see no way that*

an "outsourced" leadership development effort could have the necessary impact as the fully-engaged-in-every-session "home" CEO who already had a full portfolio of leadership development work behind him.

As Doug prepared to retire, he would leave the CEO role and commit even more time to his thought leadership efforts.

"I still had a strong desire to contribute to the leadership conversation—to help leaders be the best they can be so they can make a bigger impact on our rapidly changing world. A higher calling to empower people to lead has always been a driving force in my personal and professional life."

Doug had a plan, but he needed help. He asked his executive assistant, Diana Hansen, if she'd take a leap into the unknown with him—just the two of them, no salary for him, no guarantees. She said yes. Doug and Diana retired from Campbell's and launched a two-person thought leadership practice: ConantLeadership.

Doug's journey illustrates that there's no single "right" way to practice thought leadership. Over twenty years of working with thought leaders, we've observed three distinct models emerge—not as a hierarchy but as different answers to the same question: "In this season of your life, how will you steward the ideas you carry?" Thought leadership can be a thread running through your entire professional life, evolving as your circumstances change.

When Doug taught leadership workshops as Campbell's CEO, he practiced thought leadership as a hobbyist. We use this term with great care. Doug's thought leadership work has always been skilled and serious. At Campbell, it aligned with both his personal purpose and his plan to transform the company. So, why call him a hobbyist at that point? Simple. Doug was a CEO first and a thought leadership practitioner second.

When Doug left Campbell's with just Diana to start ConantLeadership, he became a practice owner—making thought leadership his primary work. Today, with systems, offerings, and a team in place, he has built a thought leadership business that creates impact far beyond his personal effort.

These three approaches—Hobbyist, Practice Owner, and Business

Builder—represent three different ways to engage with thought leadership:

> **Hobbyists** pursue thought leadership alongside or even within other commitments. They don't rely on thought leadership as a primary source of income. They may use it to accelerate their career, reach personal goals, or drive business results.
>
> **Practice Owners** make thought leadership their primary role. As solopreneurs or boutique-firm leaders, they are both the business infrastructure and the primary offering.
>
> **Business Builders** create thought leadership enterprises with value beyond their personal involvement. They build teams and systems where the ideas, not the individual, become the primary asset. Some build teams; others create ecosystems and partnerships.

Here's what matters: These approaches aren't stages of maturity or ambition. Don't fall into that trap. Einstein's *annus mirabilis*—his "miracle year" of 1905 that gave us special relativity—happened while he worked full time as a patent clerk. His evening and weekend theoretical work as a Hobbyist transformed physics forever.

None of these models is objectively best. However, any of them may be right or wrong for you. We have seen people pursue the wrong model, and their thought leadership work drains them rather than energizes them.

The question we want you to ask is this: "Which model enables me to live most fully while serving the ideas I carry?"

The ancient Greek philosophers called this concept *eudaimonia*: "human flourishing through excellent activity." There's no one right model here. Hobbyists, Practice Owners, and Business Builders can all achieve excellence. And your approach can change over time, shaped by your life's current realities: family obligations, financial needs, health constraints, available opportunities, and personal temperament. Your approach can also evolve based on market forces. Maybe you start as a Hobbyist, the market responds, and you expand your work and time commitment, becoming either a Practice Owner or Business Builder.

One of the easiest ways to distinguish between a thought leadership practice and a business is to ask the following question: "If the thought leader took a six-month sabbatical, what changes would we see?"

> **Hobbyist:** Very little change.
>
> **Practice Owner**: The gears grind to a halt. Clients are not served. There would be no product (the thought leader's time) available to sell. Cash flow stops.
>
> **Business Builder:** Lead generation might decrease, but with planning, the business could adapt and run well. If your ideas are supported through licensing or scalable products, the impact to the P&L statement is manageable.

You can take the thought leader out of a business, but you can't take the thought leader out of a practice. That's a key difference. In a thought leadership business, the ideas have been codified and productized. There are offerings to sell beyond the thought leader's personal time. And there are processes to keep running marketing campaigns, engage with potential buyers, scope deals, and generate revenue.

Any tension you might feel here isn't about where you are versus where you "should" be. It's about alignment: Does your current model enable you to flourish? Or are you building a business you'll hate running, maintaining a practice that exhausts you, or constraining yourself to hobby status when your ideas—and your life—demand more?

Whichever thought leadership model you choose, you will need a strategy. Doug Conant valued each of these roles. He didn't judge his teaching as "merely" a hobby or see his two-person practice as inferior to his later thought leadership business. Each model served him—and his ideas—perfectly for that season of his life. When Doug shifted from thought leadership Hobbyist to Practice Owner, he created a new strategy and executed it.

In addition to Doug, we will introduce the Hobbyist, Practice Owner, and Business Builder roles through eight people who use these thought leadership business models. They all practice thought leadership, and they all create impact. They have each found the format that serves them best in this season of their life.

The Hobbyist

As a thought leadership Hobbyist, you do not rely on thought leadership as your primary income source, although that might be your aspiration someday. You have the freedom to work on your ideas at your own pace.

For some Hobbyists, thought leadership is an evenings-and-weekends-only activity around other obligations. But we have also seen retirees invest significant time and money into thought leadership as their hobby.

It's possible to spend years, or even a whole life, practicing thought leadership as a Hobbyist. There's no requirement to become a Practice Owner or a Business Builder. You may pursue thought leadership because you love it and it brings you joy.

Let's meet three Hobbyists who practice thought leadership in different ways: Bryan Quoc Le started thought leadership in graduate school; Jeff Dellinger retired from a career as an actuary and cannot stop thinking; and Rusty Rueff uses thought leadership as one thread in a consciously crafted life.

Hobbyist: A Career Enhancer

Bryan Quoc Le was a PhD student writing his dissertation when a publisher asked him to write a book on food science. The book offer took Bryan by surprise: "I thought maybe I'd pitch a book five or ten years down the road when I have some experience."

Bryan was noticed because he'd already been practicing thought leadership for several years. In his third year of graduate school, he volunteered to write occasional articles for the blog of the Institute for Food Sciences. That led to his starting his own blog and building an audience.

"Over time, as I wrote more blog articles, I got into the nuances. How do I translate this information that's very verbose, very technical, and turn it into something that's readable for a nonscientist?" He was building thought leadership skills and making his own path.

Once the book was published, it had a snowball effect on Bryan's career. It allowed him to convey a lot of value up front to potential clients. "I was able to get a lot of long-term clients in that first year, because of the book." People started reaching out to Bryan for product development and R&D work.

"I had this knowledge base, but I could also explain it. I became really valuable because people didn't want to work with someone that was going to use highly technical terms and get into the weeds. They wanted someone that could explain things quickly and succinctly, and I was able to do that, because it was just sort of a natural way of speaking."

Bryan's entry into thought leadership wasn't part of his initial career plan, but it became a career accelerator. He got noticed. Opportunities sought him out. The early investment in thought leadership will continue to deliver a compounding effect that will propel him forward through his career.

Hobbyist: A Retiree Who Just Can't Stop Thinking

Jeff Dellinger retired from Lincoln Financial after revolutionizing its retirement annuity business. As a world-renowned actuary, he'd invented and patented two individual annuity products that generated hundreds of billions of dollars in assets. He also led Lincoln's Individual Annuities business, which became the company's largest and most profitable business line. Jeff's life's work revolved around the concept of retirement, and even after his own retirement, his passion continued.

After more than two decades at Lincoln Financial, he wanted to write a book while ideas were still fresh in his mind. So, he cold-called just one publisher—John Wiley & Sons—as a first-time author without an agent. They said yes.

When *The Handbook of Variable Income Annuities* came out, Jeff's phone started to ring. Law firms wanted him as their must-have expert witness. "I had no website, nor ever advertised. Yet, unrelated law firms would negotiate with each other for when they could 'have' me. It's not even clear how they all got my phone number!"

We met Jeff while he was writing his second book, *Another Day in Paradise: The Handbook of Retirement Income.* Free from day-to-day responsibilities and unburdened by revenue targets or client deadlines, he could finally pursue the questions that fascinated him most. This book became his masterwork—three years of meticulous research resulting in an 898-page handbook complete with formulas and footnotes. Jeff became a long-term client of Thought Leadership Leverage: We helped him craft the book launch strategy, execute it, and sustain momentum through writing and articles.

The Hobbyist model serves Jeff perfectly. He's drawn to "analytical topics, things that can be rigorously proven true." Without pressure to monetize his expertise or manage a practice, he focuses purely on the intellectual work that brings him alive.

Travel constraints due to health might limit a Practice Owner, but as a Hobbyist, Jeff uses books and articles to continue contributing solutions for those who lack time to think as deeply as he has.

Whenever Jeff talks about retirement strategy, he lights up. This joy comes not from building a business or commanding speaking fees but from the pure pleasure of grappling with complex problems and sharing hard-won insights. For Jeff, thought leadership as a hobby isn't a stepping stone. It's exactly the right approach for him to flourish.

Hobbyist: One Role Among Many

Some Hobbyists practice thought leadership not because they need to but because they cannot imagine a complete life without it. Rusty Rueff has been a business leader, Silicon Valley investor, and philanthropist. He's served on the founding boards of Glassdoor and HireVue, served as the chair of the Grammy Foundation, been a presidential appointee, and funded the Patti and Rusty Rueff School of Design, Art, and Performance at Purdue University.

By any measure, Rusty has many responsibilities and projects going on all the time. Yet thought leadership has become an integral part of how he lives. "I'd like to think that I've actually got thoughts that other people want to follow, and I could actually be thought of as a thought leader now."

Earlier in his career, Rusty authored *Talent Force* based on his understanding of his work as an HR executive. And his most recent book, *The Faith Code*, takes a deep look at life through the lenses of moral philosophy, entrepreneurship, and community building, asking questions like these: "Just what does it mean to 'live a good life'? What should we be comfortable letting go of? And where should we be doubling down?"

These questions tie back into Aristotle's inquiry into the "fulfilling life" (*eudaimonia*). And in Rusty's own words, he's spent over a decade asking himself these very questions.

So, it's particularly notable that Rusty has made thought leadership part of his life's work. He can fill his days in many ways, so why does Rusty practice thought leadership? "At the end of the day, my mind is going to deteriorate. My body is going to deteriorate. However, at the last moment of our lives, our spirit could be the strongest it's ever been in our lifetime. Spirit is the only thing that can increase while everything else decreases. I learned that."

Rusty has become driven to share this insight with others. Not to earn a living but because it aligns with his understanding of a "good life" worth living.

MOVING FROM HOBBYIST TO PRACTICE OWNER

Some Hobbyists aspire to make thought leadership their full-time professional role. And to be successful, you should have at least one of the following resources:

- An entrepreneur's confidence
- Your employer's sponsorship (if you want to practice thought leadership in-house)
- The support of a client or two lined up before you make the jump

- A reserve account that will cover the launch of your practice as well as your personal bills
- A passion or a calling to change the world

You can launch a thought leadership practice without any of these supports in place, but the transition becomes more difficult and potentially much longer. The more resources and support you have, the better.

While Hobbyists integrate thought leadership into broader life commitments, some reach a point where the ideas demand more space. Perhaps market response overwhelms their available time or their passion grows too large for evenings and weekends. When thought leadership shifts from one thread among many to the primary focus of your professional life, you enter the world of the Practice Owner.

The Practice Owner

A thought leadership Practice Owner is the principal and the primary product, much like doctors and lawyers in private practice who sell their time and earn their fees.

As a Practice Owner, you might be a solopreneur, or you may have a small team of employees or contractors. While your colleagues may know your content and have specialized roles, you are definitely the leader of the firm. People come to your practice because they have heard of your work or experienced your content themselves.

When you run a thought leadership practice, your buyers will likely conflate you (the practice lead and advocate) with your ideas. They see you as the star and your ideas as the tools you use. Clients will want *you* and seek out *your time* in the form of keynotes, fireside chats, workshops, executive coaching, consulting, etc.

Practice Owners can command a high fee for a day or even for forty-five minutes. Your time becomes your most valuable resource and your tightest constraint.

When you lead a thought leadership practice, you will likely work full time as a thought leader. But it doesn't mean you just get to work on your ideas and interact with learners. Like any small business owner, you likely wear many hats: CEO, head of marketing, and head of sales. The info@yourdomain.com emails go to your inbox. You might make the sales calls, negotiate and sign the contracts, send out the invoices, and run payroll (if you have it).

Some thought leaders who lead a practice have strong business skills, either through a formal education or years of hands-on experience inside large organizations. Yet, many thought leaders are far more comfortable with the ideas and teaching sides of the practice than the business. In fact, most Practice Owners neglect the business side, because that's not what drives them and not what gives them satisfaction.

The Practice Owner is passion driven, and that means they want to bring ideas to the world in a way that will allow them to work in their preferred modes and deliver their best. They commonly tell us they love what they do because "I get to set my own course" (agency) or "I can pick the projects I want and reject the things I don't want" (values). We'll see this mindset first through Dan Pontefract, an in-house expert who became a solopreneur, and then Hortense le Gentil, who has carefully built her practice's offerings around areas in which she personally excels.

Practice Owner: A Company of One

Dan Pontefract lists himself as the head of "the Pontefract Group—a company of one." When he became a client of Thought Leadership Leverage, we asked him why. As he told the story, we saw that the obvious tension between group and solopreneur is more than clever wordplay, and we learned how it describes Dan's approach to thought leadership. He maintains his independence while cultivating strategic partnerships that multiply his impact.

Dan's model emerged while he was an employee at TELUS, the Canadian telecommunications firm where he served as chief learning officer. He began writing thought leadership first on his own blog, and then he started writing for *Forbes* as a contributor.

He didn't seek permission. He just started doing it. Dan explains, "I have always believed in the adage that a slapped wrist after the fact is far better than a hand cut off up front."

TELUS eventually noticed his *Forbes* contributions. The company supported his work rather than stopped him. Mutual value creation became his template first at TELUS and then when he created the Pontefract Group.

At TELUS, he proposed a shift to his role. "I don't believe in holding on to a position in perpetuity," he notes. TELUS leaders listened to his pitch and supported the idea. Dan created an externally focused consulting practice inside TELUS. Dan built and led a small team that would help other organizations with culture change. The small team gave TELUS's salespeople a new way to support and serve their clients.

This hybrid model—with Dan as internal executive and external thought leader—laid the groundwork for his eventual independence.

When Dan eventually formed the Pontefract Group, he maintained strategic affiliations with TELUS. His employer became his client. TELUS retains access to Dan as a valued resource, while Dan preserves autonomy. When other partnerships violate his values (like publishers who gutted his editorial team), he exits cleanly: "I can't work with an organization that's done this to people."

For Dan, his best and most fulfilling work comes through this curated ecosystem—helping others "become better versions of themselves" while maintaining his own freedom to choose every relationship. His "Group" isn't employees but aligned partners who share his commitment to clear, consistent, real leadership.

Practice Owner: A Direct Connection Seeker

"I don't believe in keynotes." Hortense le Gentil, an author and Coaches50 honoree who works with Fortune 500 executives, laughs as she explains her unconventional stance. Instead of commanding stages as a keynote speaker, she chooses fireside chats. "I like to create experiences that connect people and the content. It's all about connection and conversation for me."

As a Practice Owner, Hortense has selected offerings that align with her strengths and her core belief about leadership itself: "We need more human leaders, not hero leaders. We need more empathy." So, rather than take the stage and speak to an audience, she chooses formats that create space for conversation.

Her commitment to dialogue shapes every aspect of her practice. In workshops—even with a thousand participants—she maintains her interactive philosophy: "After I share a concept, we do the work together right there in the room. Creating a rich, interactive experience makes it memorable and easier to apply to their daily lives."

By rejecting the traditional keynote format, Hortense ensures that her practice embodies her message. This dedication to her personal presence—every coaching session, every workshop, every fireside chat requiring her full engagement—represents how Practice Owners pursue their excellence.

Hortense's joy emerges through the irreplaceable human connections that define her practice.

As a Practice Owner, *you* are the primary product and message carrier. Therefore, people want you at your best. If you don't believe in keynotes, like Hortense, you shouldn't do them. If the thought of writing a book causes you to break out in a cold sweat, choose a different modality.

Your audience will never be more engaged with your ideas than you are. So, you need to choose modalities that allow you to work at your best. Or as Hortense says, "To unlock your highest potential as a leader, you need first to connect with your own humanity and be aligned with yourself. Then you can better connect with other people."

PRACTICE OWNER'S CHALLENGES

Many thought leader practices organize their priorities into a hierarchy that looks something like this list:

1. Serve all active clients at the highest level possible.
2. When client work runs low, start selling in a hurry.
3. Create new products (when you have time).
4. Work on your next book.

5. Follow up on contracts and invoices (especially if the bank account is low).
6. Write a social media post or publish your newsletter.
7. Explore new technologies.

You might prioritize these tasks somewhat differently, but the vast majority of thought leadership practitioners tell us five things again and again:

- They prefer talking about their ideas and enjoy making an impact.
- They are not comfortable with sales and marketing.
- They have weak sales and account development processes.
- They have a long list of products they want to create (whether or not they have a buyer).
- Their outbound marketing is inconsistent or nonexistent.

If these descriptions sound hauntingly familiar to you, then you should know that many of your peers face the same challenges, especially when they work without a thought leadership strategy.

As Practice Owners, both Hortense le Gentil and Dan Pontefract have found their pathway to excellence. They align their work with their values and choose strategic relationships. They have found balance and joy, even though many times they themselves are the product in their business. However, not every practitioner takes this path. In chapter 9, we'll explore Thought Leaders on the Run, who have a different relationship to place, pace, and personal presence.

Many thought leaders stay in the Practice Owner category their whole thought leadership career, but you may have larger ambitions. You may want to change the world or make millions through your ideas. You know there's a larger potential out there, but you may not know how to get there. That's the work of the Business Builder model.

The Business Builder

Business Builders put the spotlight on their ideas and build systems to generate revenue without their presence. Thought leadership Business Builders see themselves as both thought leadership practitioners and business owners. They know what they are great at doing and what tasks others can do much better. The Business Builder recruits highly talented professionals who implement the process and structure needed to grow the business.

Business Builder: A Shift in Mindset

When we met David Hutchens, he was a successful solo Practice Owner; his expertise was in storytelling, and he ran workshops, certified trainers, and sold participant kits. "I loved being a Practice Owner. One of my top skills is developing new content. But I made the mistake of believing new content was the same thing as growing a business."

David knew he needed a strategy to move forward and build the business he knew would be possible. Peter and Bill worked with him to craft his own story and offerings. "They helped me see that if my goal was to scale impact much broader than the twenty-four hours I had every day, I needed a whole new way of thinking." In addition to working with us on strategy, he became a long-term client of Thought Leadership Leverage. We worked with him on his sales narrative, his go-to-market positioning, and his offerings.

David started the journey of transforming his practice into a business. The strategy required him to adopt a CEO mindset and develop new skills. As David admits, "The change felt awkward at first. But I've discovered this perspective is a lot of fun. It gives me a whole new way of thinking about the impact of the 'story' skill inside big systems. I'm having fun again. I feel rejuvenated."

David recently signed enterprise-scale deals around his storytelling framework and tools. For example, he told us of a recent deal with a large consulting firm in Europe. He traveled just once from Nashville, Tennessee, to Oslo, Norway. He delivered certification training to the client's employees, and they will then teach it internally.

When we asked David about the enterprise deal, he excitedly said, "The client feels that they're getting a great discount on the per-person costs. I feel like I'm winning: They're paying for my ideas rather than me." David gets to stay at home while his ideas create value for the client.

David has been selling less of his personal time and presence. Instead, he's selling products, certification, and licensing. David now spends fewer days traveling and delivering workshops, and he focuses more of his effort on expanding within existing client accounts and growing his business. His transition has taken time, but it's given him new challenges and renewed joy.

Business Builder: Harmony and Disruption

"Can you actually promote and lift up two brands at the same time?"

Charlene Li faced this question when founding Altimeter Group after years as a principal analyst at Forrester Research. While many thought leaders jealously guard their personal brand, Charlene took the counterintuitive path: building a company brand that could thrive independently of her own reputation.

"A lot of people know Altimeter and don't know me. Other people know me but don't know Altimeter," she explains.

This dual-brand strategy required recruiting partners who understood that personal and company brands must live "in harmony with each other"—not an easy balance when dealing with accomplished thought leaders. "You need a special kind of person who understands what a *brand* means." She needed people who could grow their own personal brand and also advance the company's voice. Not easy.

"It was counterintuitive, and it worked brilliantly" for her and the other partners.

Charlene's systematic approach transformed insights into business value. Starting with research and writing focused on specific problems, she built a pipeline: "When somebody reads about that problem, then they call me like, 'Hey, you seem to know something about my problem. Can we talk?'" This led naturally to speaking engagements and then deeper consulting relationships through Altimeter's team.

When Prophet acquired Altimeter, Charlene had achieved what many thought leaders only dream of—building enterprise value beyond personal reputation. She stayed on because the cultural fit aligned with her values, but the business she built could operate without her daily presence.

Charlene's excellence comes through creating something larger than herself: an organization where multiple thought leaders could thrive while building collective value that exceeded any individual contribution.

Business Builder: From Accidental to Commercially Successful

Kim Scott was lying on the floor in the green room, exhausted after delivering her third speech of the day. Yet, she was still eager to learn. When another speaker asked about her fees, she sat up. "Charging? I didn't know that was a thing!"

When Kim now reflects on her entry into thought leadership, she admits, "I had no strategy." Kim's persistence had created overwhelming demand for her ideas—now she needed systems to scale them beyond her personal delivery.

Kim had aspired to be a novelist, and she had become a leader at Google and then Apple. She was designing a "Managing at Apple" course for Apple University when ex-CEO of Intel Andy Grove suggested she write a book about management "because it's got all the drama of a novel."

Kim coached CEOs at Twitter, Dropbox, and Qualtrics. Her book, *Radical Candor*, was an attempt to share what she couldn't scale.

As demand exploded, Kim tried everything. Other executives offering to teach? Her children suggested a 70/30 split over breakfast. Give the executives 70 percent, and she would keep 30 percent. Kim took her young kids' suggestion without doing much research. Over time, she found that giving executives such an above-market share made it impossible for her to grow the business. She had to adjust.

Software to scale the ideas? "We built one app, we built another app, we built a third app. They all failed."

After burning through $2 million, many would have retreated to the safety of corporate life. Instead, Kim chose the harder path of persistence.

She published a brutally honest blog post analyzing what worked (talks and workshops) and what didn't (apps).

That transparency attracted exactly the right partner. Jason Rosoff read that post and reached out: "Let's build a company that's doing what you should have been doing all along."

Together they built Radical Candor, Inc., delivering workshops worldwide and teaching managers to care personally while challenging directly.

For Kim, her fulfillment comes through solving the problem that mattered most to her—reducing workplace misery—while building a structurally sound business that allowed her to prioritize time with her family over three keynotes in a single day.

Finding Your Season

Your thought leadership model can and probably will change over time. Each shift is a business model transformation. And like any change, you can implement this shift smoothly over time with a clear strategy, or you can make a sudden change. In our experience, both clear strategy and purposeful execution help the shift happen more smoothly.

When Doug left Campbell's, he had the opportunity to ask himself, "If I could do anything in the world, anything that I wanted, what would I do?" The CEO who carved out time to teach seventy-five high-potential leaders discovered that teaching leadership was the work for the next season of his life.

Doug shifted from being a thought leadership Hobbyist to a Practice Owner with a two-person team (himself and Diana) and some ten social media followers for ConantLeadership. Now, he's a mission-led Business Builder with a team of eight leadership development professionals. They deliver boot camps and summits and even publish free resources to leaders worldwide.

How does Doug measure success? He's touched hundreds of companies. By his estimate nearly one hundred leaders who have studied Doug's BLUEPRINT framework over the years have become CEOs or CXOs. But on a deeper level, Doug is driven by four simple words: "How can I help?"

Doug still doesn't draw a salary, and ConantLeadership has donated over $1 million in profits to charity. Would he do it all again? "My answer then, as it remains today, is that I would be doing exactly this work."

Hobbyist, Practice Owner, and Business Builder are not rungs on a ladder. They are each different ways for you to engage with ideas and take them to the world. If you ask why you're still "only" a Hobbyist or someone is "already" a Business Builder, you're likely asking yourself a flawed question.

The real question is whether your current approach enables you to work at your best—to practice what the Greeks called excellent activity within your actual circumstances. Each season of your life will present its own constraints and opportunities.

You will likely need to adapt your model between Hobbyist, Practice Owner, and Business Builder at least once, perhaps even more often.

You've now considered *how* you might practice thought leadership. The next essential question is *what* your thought leadership contains. Just as choosing the right model matters, so does understanding the fundamental elements that transform expertise into impact.

Chapter 4 explores these Four Elements—the building blocks every thought leader needs, regardless of whether they practice as Hobbyist, Practice Owner, or Business Builder.

Chapter 4

The Four Elements of Thought Leadership

Lisa Bodell's full-day innovation workshop wasn't going well.

She'd done her homework on the organization, prepared with the sponsor, and customized her materials. Yet as the morning progressed, the participants seemed increasingly disengaged. "Nobody in the room was listening to me. They were going through the motions. They were checking their phones. And as I'm presenting, I'm asking myself, 'Well, why am I here?' I felt irrelevant."

The feeling was familiar. After years of teaching innovation to Fortune 500 companies, Lisa had noticed a disturbing pattern. Executives would hire her to teach breakthrough thinking and then resist any actual breakthrough. They wanted innovation, but not *that much* innovation. They wanted change, but not *that much* change.

During the break, Lisa pulled the client's leader aside. "No one is listening. I'm giving my all here. What's going on?"

His response stopped her cold: "Oh, don't worry about it. They hear what you're saying. They just don't believe they can act on it."

At that moment, Lisa faced a choice. She could continue delivering her prepared content to an audience that had already checked out. She could collect her fee and move on. Or Lisa could take a risk and pivot mid-session.

"So that's when I decided to actually shake it up. I brought everybody back into the room, and I said, 'All right, you know what we're going to do? We're actually going to put this idea into practice. You want to innovate? We're going to start innovating by getting rid of your own company!'"

Across the audience, eyebrows twitched upward.

What would Lisa say next? The audience wanted to know, and so did Lisa. Years of teaching innovation had led her to this moment of improvisation.

"Let's kill the company," she told the participants, and her impromptu words brought the room to life. Participants set down their phones. They weren't sure where Lisa was going or even what she meant, but this sounded interesting.

Lisa's choice of words surprised her as well. "It was like an epiphany. It was simple. It was provocative." Lisa scrapped her planned innovation workshop and leaned into the "kill the company" language—developing new activities and insights.

In that session, Lisa Bodell made the idea clear and urgent to her audience. She had found her platform identity.

Beyond Instinct and Intuition

Lisa Bodell, in a moment of desperation, found the right words, the right framing, and the right provocation. She transformed a dead workshop into a living laboratory.

You shouldn't have to wait for a crisis to discover what makes thought leadership work. There's a strategic, systematic way to evaluate and strengthen how you share your expertise. And this format gives you the time to reflect, evaluate, and refine.

Over twenty years, hundreds of practitioners asked us to evaluate their work. Working with each client, we saw patterns emerge.

The Four Elements framework crystallized from those patterns, giving us a practical vocabulary for what makes thought leadership effective.

Just as thought leaders equip their audiences with frameworks to navigate complex realities, this handbook offers tools to navigate the discipline of sharing expertise itself. The Four Elements—core ideas, content library, market offerings, and platform identity—reveal the pattern beneath Lisa's intuitive breakthrough.

The Four Elements

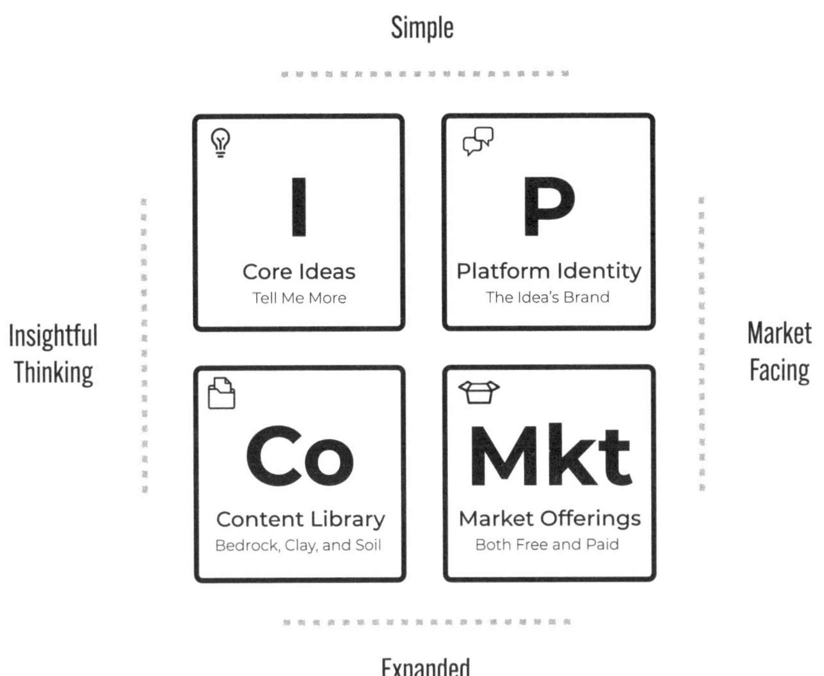

Most experts pursue domain knowledge. Fewer study how to share their insights effectively.

We're not suggesting that you reduce your knowledge to formulas or betray its complexity. We're recommending that you become as deliberate in your sharing as you are in your learning. After all, what good is your understanding if no one understands you?

I Core Ideas

Core ideas are the foundation of thought leadership. They support your entire body of work. If you do not have strong core ideas, you are not practicing thought leadership at all. You are just adding to the noise. Clearly defined core ideas will help you break through the noise and be heard by the right people.

So what exactly is a core idea? And how is it distinct from an everyday idea?

Not all ideas are thought leadership. "Let's get lunch" is an idea. "We should raise our prices" is an idea. "My calling in life is around negotiation skills" is also an idea. None of them are thought leadership.

In our Four Elements framework, a core idea is a short, provocative, generous, and distinctive statement. It catches your target audience's attention and causes them to say, "Tell me more." Core ideas are a starting place for your audience; however, it may take you a lot of work to polish an insight into a core idea. Here's what we look for in a core idea:

- **Provocative:** It aligns with your passion and attracts your audience's attention.
- **Generous:** It offers an insight rather than just a critique.
- **Distinctive:** It sounds like you (rather than other people).
- **Short:** It uses fewer than twenty words and makes each word count.

As a thought leader, you don't need dozens of core ideas. In fact, you might only need three to five carefully chosen core ideas to support your entire body of work.

David Komlos and David Benjamin had studied complexity. They'd spent years helping senior executives at Fortune 500 companies solve their most challenging problems, deploying sophisticated methodologies for what they called "Syntegration"—an algorithmic approach to generating focused conversations among a carefully curated group of people with varying backgrounds and expertise.

They had a smart way to solve complex problems. Except, few people intuitively understood what "Syntegration" was.

The two Davids became clients of Thought Leadership Leverage while they were finishing a book manuscript. We traveled to Toronto to help them shift the book from a project into a business growth catalyst. They came to Las Vegas multiple times to work on go-to-market language and products at different price points.

Walking to brunch in Las Vegas one day, David Benjamin was thinking ahead to the book launch campaign. "What should we talk about on our book tour?" he asked Bill.

"Start with one of your core ideas: Simple, complicated, and complex problems are different and require different solutions," Bill replied. "And then explain why you'll never solve a complex problem using tools designed to solve complicated problems."

David Benjamin pushed back. "Is that enough? It seems so basic." He worried that he might demean his audience's intelligence.

"You've spent years in this field, but your audience hasn't," Bill explained as they walked. "You know that complicated problems are the domain of experts. They use well-defined processes that lead to specific outcomes. Complex problems offer many viable options that affect many stakeholders and rarely have a single correct answer. Therefore, complex problems require different solutions. That's a fresh idea for most people. We've all faced problems that resist solutions. But we don't know why. You do. Start at the beginning. Share your core idea. Keep it simple. Invite your audience into the conversation."

When David Benjamin and David Komlos went out on their book tour, they led with their "basic" distinction. Complex problems required specific tools to solve them.

Audiences leaned in. That simple idea opened doors to deeper conversations about their methodology—conversations that never would have happened if they'd started with "Syntegration."

Your Core Idea: A Reality Check

Write down your core ideas. You may have more than one. Circle whichever one feels the most foundational to your work. Then test it against these criteria:

- I can state my core idea in under twenty words.
- People lean in when I share my core idea.
- My core idea solves an actual challenge.
- My core idea adds to the conversation.
- My core idea emerged from something I personally struggled with or discovered through deep study.
- I find new energy—not exhaustion—when explaining it for the

five-hundredth time.

- My core idea aligns with my purpose or my passion.
- My core idea is supported by research or expertise.
- My core idea is unique to me.
- My target audience values my core idea.

You don't need to check all these boxes to have a core idea. But you should be able to check most of them.

A provocative core idea opens the door, but without evidence to support it, even the best ideas wither. Your audience's initial curiosity—that "tell me more" moment—demands substantive follow-through. That's where a content library becomes essential.

Co Content Library

An idea alone can't create impact. Ideas provoke; content persuades. We view "content" differently than content marketers. They see finished products to post online; we see content as the individual reusable assets within your content library.

Your content library includes the stories, frameworks, case studies, and insights that support your core ideas. A conference anecdote that perfectly illustrates your point. The dataset that supports your framework. The client transformation that shows what's possible. All are part of your content library, waiting to be deployed.

The 2.6-Million-Word Wake-Up Call

When Peter and Bill started writing this book, we thought we'd quickly gather the gold from our podcast. Eight years—650 episodes.

Our book would focus on our thought leadership frameworks. The podcast stories would support them. Easy. With over 650 hours of recorded conversations, there was plenty of material. How hard could it be?

Peter asked Bill, "What are our best stories and quotes?"

"I have a few really good stories, but most of them come from recent episodes. Peter, what do you remember?"

And that's when it hit us. Our guests had entrusted us with profound moments of vulnerability, but our memories were imperfect.

We stared at each other over Zoom. We had uncovered a massive 2.6-million-word problem: We had accumulated eight years of content library debt.

Some episodes had transcripts. Many didn't. Others had autogenerated text where "Thought Leadership Leverage" morphed into "taught meter ship beverage." Every guest's insight was recorded but adrift in an ocean of 2.6 million words.

Our work on this book couldn't proceed until we rediscovered what we had already been told.

Six weeks. That's what it took us.

We built AI-augmented workflows. Our team transcribed and tagged. We searched for patterns and extracted insights. When we uncovered what we'd forgotten, the discoveries humbled us.

Janet Foutty, former US board chair of Deloitte, had described "maybe one of the scariest moments I've had professionally." She'd sent emails to twenty-two senior clients, asking them to share their truth for her book on women's leadership. That fear about risking her most valuable relationships. Essential for chapter 7 about Growth-Minded CEOs.

Stephen M. R. Covey, son of the legendary Stephen Covey and author of *The Speed of Trust*, had admitted his deepest fear of getting into thought leadership: "I thought I'd just be, no matter what, just a poor man's comparison to my father." His honesty anchors a discussion of the Impact Equation in chapter 5.

Jayshree Seth, 3M's first chief science advocate and holder of eighty patents, had broken down reading academic research about why some people don't feel like "the science type." "I'm literally in tears. I feel validated." This moment showed exactly how In-House Experts bridge worlds. It became the keystone of chapter 10.

If we had written this book faster, it would have contained a bare handful of stories and omitted much of our guests' hard-earned wisdom.

From Debt to Asset

Content library debt slows projects. It prevents ideas from reaching your audiences. In most cases, your challenge isn't scarcity. You've likely said or heard something relevant. Abundance is your obstacle.

A folder full of PowerPoints isn't a content library any more than a garage full of car parts is a working vehicle. Unless your content library is organized, tagged, and searchable, your own best insights will fade from your memory. What's the state of your content library?

Your Content Library: A Reality Check

- My content library contains persuasive material for each of my target audiences.
- I can find any story or example in under two minutes.
- I could create a complete list of my stories, frameworks, data, and examples in less than a day.
- My insights live in a well-organized content library (not buried in random files from past projects).
- My frameworks and unique terms are stable and consistent.
- I actively collect and test new material.
- I retire assets from my content library when they no longer create breakthroughs for others.
- My team creates assets without needing me to feed them content.
- My references and data are current or timeless.
- Whenever I use an asset from my content library, it remains consistent across speeches, workshops, and writing.
- I can deliver the same concept at 101, 201, and 301 levels.
- Each asset in my content library supports at least one of my core ideas.

What really are your best stories, data, and examples? If you work in isolation, you may struggle to evaluate your own material. That's why we find ourselves invited into so many of our clients' intellectual attics, helping them sort years of content. A good content library reduces stress and moves projects forward. It certainly did for us.

Yet core ideas and assets in an organized content library tell only half the story. Your assets—the stories, data, and frameworks—need to be packaged and delivered. You need market offerings that match your strengths and your audience's preferences.

Mkt Market Offerings

Market offerings are how you package your ideas and deliver them to your target audience. Your offerings may be simple and free (a LinkedIn post) or robust and expensive (an organizational diagnostic or licensed learning program). Many thought leaders stumble at this point. They create market offerings that serve their own interests rather than meet their market's needs.

Imagine an Amazon warehouse team that ships packages without the correct products. The warehouse team grabs something—literally anything—from the shelves, picks an address, and ships it for delivery. Maybe the box will contain what the people at that address want. Seems doubtful, right?

And delivery isn't the only problem. We've visited many clients' expensive market offerings graveyards and participated in their success stories.

Market offerings can be tricky. We've seen too many thought leaders spend money and time creating new market offerings that become abandonware, either because they lose interest or because the market doesn't want the idea in that format. Many practitioners love to create new market offerings. But to be successful, they must think like CEOs and end experiments that have become too costly. Here's what we've learned from working with hundreds of thought leaders:

1. **Test demand before investing heavily:** One thought leader with a million LinkedIn followers invested six figures in a course that sold fewer than ten units.
2. **Finish and pitch your work:** Another thought leader built 80 percent of a diagnostic tool as a "summer project" but never pitched it to buyers.

Action > perfection.

3. **Minimize up-front investment:** We sold a six-figure video series with just three short videos filmed in a single day. Think minimum viable prototype.
4. **Consider licensing or partnering:** We helped a client license five of their PowerPoint slides for six figures on a multiyear deal to a single organization.
5. **Design for delivery at scale:** We've sold thousands of self-assessments on behalf of our clients, generating revenue without requiring our presence for each sale.

Tim Sanders's love of technology and people lit up every stage he touched. Tim had been involved in the early days of live streaming with Mark Cuban at Broadcast.com. Then, as Yahoo!'s chief solutions officer, he was instrumental to their largest marketing partnerships, including Sony, HP, Barnes & Noble, and Kmart.

Tim's first book, *Love Is the Killer App: How to Win Business and Influence Friends,* launched on February 14, 2002, with Tim on the cover of *Fast Company* magazine holding a giant pink heart. The article and book talked about how sharing your knowledge and your network and showing compassion drive business success.

He was in demand as a keynote speaker, and off-the-shelf learning programs seemed a logical next step. That's how Bill and Tim first met in 2005, and Tim became a client. Tim mentored Bill on the ideas in his book, and then Bill and the team spent months building a curriculum based on Tim's message and core ideas. We tried to capture Tim's magic into scalable workshops. But despite a strong pilot and a few initial buyers, we saw little demand.

Tim tried five times over the first twenty years to create a profitable training program, investing heavily: "I've lost a quarter million dollars chasing that model." Each of the corporate learning programs failed.

The problem wasn't the quality of the core ideas or even the content library; it was the distribution method. Training programs need to work independently, without the founder's charisma. Tim's strength in thought leadership was his in-person presence and expertise. And if you took that away, it became difficult to sell the market offering.

Tim shifted his focus to training firms that had already built distribution systems, such as Skillsoft. "That approach—using someone else's sales distribution—completely changed the profitability of my training business. I've recovered the $250,000 loss and am now up an additional $250,000 in training income. The royalties keep coming in."

Tim also heeded Tom Peters's warning about "fresh-cut flower syndrome." Tom warned that speakers who leave business eventually become performers instead of active businesspeople. Tim applied this lesson to his own work. He balances his keynoting with taking in-house roles and advocating technology's evolution. "Every project must provide insights that make me more relevant and on-platform," he explains—meaning it must be aligned with his core ideas and platform identity.

Today Tim is actively into AI transformation, not reminiscing about early internet days at Broadcast.com and Yahoo! Tim thrives because he applied selective excellence. He now alternates between inspiring audiences and solving real problems as VP of research insights at G2 and serving as an executive fellow at Harvard Business School. Some thought leaders scale through systems. Tim scales through selecting.

There's often a gap between the market offerings we want to create and the way buyers (and audiences) want to consume content. We call this tension between creation and consumption the "Comfortable Corners of Thought Leadership," and we revisit it in section 4.

Every market offering requires your audience's most precious resource: their attention. Whether it's a LinkedIn post or a licensed program, they must receive more value than the time (and often money) they invest. A five-hundred-page manuscript sent unsolicited remains unopened. But a compelling social media hook that speaks directly to their needs? They'll click "See More."

Your Market Offerings: A Reality Check

- My audience can easily find my market offerings when they need them.
- Each market offering creates more value than it costs (time or money).

- I test demand before major investments in new market offerings.
- I presell before investing big money in product development.
- I create market offerings based on audience preferences, not my comfort zone.
- I recruit expert help for building market offerings in uncomfortable or highly technical formats.
- I make small experiments with new and emerging formats.
- My market offerings actually solve challenges that my audience struggles with.
- I measure success by measurable audience behavior change, not just positive feedback.
- I retire offerings in formats that the market no longer wants.

Lisa Bodell discovered how to bridge this gap by developing a portfolio that served different needs and price points. "I wanted to have things that facilitated buying my thought leadership," she said. "It's the book and the speech that ignites the thinking; it's the training that ignites the skills; and it's the tools that let them scale across the company."

Scaling Content in Organizations

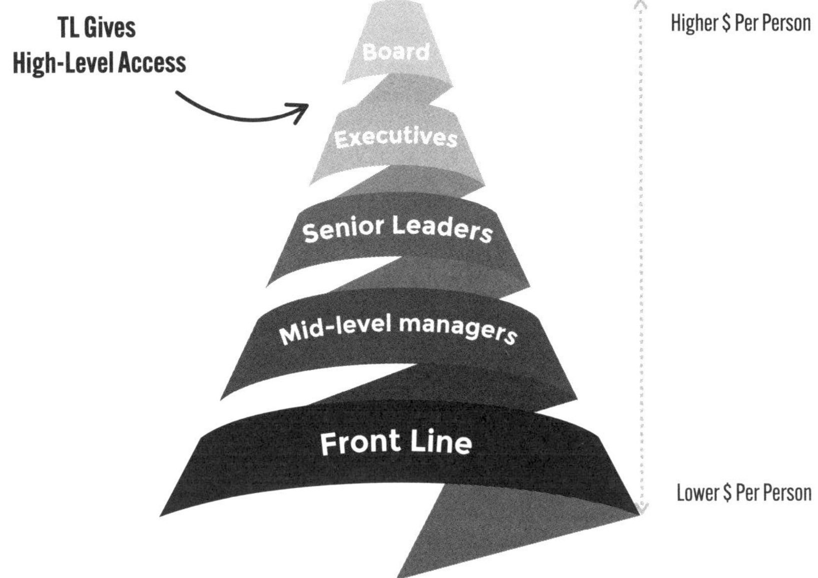

At the enterprise level, you must match market offerings to budgets. An executive committee will pay your full day rate for strategic insights. But for frontline employee training, they might spend only one-thousandth of that per person. Your offerings must scale accordingly. You need the right balance of high-ticket/low-volume market offerings (like a keynote or consulting) and low-ticket/high-volume offerings (like individual assessments).

Think like both a product manager (*What should exist?*) and a warehouse manager (*How do we deliver it efficiently?*). That discipline transforms offerings from expensive experiments into engines of impact.

P Platform Identity

How do people describe your work when you're not in the room?

If you don't know—or don't like what you hear—you have a platform identity problem. And like most thought leaders, you probably don't realize you have this problem.

So what exactly is a platform identity? And what makes one strong versus weak?

Your platform identity is the language people actually use when describing your work to others. You can strategically design and test this language, or you can leave it to chance.

A strong platform identity has four characteristics:

- **Concise:** It consists of two to four words that fit on a book spine, conference program, or in casual conversation.
- **Clear:** People understand it immediately without explanation—not jargon, technical terms, or clever wordplay that requires decoding.
- **Signals what it solves:** Your target audience knows within five seconds whether your work addresses their specific challenges. "The Experience Economy" solves understanding new value creation. "Trusted Advisor" solves building client relationships. "Crucial Conversations" solves difficult discussions.
- **Distinctive:** It is your own term or phrase—not generic field language or another practitioner's proprietary brand.

When your platform identity works, what you call your work and what others call it align perfectly. When it doesn't, you'll hear a dozen different descriptions—or, worse, confused silence.

In Bill's undergraduate theater program, he wrote a long one-act play. Once the first draft was ready, his mentor convened actors for a table reading. Bill was allowed to attend but was told he must remain silent during the reading and the following discussion. His mentor asked the actors questions: "What's the author's big idea in this script?" "What is the author trying to communicate here?" "What seems confusing?" And all the while, Bill sat quietly, listening to others talk about his work.

What was clear to Bill as the author was not clear to the actors. It was a humbling experience, but it showed him how others perceived his work. And it guided his script revisions. This is how platform identity is built: by creating opportunities to hear the language others actually use when describing your work.

We will see in chapter 5, "The Impact Equation," that a weak platform identity reduces how far and fast ideas spread. So our work with clients typically begins with defining or refining their platform identity.

Jane Hyun excels at building platform identities. Over her career, she's built and sustained two distinct ones—when most thought leaders struggle to sustain even one.

When Jane moved from Korea to New York at age eight, she saw a classmate challenging the teacher. Internally, Jane thought, *That boy is going to get in trouble*. But instead, the teacher praised him for sharing his opinions.

This formative moment stayed with her throughout her corporate career. Her learnings shaped her desire to teach these concepts to others, regardless of background, as she moved into thought leadership.

Jane's initial platform identity comes from her first book, *Breaking the Bamboo Ceiling*, published in 2005. The question it addresses is this: How can people with Asian cultural values navigate Western corporate culture? Jane focuses on identifying misunderstandings and overcoming challenges so that her audience can leverage their strengths to advance their careers and help their organizations thrive.

Unlike Lisa Bodell, who came to her platform identity, "Let's Kill the Company," in a moment of serendipity, Jane listened to the challenges her audience faced and tested her "Bamboo Ceiling" platform identity with focus groups.

According to Jane, "I gave them a few options and said, 'Hey, I'm writing a book about this content. Which of these titles resonate with you?'" They unanimously chose the "Bamboo Ceiling" to describe her work, because it gave a name to something they experienced but lacked a term to describe. "They felt that it was a nod to the Glass Ceiling term, while being specific to the Asian experience."

Jane understood that effective platform identities must acknowledge complexity while remaining simple enough to communicate the idea. After twenty years of work around the "Bamboo Ceiling" (and her recent sequel, *Leadership Toolkit for Asians*), Jane has earned the respect and attention of her audience.

They connect strongly with the language she legitimized.

If you're an emerging thought leader, learn from Jane: Actively create opportunities to test potential platform identities and discover how others describe your work. You can test language in a keynote vignette, in comments on LinkedIn posts, or in responses to *Harvard Business Review* articles. Few take advantage of these opportunities consistently.

Again, you serve as the CEO of your thought leadership. Platform identity testing and refinement is an essential risk management strategy.

Jane built a second platform identity for today's multicultural workplace: "Cultural Fluency." Few people are trained to lead across differences—whether culture, ethnicity, gender, ability, or age/generation—yet this skill is critical for any go-to-market strategy or people initiative. Few are offered formal training on how to make sense of and respond to differences or taught how to forge relationships to move the business conversation along.

"Cultural Fluency" speaks to developing these essential skills. The framing is itself brilliant—it connects cultural fluency to language fluency, a skill that people know takes time and ongoing practice. The platform identity of "Cultural Fluency" also signals broad utility; it's something every leader, aspiring leader, and team member can benefit from. Jane methodically tested the language with focus groups—listening to their responses and then using the term again and again to help people encounter and embrace it.

Earlier in this chapter, we talked about David Komlos and David Benjamin and how they struggled for traction while they used a technical term, "Syntegration," as their platform identity. The two Davids understood what this concept meant, but it confused their target audiences.

Using "Cracking Complexity" as their platform identity made it easier for people to talk about and immediately understand their work.

The idea didn't change. The platform identity did.

Do you know how people describe your work? You may not be able to eavesdrop on conversations, but you can ask others to describe your work in just two to four words. If you can, convene a few people and have someone else moderate a discussion.

Stay silent (or even on mute). Keep your facial expressions neutral, and take lots of notes.

Jane's two platform identities each solve for *X* with crystal clarity. "Breaking the Bamboo Ceiling" solves for Asian professionals navigating Western corporate culture. "Cultural Fluency" solves for leaders managing diverse teams.

What does your work solve?

Your Platform Identity: A Reality Check

- I know how people introduce my work to colleagues when I'm not in the room.
- I have made it easy for others to quickly introduce my work.
- I am happy with how people describe my work to others.
- Others describe my body of work with the same language I use.
- I have tested my platform identity with actual target audience members.
- My platform identity signals clear relevance to my exact audience.
- Someone would know within five seconds if my work is for them.
- My platform identity works well in writing.
- My platform identity works well when I explain it verbally.
- My platform identity can stand alone on a book spine or conference program and still attract the right people.
- I have optimized my platform identity for clear over clever.
- People who use common search terms will recognize my work as relevant to them.

If you checked fewer than half these boxes, you're in good company—but you're also leaving impact on the table. Your core ideas deserve a platform identity strong enough to carry them into rooms you'll never enter, conversations you'll never hear, and organizations you'll never know.

That's the work ahead.

Listen to how your friends, fans, and clients interpret your work. Do they all align around a single phrase? Or do you get a wide range of terms? Where do they find the greatest meaning and value? Do the people who most love your work still struggle to summarize it? If so, that's a clear sign they are not talking about your work. And you are likely missing referrals and opportunities.

It may be difficult to listen to others without interrupting them. It may be painful to hear them misrepresent your core ideas. But, like Bill rewriting his one-act play, you have to listen before you can revise and polish your platform identity.

The Four Elements in Action

The Four Elements framework doesn't demand prelaunch perfection. It reveals the pattern beneath breakthroughs like Lisa's, giving you a systematic way to develop what she discovered through necessity. You can build these elements consciously, refine them deliberately, and—most importantly—begin sharing them before they're perfect.

When Lisa Bodell proclaimed, "Let's kill the company," she unconsciously deployed each of the Four Elements. Her core idea provoked attention. Her content library—stories of organizational inertia—provided evidence. Her market offerings gave participants a way to engage. And "Kill the Company" became her platform identity, a phrase that traveled even when she wasn't in the room.

Your ocean of expertise is vast. Your understanding will always be partial. Your explanations will never capture everything you know. But somewhere, someone is drowning in complexity, just as Lisa's workshop participants were that day. They don't need your entire ocean of knowledge. They need exactly the drop of insight you can provide: simple enough to grasp, profound enough to matter, and clear enough to act upon.

Chapter 5

The Impact Equation

In the 1980s, Stephen Covey was working on what would become one of the most influential business books of all time: *The 7 Habits of Highly Effective People*. He had been teaching these concepts since 1979, developing audio tapes and refining his material. But when he considered publishing a book, he faced significant pushback.

Some business consultants were saying, "You know what? Don't put this into a book," recalls his son, Stephen M. R. Covey. The advisors had another worry: Who would hire Covey if they could get his ideas for the price of a book? Even within their own family business, debate continued about whether publishing would cannibalize their speaking and training business.

Covey faced a fundamental thought leadership dilemma: Should he guard his intellectual property to maximize its commercial value or share it widely to maximize its impact?

The business consultants saw scarcity. Every reader who bought the book was one less potential client for a workshop.

Covey saw abundance. It wasn't an either/or choice between the workshop and the book. It might even be a both/and choice. The person who spends a nominal amount on a book might later pay to attend a workshop or recommend that their organization bring Covey in. Covey understood that the total audience for the idea was larger than he could ever humanly reach himself through speaking and workshops. He chose abundance, and he went forward with the book.

"This idea will come back a hundred times and more," he predicted. The subsequent success of *7 Habits* proved Covey right, though his son admits, "It looks obvious today, but at the time it wasn't so clear cut." The book alone has sold more than forty million copies.

This choice—between hoarding and sharing, between scarcity and abundance—determines whether ideas create impact or die in obscurity. In this chapter, we look at the very tricky concept of impact in thought leadership. What is it? How is it created? And how do you create more of it?

A Certain Slant of Light

Emily Dickinson's poetry is a literary miracle. Yes, her unique style defied nineteenth-century conventions. Her poems twisted nouns into verbs, used quirky punctuation, and favored imperfect rhymes. But it's amazing that we can talk about her poems. She barely published in her lifetime. She kept the poems locked in a chest in her Amherst bedroom. One of the most innovative bodies of work in American literature could easily have become ash or, at best, a family heirloom. How these poems survived is documented in Lyndall Gordon's *Lives Like Loaded Guns* and Millicent Todd Bingham's *Ancestors' Brocades*.

When Dickinson died in 1886, her sister, Lavinia, cleaned out the room and burned Emily's private papers. But when she came to the locked chest, she discovered a wonder: nearly eighteen hundred poems crafted with meticulous precision, single words revised across multiple drafts and then bound in handsewn fascicles. Lavinia refused to put her sister's poems into the fire. Instead, the poems lit a fire in her.

Emily Dickinson's literary legacy exists because Lavinia advocated the poems in a way her sister never did. She searched for a manuscript editor; two said no before a third said yes. She navigated the publishing world, overcoming rejection from Houghton Mifflin. She self-financed publication. A small Boston publisher agreed to print Emily Dickinson's *Poems*—if Lavinia would pay for the cost of the printing plates and waive the royalty on what they expected would be the first (and only) print run.

On the first day, the publisher's entire print run—five hundred copies—sold out. Eleven printings in the first year. First-year sales for Emily Dickinson's *Poems*: eleven thousand copies. Remarkable for a first-time author's book of poetry.

Why did Lavinia care? *Ancestors' Brocades* preserves a letter Lavinia wrote to a family friend and editor at *The Atlantic*:

> I have had a "Joan of Arc" feeling about Emilies poems from the first & their reception convinces me I was right. As all Emilies possessions were given to me, years before her death, I recognize the right to magnify her name as she deserved.

If Lavinia had chosen another course, we would have no "Because I could not stop for Death," no "I'm Nobody! Who are you?" Emily meticulously crafted the poems over decades. Lavinia built the systems to share them. Both mattered.

"I Most Cordially Hate the Lecture Field"

Mark Twain spent decades as an accomplished speaker on the lecture circuit, but it pushed him beyond his limits. Biographer Ron Chernow's *Mark Twain* notes that Twain periodically "would reach the end of his tether and say, 'I most cordially hate the lecture field.' Throughout his life, Twain would swear that he was through with the stage only to renege on his pledge under money pressure." Twain found speaking easier and more profitable than writing, even as it wore him down through fatigue and illness.

This pattern started on October 2, 1866, with his first paid speech. Chernow describes how Twain had arrived two hours early, planted shills in the audience to laugh at his jokes, and found the hall silent and gloomy. When the show began, Twain stood silent for two full minutes. Then he opened with a line that promised escape: "Ladies and gentlemen . . . this is the first time I have attempted to speak in public, and if I know myself as well when the lecture is over as I do now, it will be the last." He won the audience over that night and launched his career.

Twain lectured at a pace that remains impressive by modern standards—and he achieved it in an era when the fastest travel was by train and steamship. His 1871–72 lecture season hit at least seventy-seven engagements. His 1884–85 "Twins of Genius" tour with George Washington Cable logged over one hundred performances across North America.

Twain juggled speaking engagements while writing prolifically. Over his lifetime, he produced twelve novels, ten travel books, hundreds of short works and essays, thousands of newspaper articles and letters, and a three-volume autobiography. He operated as journalist, novelist, essayist, and correspondent simultaneously—feeding fresh content to multiple publications while living out of hotel rooms.

He sustained a grueling pace of production and travel that would challenge any practitioner. The personal cost showed itself in dark humor: "I wouldn't want any better fun," Twain wrote, "than writing obituaries for chambermaids"—those hotel workers whose morning wake-up calls interrupted the sleep of a perpetually exhausted man.

At age sixty, Twain went on a global speaking tour—not as a victory lap but to repay debts. The fifty-three-thousand-mile tour took him to seventy-one cities across the world: North America, New Zealand, Australia, India, and Africa.

In Vancouver, Canada, he delivered a postponed lecture mostly in a whisper. Twain felt the pressure of the tour on his aging body:

> I do not enjoy the hard travel and broken rest inseparable from lecturing, and if it had not been for the imperious moral necessity of paying these debts . . . I should never have taken to the road at my time of life.

Twain put his ideas and himself out into the world continuously, a counterpoint to Emily Dickinson. He knew he could make audiences laugh, but he also wanted to leave them with a lesson. He wanted to create impact. But few people heard his moments of self-doubt. He once confided to a friend, "As a lecturer, I'm a fraud, aren't I?"

After one particularly successful event, Twain dismissed his work privately to his colleague:

> Such a triumph? A triumph of the moment; but those people are going home to their beds, glad to get there, and they will wake up in the morning ashamed of having laughed at my nonsense.

Twain became one of the most recognizable figures of his era. His relentless personal effort created substantial impact: global fame, cultural influence, and financial recovery. People loved his writing; he sold hundreds of thousands of books. But even more people wanted to see him and hear him. He could never satisfy the public's demand for Mark Twain (the icon) he had carefully constructed.

When Twain couldn't show up or his health prevented him from speaking, momentum slowed. His career demonstrates both personal effort's incredible power—and its inevitable ceiling.

The Impact Equation

If you practice thought leadership, you probably want to create more impact. But that leads to two difficult questions: What is impact? How do you create it?

That's where the Impact Equation becomes essential. It reveals the relationship between sharing and influence, between velocity and reach. It provides a guide for you as a practicing thought leader to evaluate what's working and what's not—and, more importantly, where you need to apply effort.

First, let's acknowledge an obvious challenge. The word *impact* is incredibly slippery because it conflates intent, effort, and outcomes. In the Impact Equation, *impact* measures the outcomes your ideas achieve—the actual results, not just your effort or intentions. The equation separates what you control (the inputs) from what you measure (the output).

You get to decide the impact you want to pursue. It can be any combination of business growth, social transformation, behavioral change in individuals, reputation, or personal legacy.

You can't create impact if your work is locked in a chest. And you risk recurring burnout or illness if you try to take your ideas everywhere.

The Impact Equation itself is deceptively simple:

IMPACT = ! x ✓ x V→ x %

!	✓	V→	%
Idea Simplicity	Audience Relevance	Velocity	Audience Share

1. You don't need to enter exact numbers into the equation. It's not that kind of equation. Instead, it's designed to give you directional guidance.
2. The factors multiply rather than add. If any factor is zero, your *impact* becomes zero. All factors matter equally.

We've deliberately omitted idea quality from the equation. We've seen plenty of good ideas flourish, and we have seen amazing ideas languish unseen in a file drawer. The Impact Equation explains, in part, why that happens.

Now, let's turn our attention to the variables that you, as a thought leader, can influence.

! *Idea Simplicity*

Idea simplicity describes how easily the idea can be communicated between people.

In the early days of your thought leadership, you will be the one communicating your core idea. And it's not how quickly you can say the idea. We can all create jargon-laden six-word sentences. Can you, in a sentence or a quick doodle, get someone else to understand the core of your idea? That's the first hurdle.

As the idea's simplicity increases, the time to initial comprehension decreases. We live in a world where people quickly scroll through their inbox or social media to evaluate if the idea is relevant or interesting to them. They'd rather be fast and sometimes wrong than slow and always right. Your core idea needs simplicity, or it won't break through the noise.

Idea simplicity also helps others share the idea on your behalf. If your core idea seems too complex, they won't try.

Audience Relevance

Audience relevance describes the value your target audience places on your idea.

Whenever someone encounters your core idea, they quickly evaluate four types of value:

- **Time:** "How much of my time is this idea worth?"
- **Effort:** "How much of my effort (or my team's effort) is this idea worth?"
- **Resources:** "How much money is this worth?"
- **Reputation:** "How much of my reputational capital will I put into this idea?"

When you first introduce a new idea to your target audience, they may give you a few scant moments of attention.

Your idea asks people to invest scarce resources—their time, effort, money, and reputational capital. Therefore, it's on you (and the systems you create) to demonstrate rapid and increasing audience relevance.

If you want to create any *impact*, you need to quickly signal audience relevance. Give people the information they need to make a fast decision.

If you do it right, a well-defined target audience member will say, "Tell me more," while everyone else will give a fast no and move on. That's exactly what you want.

V→ Velocity

Velocity describes how frequently people encounter your core idea. There are, broadly, two ways to generate velocity:

> **Personal velocity:** You advocate for the idea through your own direct effort. Every speech, every article, and every conversation creates personal velocity. But it comes with a ceiling. Even when you are passionate about the idea, you have only so many hours and can do only so much yourself.

> **System velocity:** The effort comes from outside you. It can be supplied by team members, fans and protégés, products (such as books and online courses), licensees, and certified facilitators.

The list of ways to create system velocity is nearly infinite. The key way to identify system velocity is "not you."

To understand the velocity transition, consider the ratio between personal and system contribution. This ratio typically evolves over a thought leader's career, with legendary impact occurring when systems consistently generate almost all velocity.

VELOCITY SOURCES	KEY OUTCOMES	IMPACT LEVEL
0%–30% system	• Ideas gain attention while you're present. • Impact depends on your ongoing involvement.	Limited
40%–60% system	• Ideas start spreading through others. • Systems amplify your personal efforts.	Significant
70%–100% system	• Ideas travel widely and independently. • Impact continues long after you step away.	Legendary

Emily Dickinson and Mark Twain provide examples at the extremes. Dickinson created minimal personal velocity and no system velocity in her lifetime, but Lavinia pushed hard—recruiting editors, advocating relentlessly, and even self-publishing her sister's work. She provided the personal velocity needed to create legendary system velocity. Mark Twain maximized personal velocity. Like Sisyphus, he had to keep pushing, and whenever he stopped—for a day off, exhaustion, or illness—he lost velocity.

Over time, the most successful thought leaders transition from generating 100 percent of velocity personally to having systems generate most of it, enabling ideas to spread without their constant involvement.

If you want to increase your impact and preserve your well-being, build the systems that allow other individuals and organizations to add velocity to your core ideas.

% *Audience Share*

Audience share is the percentage of your target audience that is engaged with your idea. When we ask thought leaders about their target audience, we ask two questions: "Who is your target audience?" and "What percentage of that audience is listening to you?"

We have heard people tell us that their leadership content is "for anyone, whether they're at work, at home, or in their community." And we ask for clarification: "Do you mean everyone in the United States? Or do you mean everyone alive in the world?" Unless you have an incredible amount of system velocity and support from others, your audience share is likely to be effectively 0 percent.

The larger your target audience, the smaller your audience share. And that makes it harder to signal audience relevance to any individual or group. Impact diminishes.

Therefore, we encourage our clients to think more narrowly around their potential target audience. Perhaps you want to focus on leaders in healthcare. Or perhaps physician leaders. You could even narrow your target audience by geography, training, role, or even experience level.

Here's the paradox: Narrowing your target audience increases your audience share, which ultimately expands your total reach. Thought leadership achieves massive audiences through careful narrowcasting, not broadcasting.

Legendary Impact: The Universe in Five Symbols

Walk into any college dorm, science museum, or novelty shop, and you'll find Albert Einstein's wild-haired, tongue-out image alongside the equation $E = mc^2$. A patent clerk's equation from 1905 became the cultural shorthand for genius itself. Why?

Einstein didn't understand how he became a cultural phenomenon. In 1942, Einstein's colleague and successor at the German University of Prague—physicist

Philipp Frank—asked him to write a foreword for a biography. Einstein agreed and wrote candidly. As Robinson records in *Einstein: A Hundred Years of Relativity*, Einstein confessed:

> I never understood why the theory of relativity with its concepts and problems so far removed from practical life should for so long have met with a lively, or indeed passionate, resonance among broad circles of the public. . . . What could have produced this great and persistent psychological effect? I never yet heard a truly convincing answer to this question.

Einstein's candor wouldn't see print until 1979. Publishers cut it from both the American and German editions of Frank's book. Perhaps his reputation had already grown too large for such contemporary vulnerability. And so Einstein's self-reflective question remained silent until long after his death.

His puzzlement illustrates a core idea in this book:

Expertise in a field ≠ expertise in thought leadership

Einstein understood relativity. He couldn't explain why it resonated with "broad circles of the public"—but the Impact Equation can.

$E = mc^2$ didn't just explain the universe. It demonstrated every element of our framework at work:

> **Idea simplicity:** $E = mc^2$ communicates profound truth in five memorable characters.
>
> **Audience relevance:** "Energy and mass are equivalent and interchangeable." That statement reshapes how people think about reality.
>
> **Velocity:** Einstein's equation traveled from academic journals to high school textbooks to popular culture. Educational systems, media,

and merchandising created massive system velocity that no longer requires Einstein's involvement.

Audience share: Initially published for theoretical physicists, $E = mc^2$ now reaches every student taking basic science.

In thought leadership terms, $E = mc^2$ provides an idea simple enough for systems to amplify long after Einstein himself has gone.

How Can You Create More Impact?

So, let's return to you and your work. You do not need to become the next Einstein. You do not even need your own "wonder year" to redefine your field. You may aspire to become the next Covey.

Your impact goals may be more immediate and short term.

Launch your core idea before it's perfect. Feedback improves both quality and impact.

- Pursue greater **idea simplicity**.
- Sharpen **audience relevance**.
- Increase **velocity**.
- Expand **audience share**.

Evaluate each component, and identify where changes—large or small—could multiply your impact.

As both the author of *The Speed of Trust* and the son of Stephen Covey, Stephen M. R. Covey discovered that inherited system velocity still requires an initial personal velocity input. Even the most sophisticated systems cannot create velocity until you put work into your own ideas.

"It was almost easier to say, I'll carve my niche out on the business side. And my father will be the thought leader," he admits. "I did have a little bit of fear, honestly, of the other side, because I thought I'd just be—no matter what—just a poor man's comparison to my father."

This positioning seemed logical. Why struggle to generate personal velocity when his father had crafted ideas that had broken through and were supported by powerful organizational systems?

Stephen's transformation came when he developed his trust framework: the twin concept of a trust tax and a trust dividend. Simple, memorable, and useful. "Speed of Trust" offered a simple platform identity that individuals and organizations could remember. "Once I found this trust message, it literally changed my paradigm. It also gave me the courage to follow in my father's footsteps and to have the audacity to write a book."

But before he could leverage system velocity, he needed to invest independent effort: "I knew I had to put it into the form of a book. I had to codify it, and then we could productize it."

Stephen's experience illustrates the Impact Equation's idea simplicity and velocity components in action: "I first really had to find my contribution, my voice that I felt passionate about, and then also that I had a distinctive approach to."

While Stephen faced the challenges of building idea simplicity and personal velocity despite inherited systems, Dorie Clark faced different challenges of audience relevance and audience share.

Dorie Clark, author of multiple books, including *Stand Out*, *Entrepreneurial You*, and *The Long Game*, recognized a fundamental vulnerability in her thriving thought leadership practice. Despite commanding significant speaking fees and maintaining a robust calendar, she faced what many successful practitioners eventually confront: the fragility of pure personal velocity and the risk of external shocks to demand.

"I was making a significant amount of my money from speaking," Dorie explains. "The perils that I foresaw were either that there would be a recession and so nobody would want to have conferences or that maybe I might get sick and just wouldn't be able to deliver, right? And so I was like, OK, well, that would be a problem. So I need to diversify."

Rather than waiting for a crisis, Dorie began deliberately building system-driven velocity through online courses and digital offerings. She blended her virtual presence with recorded material. Each online cohort helped her sharpen audience relevance and make her value proposition clearer. Dorie's foresight proved transformative when the 2020 pandemic eliminated live events globally.

"I felt very fortunate that for the past several years prior to that, I had been kind of, you know, tilling the garden in terms of creating online courses," she reflects. While colleagues scrambled to pivot digitally, Dorie had already established systems that generated impact without her physical presence.

Her strategic approach illustrates the Impact Equation in action: focusing on high audience relevance and creating new market offerings that gave her different ways to expand her audience share.

Different thought leadership avatars may prioritize different types of impact, but all must work within the Impact Equation to achieve results.

The Power of Compound Impact

Stephen Covey's choice to share rather than hoard didn't just create a bestseller—it created a multigenerational impact that proves the Impact Equation's deepest truth. His son Stephen M. R., who once feared being "a poor man's comparison," found his own voice precisely because his father chose abundance. The ideas in *7 Habits* didn't diminish through sharing; they multiplied through millions of readers, thousands of certified facilitators, and a second generation of Covey thought leaders.

The business consultants who advised against publishing saw only subtraction. Covey saw multiplication. His abundance thinking created the very systems that continue generating velocity today, decades after that initial choice. That's the promise—and the proof—of the Impact Equation: When you choose sharing over hoarding, *impact* compounds in ways that scarcity thinking can never imagine.

Self-Reflection Activity: Assessing Your Impact

1. **What ideas are you perfecting in private instead of sharing?** Name three insights you've developed but have kept locked away.

2. **If you had to multiply your velocity by ten through personal effort alone,** what would break first—your calendar, your health, or your relationships?

3. **Estimate your current velocity sources:**

   ___ percent from your personal effort
   ___ percent from systems that work without you

4. **What would advisors tell you not to share?** Where might their scarcity thinking limit your impact?

5. **Test your Impact Equation:**

   - **Idea simplicity:** Can someone explain your core idea after hearing it once?
   - **Audience relevance:** What problem does your idea solve that keeps people awake?
   - **Velocity:** What system could you build in ninety days to spread ideas without you?
   - **Audience share:** Are you trying to reach everyone (and therefore no one)?

6. **Who would champion your core ideas if you died tomorrow?** Have you made it possible for them to do so?

Next Steps

Chapters 4 and 5 gave you the fundamental frameworks: the Four Elements to organize your work and the Impact Equation to multiply its reach.

But thought leadership isn't one size fits all. In the next section, you'll meet the Five Avatars—five distinct approaches to thought leadership, each with unique motivations, strengths, and challenges.

In chapter 6, you will meet all five avatars. Identify which one most closely matches why you practice thought leadership and then turn to that avatar's dedicated chapter. Understanding your avatar will help you make smarter, strategic choices that align with your motivations.

SECTION TWO

THE FIVE AVATARS

Growth Minded CEO

Impact & Legacy Executive

Thought Leader on the Run

In House Expert

Hall of Fame Thinker

Chapter 6

Meet Five Thought Leadership Avatars

"Five thought leaders walk into a barbershop in Las Vegas." It sounds like the setup to a niche joke, but what happened next changed how we understand the field of thought leadership.

The Barbershop at the Cosmopolitan doesn't look like a place where breakthroughs happen. You walk through a working barbershop, step into a janitor's closet, and find yourself inside a speakeasy-themed bar with exposed brick, bartenders in sleeve garters, and a live band. On this particular evening in 2018, we'd gathered five successful thought leaders there, not realizing we'd accidentally assembled the entire thought leadership ecosystem in miniature.

Bill was halfway through his whiskey when the pattern emerged. The CEO who'd sold his firm to a billion-dollar think tank was now about thirty days into his first book tour, and he confessed that he'd started to feel tired saying the same things to different audiences. The former hotel executive laughed. "Mate, you're going to be talking about that book for years." Meanwhile, the technology executive was already thinking ahead to tomorrow's video session, and he asked Peter for on-camera delivery tips.

Over in the corner, a keynote speaker had just received editor's feedback on her first business book. She was looking at the markups on her phone and chatting with a veteran author of fifteen books about the journey ahead.

Five successful professionals. Similar tactics. Shared struggles. Completely different reasons for being there.

For twenty years, we'd organized thought leaders by their role: Speaker. Author. Consultant. Coach. But watching this group interact, Bill saw what we'd been missing for twenty years.

They weren't divided by *how* they practiced thought leadership. They were distinguished by *why* they practiced it at all.

That night marked a turning point in how we understood our field. The question that unlocked everything was surprisingly simple:

Not "*How* do you practice thought leadership?" Rather, "*Why*?"

Each of our five guests that night embodied a different answer, working toward a different goal. And over the following months, we reflected on the hundreds of practitioners we'd known and worked with. Five distinct patterns became clear to us:

- The Growth-Minded CEO
- The Impact and Legacy Executive
- The Thought Leader on the Run
- The In-House Expert
- The Hall of Fame Thinker

Each of these Five Avatars practices thought leadership. They all devote intense effort to polishing and communicating ideas to their audiences. And on a deeper level, it's often how they find meaning in their work.

These categories aren't permanent. They describe *why* people practice thought leadership. We've seen people shift naturally and fluidly between avatars as their goals change and their career evolves.

As you read this chapter, you may see yourself in one or more of these Five Avatars. And that's similar to our Las Vegas guests, who immediately recognized parts of themselves in each other.

The Growth-Minded CEO

I practice thought leadership to help my core business grow.

When you ask a Growth-Minded CEO *why* they practice thought leadership, their answer typically reveals sophisticated strategic thinking. They don't see thought leadership as basic content creation. They see it as a strategic lever for asymmetric competition. Here are some actual responses we've heard from CEOs who practice thought leadership:

- "I use thought leadership to get in rooms my sales team can't get to on their own."
- "We need to shift how the market perceives us—from commodity to premium solution."
- "We're competing against much larger organizations with vast marketing budgets."
- "Our startup is creating a new category. We need to educate buyers before we can sell."
- "We use thought leadership to deepen our relationships with existing customers."

The Growth-Minded CEO recognizes that when you can't outspend competitors, you must outthink them. Often you need to shift how your buyers think about a topic before you can even begin a sales conversation.

The Growth-Minded CEO who practices thought leadership can serve in many different roles and types of organizations:

- Founders of technology startups who list thought leadership as a dedicated use of venture capital funds
- Fortune 500 CEOs whose boards see direct return on investment from their public thought leadership
- Nonprofit CEOs who advocate for their cause with corporate and government partners

- Division presidents within larger organizations who use ideas to differentiate their business line within the marketplace

If you're a Growth-Minded CEO, you've assumed the additional responsibility of being a public voice for your organization. If you run a larger organization, you may have marketing teams and PR firms supporting you. If you're bootstrapping a startup, thought leadership may be one of many hats you wear.

Growth-Minded CEOs balance the very real constraints of time, energy, and competing priorities. They know that thought leadership is worth their time and their team's time. But their business school classes didn't cover thought leadership, and they didn't do a rotation as the head of thought leadership. Therefore, they often seek strategic clarity around where to put their efforts for maximum business impact.

The Impact and Legacy Executive

I'm either on my way out of my current role or I have retired. But I'm not ready to ride off into the sunset.

Impact and Legacy Executives have proven they know how to lead and create impact within organizations. They face a jarring transition as their departure date approaches or has already arrived. The entire machinery that has amplified their ideas, implemented their vision, and created velocity for their initiatives now responds to someone else.

The Impact and Legacy Executive practices thought leadership to navigate these profound shifts. When you ask them *why*, their answers reveal both ambition and vulnerability:

- "I want to share what I learned during my career—the things nobody taught me."
- "I've proven I can run a large company. Now I need to prove I can be relevant without the title."
- "Someone needs to advocate for this issue. I finally have time to do

it right."

- "I see thought leadership as giving back to the next generation."
- "I want to stay intellectually engaged while I figure out my next chapter."

When we say "retirement," we use the term broadly. This category also includes founders who have had successful exits, executives moving from corporate life into small-practice consulting, and those affected by restructuring and even unplanned and forced exits.

These executives don't lack postretirement options. They could join boards, play golf, or simply enjoy their success. Many do all these things, but Impact and Legacy Executives also find themselves attracted to thought leadership. Some are experienced with thought leadership—they practiced thought leadership in the C-suite. But for others, it is a new challenge—something they wanted to do but didn't have time for while leading their organization.

The Impact and Legacy Executive pursues impact through ideas rather than institutional authority. They're fluent in business, and they can leverage these skills. They often discover that thought leadership requires different muscles. They often seek continued relevance and the intellectual vitality that comes from grappling with important problems and sharing hard-won wisdom. Impact and Legacy Executives must learn to generate their own velocity in a world that no longer automatically amplifies their voice.

Sponsoring ideas without infrastructure becomes their next—and perhaps most challenging—leadership assignment.

The Thought Leader on the Run

I started studying a topic because I wanted to understand it better. Now people see me as an expert and will pay me for my insights.

Thought Leaders on the Run practice thought leadership everywhere—planes, trains, automobiles, conference stages, and virtual sessions. They've often stumbled into this life through curiosity about a specific challenge. And then it grew into a career.

When you ask them *why* they continue despite the demanding travel schedule, their answers reveal genuine excitement about their ideas. Their work is very integrated with their sense of self:

- "I can't stop talking about this idea. It changed my life, and it will be helpful to others."
- "Every time I deliver this content, someone has a breakthrough."
- "Organizations use my frameworks and see measurable results."
- "I'm living proof that this approach works."
- "The market keeps pulling me forward. I couldn't stop if I wanted to."

The Thought Leader on the Run typically operates as a solopreneur or with minimal support. They are simultaneously the product, the sales force, and the delivery mechanism. Their personal brand and their idea's brand become so intertwined that separating them seems impossible.

This creates a fundamental challenge: Their impact depends entirely on their personal velocity. Every speech, workshop, and consultation requires their direct presence. Success creates greater demand, which requires more travel, which demands more energy.

The Thought Leader on the Run has built something valuable—and exhausting. Yet the passion that sparked their curiosity still burns brightly. They genuinely love seeing their ideas create breakthroughs. They often can't imagine doing anything different.

Many Thought Leaders on the Run privately wonder about sustainability. How long can they maintain this pace? What happens when they need a break? Is there a way to create impact that doesn't require constant motion?

These questions become more urgent with each passing year on the road, especially when they realize that their greatest strength—being personally indispensable to their ideas—has become their deepest trap.

The In-House Expert

I practice thought leadership on behalf of my organization.

In-House Experts live between two worlds. When they step onto a stage or publish an article, audiences see both a company logo *and* a human being with distinctive insights. Their company's logo helps them get onstage or into print, but the audience wants to hear what they really think rather than what marketing has approved.

This dual identity defines their work. One moment you're the trusted industry voice everyone seeks out at conferences. Then, you're in an internal meeting with marketing and legal, finding the balance between what you'd love to say with what they consider "on message" and defensible.

In-House Experts are often highly social and charismatic. They constantly switch between internal champion and external evangelist. When you ask In-House Experts *why* they practice thought leadership, their answers reveal this unique balancing act:

- "I bridge what we know internally with what the market needs to understand."
- "My CEO wants me to shape industry conversations, and they also want me to stay on message."
- "I'm building my own reputation while advancing our company's ideas."
- "Half of me represents the company; half of me is just me."
- "I translate our technical genius into stories that make executives lean forward."

In-House Experts must constantly calibrate. They must maintain an authentic voice while speaking for an organization. They build strong personal brands without overshadowing company objectives.

They need enough personal credibility to be invited to speak, but not so much that they eclipse their organization. They must be provocative enough to get attention and careful enough to protect corporate interests. They're simultaneously the company's voice and their own person.

The most effective In-House Experts transform these tensions into advantages. Their organizational backing provides resources and reach that independent thought leaders envy. Their position between internal knowledge and external need lets them spot patterns others miss. They become bridges, making valuable connections visible while navigating demands that would exhaust most people.

Building a personal brand while serving organizational goals is the In-House Expert's daily tightrope walk. One wrong step, and they're either "too corporate" for external audiences or "too independent" for internal comfort.

The Hall of Fame Thinker

I want my ideas to outlast me.

Hall of Fame Thinkers have reached thought leadership's summit—their ideas shape industries, their books sell millions, and their frameworks enter MBA curricula. Yet when you ask them *why* they continue, their answers reveal a profound shift in motivation:

- "I'm not building a personal brand anymore. I'm ensuring that these ideas survive without me."
- "After twenty-five years of advocating for this concept, I'm focused on who will carry it forward."
- "The accolades were nice. Now I measure success by how independently my ideas travel."
- "I used to generate all the momentum myself. Now I'm building systems that create their own velocity."
- "My mortality is real. My ideas don't have to be mortal."

This focus on idea independence—rather than personal recognition—distinguishes Hall of Fame Thinkers. They've discovered that lasting impact requires transitioning from being the primary source of their ideas' momentum to creating systems that generate velocity independently.

Hall of Fame Thinkers share a distinctive persistence in promoting ideas while also systematically reducing their own necessity. They build certification programs, establish institutions, and cultivate next-generation advocates. They shift from being the star to being the architect of their idea's future.

One Hall of Fame Thinker told us, "I'm coming up on the twenty-fifth anniversary of my first book. The first ten years after it was published, I felt ahead of the conversation. Now, as I'm looking toward retirement, I see the idea that I advocated has been embraced."

What started as an outlier idea became part of the general business lexicon, but it didn't happen overnight. They spent years as a Thought Leader on the Run, taking their ideas anywhere people were willing to listen. Then, the idea started to gain system velocity and traveled without them.

The Hall of Fame Thinker has carried their ideas for years, if not decades. They have spoken about them to thousands of strangers. The person and the idea have become a symbiotic pair. They nourish and benefit each other. Ideas need the person to replicate in the world, and the person draws livelihood and purpose from the idea. It can sometimes be difficult to see where the person ends and the idea begins.

Yet, Hall of Fame Thinkers must embrace their professional mortality. If they are lucky, their idea will endure long beyond them.

Who Are You?

That night in Las Vegas, watching five successful professionals discover they weren't alone in their particular struggles, we realized something crucial: They'd been invisible to each other because the field organizes itself by tactics—author, speaker, consultant, coach—rather than motivations.

Each avatar you've just met can practice thought leadership through any modality. Growth-Minded CEOs aren't always keynote speakers; some write influential articles or host industry roundtables. Thought Leaders on the Run aren't always solo consultants; some are bestselling authors or workshop facilitators. In-House Experts might never write a book but instead reshape industries through conference presentations. Your *why*, not *how* you practice, determines your avatar.

You might have recognized yourself immediately in one of these descriptions. Or perhaps you see elements of several. That's natural, as people often transition between avatars as their careers and motivations evolve. The Growth-Minded CEO who sells their company might become an Impact and Legacy Executive. The exhausted Thought Leader on the Run might join an organization and become their In-House Expert.

In the next five chapters, we explore each avatar in depth: their unique challenges, their paths to success, their common pitfalls, and the choices they face. While you could read straight through, we encourage you to turn directly to whichever chapter calls to you. After all, understanding your *why* is the first step to creating meaningful impact through thought leadership.

Just as our Las Vegas guests found their real peers once they understood their deeper motivations, you'll find that your path forward becomes clearer when you recognize which avatar's journey most closely mirrors your own.

Chapter 7

The Growth-Minded CEO

Simple Truths

Kara Goldin was ready to throw in the towel.

The senior Coca-Cola executive had taken her call, and his response confirmed everything she feared. Fruit-infused water needed preservatives. Without them, her business, Hint Water, would never grow beyond farmers markets and local distribution.

I have no idea what I'm doing, Kara thought. *I know nothing about this industry. This is all way beyond me. Why did I ever get involved in the first place?*

She offered to hand over the company. "Why don't you just take over? I don't care if you pay me anything. I just want to get this product category out there, and you seem to have the resources to take on the challenge."

"Listen, sweetie," he said with a chuckle. "I've been in this business a long time. There's one thing I know. Americans want sweet drinks. Sure, you might sell your fruit drink in places like San Francisco, but outside of your friends in Marin County, no one really wants unsweetened drinks."

All she heard was "sweetie."

Hint Water had started in Kara's kitchen. She gave up her eight-can-a-day diet soda habit. She started slicing fruit into water. Her own health choices had led to a growing business.

When her husband concluded that shelf life without preservatives was impossible, Kara asked, "Well, what *can* we do?" They could deliver locally. Build their own solution. Work within constraints.

That's why the call to the Coca-Cola executive mattered so much to her. Was there something she had missed?

She had gotten her answer.

"I recognized all the politics behind how many of these brands are built," Kara would later explain. "Large companies can't really talk about health because they start to undo the rest of their products."

She thanked him. Genuinely.

He'd shown her what the giants couldn't do.

She now saw bigger possibilities. Kara couldn't outspend Coca-Cola. She couldn't outdistribute them. But she could say what they couldn't say. Champion health while they protected sweetness. Tell her kitchen story while they hid behind corporate messaging.

As Hint Water gained traction, tech companies started inviting her to speak—an AOL executive who'd left to start a beverage company was an irresistible Silicon Valley story.

Kara turned these speaking invitations into distribution strategy. "You need to stock Hint before I'll come," she'd tell organizations. "It's going to be really awkward and embarrassing for me to come and talk about this great product and you guys don't actually have it."

Tech companies stocked their refrigerators. Speaking engagements opened doors. Her founder story transformed Hint Water from commodity to premium.

"I don't sit there and ask myself, 'What would be a really good way to get a client from this?'" she explained. "I try to create something that's valuable to someone else."

The executive who had called Kara "sweetie" had revealed her advantage. While billion-dollar brands remained trapped by their own success, she would build her company on a simple truth they couldn't speak.

Health mattered more than sweetness. Kara had nothing to lose by saying so. They had everything to lose by admitting it.

The Power of Discretionary Speech

Every CEO has obligations to speak. Earnings calls, board presentations, regulatory filings. These requirements come with the office. Kara chose to speak beyond requirements. She told her kitchen story at tech conferences. She championed health while giants protected sweetness. She filled the space they couldn't enter.

Growth-Minded CEOs—whether they are CEOs, presidents, business unit heads, or CXOs—use thought leadership to drive business growth. They add voluntary advocacy to mandatory communication. They write books about transforming industries. They develop frameworks for others to follow. They speak at Davos and TED about the futures they want. They make the possible more probable. Whether boards push them or they push themselves, they've discovered what required speech will never accomplish.

Required speech keeps companies operational. Discretionary speech transforms them. The Growth-Minded CEO sees the difference everywhere: which key talent joins their organization, which peer CEOs take their calls, and how they position against shifts competitors miss. When they can't outspend rivals, they outthink them. When distribution is limited, stories travel where products can't.

The CEO role is always temporary. Fortune 500 CEOs inherit institutional amplification that vanishes at retirement. Founders like Kara slowly build their own amplification, but even this relies on their active presence. The voice that comes with any position—built or borrowed—belongs to the position. When the CEO leaves, the amplification stays behind.

For Growth-Minded CEOs, this temporality creates urgency. Every day in the office brings them closer to leaving it. Every speech chosen means another forgone. They could advocate for sustainability, transformation, workforce development, or stakeholder capitalism. They can't champion everything.

When Growth-Minded CEOs stay silent, others fill the vacuum. Consultants define best practices. Competitors shape expectations. Activists frame problems. Regulators set agendas. The conversation continues with or without them.

Kara could have championed the safe topics of business school case studies: supply chains, consolidation, or operational excellence. She chose health over sweetness. Year after year, speech after speech, that choice revealed what mattered most. Not through mission statements or values posters but through the scarce currency of executive attention.

Limited voice reveals what you value most.

I'm Glad You Asked

Janet Foutty, US board chair at Deloitte, worried about sending the emails. She described the moment as "maybe one of the scariest moments I've had professionally."

To understand why Janet—who led Deloitte Consulting through $10 billion in growth while she was CEO—felt such strong fear, you need to understand both what she was risking and why she was risking it.

"In professional services and consulting, thought leadership is part of what we do every day," Janet states. She'd done it her whole career—developing perspectives about markets, crafting frameworks for clients. That was all required speech. Part of the job.

But writing a book? "That was not in my grand life plan whatsoever," she admitted to us, first as a guest on our podcast and then later as a client as we worked on her thought leadership strategy.

The book project first began when Simmons University approached her. Its new president, Lynn Perry Wooten, was one of the few Black women university presidents in America. Its teams suggested Foutty and Wooten write a book together on women's leadership, along with a third coauthor who brought leadership coaching expertise.

Janet's first thought was dismissive. *Really? That's what the world needs—another book on women's leadership?* The market was saturated. Her calendar was full. This wasn't required speech for a consulting company's CEO.

She took the first conversation begrudgingly. But when the three women talked—academic, consultant, and coach—they began a weeks-long search for what wasn't already being said. Then Janet identified it.

"There's so much written around 'How do you get there?'" she observed. "But once you're there, how do you thrive?" Books explained arriving into leadership. None explained thriving once there. *Arrive and Thrive* would address that silence.

To fill that gap authentically, they couldn't just write from their own experience. They needed senior executives to share their truth. Which brought Janet to this moment where she faced the Send button. She had identified twenty-two of her most accomplished clients. She wanted to interview them for the book.

"Senior people are very careful about where they lend their names," she says. These executives ran major corporations. They could easily decline. Or delegate to assistants—professional courtesy at arm's length.

She emailed them rather than called. It was "less fearful than picking up the phone," she admitted. She offered two options: "Write up your thoughts, or do a live interview." She sent all twenty-two messages.

She expected written responses, probably drafted by staff.

The first response came back: It was a yes. The executive wanted a live interview.

The second: another yes. Live interview. "I don't want to just talk about one or two of these practices. I want to talk about all of them!"

By the end, all twenty-two executives had said yes. All but one wanted live interviews.

"What shocked me was that we got yes responses to all of them," Janet recalled. The gap she'd identified wasn't theoretical. These executives had been waiting for someone to ask about thriving, not just arriving.

The book's impact surprised her further. Deloitte partners started buying copies for clients. Not to showcase Deloitte methodologies. Not to pitch services. But to start different conversations with their clients.

Partners reported buying copies for clients, "opening conversations they would not have been able to have." These weren't about digital transformation or operational efficiency. They were personal conversations about struggling with success, about the isolation that comes with thriving.

"I had not thought about something that I had written being helpful to them in a very personal moment with their clients," Janet reflected.

A Fortune 250 CEO speaks with a borrowed voice. The amplification belongs to the office, not the person. Janet could have spotlighted any initiative, championed any methodology.

Janet chose women who thrive in leadership. Not Deloitte's core expertise. Not the $10 billion growth story. She invested time she couldn't reclaim. She risked relationships she had spent decades building.

Each interviewee could also have said no. Their executive time and voice were precious resources.

They all said yes.

Their stories and the book became a catalyst for conversations.

Knocking on Doors

Kelly Breslin Wright joined Tableau one month before it launched version one of its visual analytics platform. She had never been at a big public technology company before. "We were figuring out things on our own, like how do we go build this?"

Kelly started her sales journey in college, running her own business selling educational books door-to-door. She carried a twenty-five-pound book bag. A no came in many forms: "Not interested" was the most kind. Hundreds of doors slammed in her face. Dogs were let loose on her. Police were called.

Kelly learned to create conversations from cold encounters, setting sales records because she connected with people as people. But she also learned that not everyone would listen or say yes—a lesson that would shape everything she built at Tableau.

Over twelve years, they figured it out. Kelly built Tableau's sales organization from zero to almost $850 million in revenue. But the real discovery wasn't in the revenue numbers. It was in understanding how they'd achieved them.

"We were trying to do thought leadership before we even knew it was called thought leadership," Kelly muses. Tableau's mission "to help people see and understand data" shaped every customer conversation. Not because leaders mandated it but because employees genuinely believed in the mission.

Kelly noticed something about her top performers. "If you look at the top sales leaders and then top salespeople, they're really great at thought leadership." They weren't reciting features and functions. They were challenging how companies thought about data. They articulated the status quo, identified its problems, and painted a picture of transformation. They told stories that mattered: why they personally joined Tableau, why the company existed, and why the customer's future could be different.

It was easy to teach product specifications to new salespeople," Kelly says. "The much more challenging part is to be able to tell a story: Why does this matter? Why should customers even care?" Most companies skip this part of sales education because it's hard work and everyone's moving fast. New employees get taught the *what* and *how*, but it's much harder for them to grasp the *why*. If they don't fully get the *why*, how can they persuade the customer to change? But Kelly saw that the confusion about *why* extended far beyond frontline salespeople all the way to the top of organizations.

After leaving Tableau, Kelly met with 130 technology CEOs, founders, and investors in eighteen months. Each conversation revealed the same disconnect. When she asked about mission and vision, many executives struggled to answer, even when their statements were written in bold on their corporate websites. Worse, when she asked different executives from the same company to explain their company story and their *why*, their answers didn't match. Yet, when Kelly suggested that culture drove sales performance, they dismissed it.

"Kelly, we don't want to have a conversation with you about mission and vision. We want to have a conversation with you about operational efficiency."

"I literally just don't understand where they're coming from," Kelly explains. "Their alignment problems were obviously cultural. But they couldn't see it."

Kelly had built a culture-driven sales organization at Tableau. She could consult with companies individually. But could she frame these ideas in a way that didn't require her presence? Could she help companies connect culture and sales without being on their executive team or a board member?

Kelly believes that company mission, vision, and values are the basis for the company's *why*. They provide the foundation for the company culture. This culture helps the company emotionally connect with customers. She explains the cascade this way: "If execs aren't aligned on culture, they aren't aligned on their *why*. And if they aren't aligned on their company story, how in the world could they expect top sales results from their go-to-market teams?"

Kelly came to Peter and Bill with questions about her own thought leadership and strategy. She was already teaching at the University of Washington about culture in sales. She had stories and insights from years of building sales teams.

We explored her content library together, and as outsiders, we saw a pattern. "Culture-Driven Sales" wasn't just an observation. It could serve as the platform identity for Kelly's thought leadership. The three stories every salesperson needs. The priority of people over metrics. These insights could form a systematic approach for companies and individuals to implement without her.

Kelly qualifies her thought leadership audience exactly as she taught salespeople to qualify prospects. "Not everyone is going to buy what you're selling," she acknowledged. "Much of my time was focused on people who already believed mission and culture were critical. I had a harder time making an impact in organizations that didn't already believe what I believed."

This wasn't failure but strategic focus. With limited bandwidth, Kelly chose depth over breadth. By redefining her target audience, Kelly created greater impact with the same amount of effort.

"That's why it's called thought leadership. If everyone already believed it, there wouldn't need to be thought leadership around it."

Today, Kelly champions "Culture-Driven Sales" through her teaching, consultancy, and board work, with a future book planned. She knows the leaders who want operational efficiency aren't wrong. Operations matter. But Kelly had learned something at Tableau that she couldn't unsee. Culture is the story. It motivates employees, attracts customers, and grows companies. When salespeople tap into this culture to challenge worldviews rather than pitch products, they create a competitive advantage no budget can buy. Someone has to tell the company's story and the idea's story.

We Put Almost Everything in the Books

"We hated your books."

That's the review every author fears.

This critique came from a competitor—a European entrepreneur who'd built a networking organization to compete with Dr. Ivan Misner's BNI. It didn't work as planned. The entrepreneur split with his business partner, and he arranged a meeting with Ivan.

Ivan had founded BNI (Business Network International) in 1985. The concept was simple. Business owners meet weekly to exchange referrals. By 2025, BNI had grown to over 11,400 chapters worldwide with 335,000-plus members. Each chapter is part of a franchise using BNI's system and brand.

Why would Ivan's books create business nightmares for BNI's competitors?

The competitor explained that the books were everywhere.

"We would walk into groups, *our groups*, and they would have your books. Our members would ask us, 'How come you guys aren't doing this?' They told us we needed to give them better stuff. 'This guy, Ivan Misner, is telling us how to network. You guys are throwing us in a room, and you're not telling us how to network.'"

The competitor's members owned Ivan's books, and they wanted what only BNI delivered.

This feedback validated Ivan's forty-year strategy of giving generously. As founder and chief visionary officer, he led BNI. For most of his forty years, no board restricted his topics. No shareholders questioned his choices. He could have protected every framework and charged for every insight. Instead, he'd published thirty books revealing virtually everything.

The books explained his core principles. How giving referrals creates reciprocal value. Why accountability drives network success. How to structure meetings for maximum referral generation. These weren't generic networking tips. They were BNI's crown jewels, the foundation that franchisees paid to access.

Anyone could buy the books. Anyone could visit a BNI chapter as a guest. Ivan held back only the operational mechanics.

"Things that are very, very BNI centric, such as how we run a meeting and the 'behind the drapes' processes, we don't share publicly," Ivan explains. "But otherwise, everything's fair game."

He gave away the *why* and *what*. He only protected the precise operational *how*. Competitors could learn the philosophy of "Givers Gain." They couldn't replicate forty years of embedding it into organizational culture.

The strategy began with failure. His first book, *Networking for Success*, was published in 1989. "If you don't recognize it, it was because I think I sold twenty copies." That humiliation taught him something unexpected. "I discovered that the media will interview anyone with a book. And now I have thirty books."

Books didn't generate direct wealth: "I'm not sure I've ever made a lot of money on book sales through bookstores," Ivan admits.

The books served different purposes. Media interviews opened doors. Speaking opportunities reached potential franchisees. Most importantly, books prequalified prospects. Readers who embraced his philosophy became franchisee inquiries. They understood what they were buying before BNI ever made a sales call.

Every Wednesday, Ivan writes. "I set at least a day a week aside. That's my writing day. I write all day. Usually on Wednesdays." He faces no deadline. No assignment. As a founder with his own corporate voice, he could write about anything. He's written about networking for forty years.

His calculation was deliberate: "Very few people will go through all the stuff I've ever put out, compile it together, and then create a business that will compete with me." Even if they tried, he says, "You can steal stuff, you can steal people's ideas, but it's hard to steal culture."

Competitors proved this repeatedly. They'd announce, "We're BNI without the rules" and fail. "It's like hockey without rules would be boxing on ice," Ivan observes.

BNI's growth validated Ivan's thought leadership strategy. In the first eleven years, BNI formed five hundred chapters. After embracing radical content sharing, the next eleven years added five thousand chapters.

Each new book expanded the market of people who understood structured networking. Franchise inquiries followed book releases. Member recruitment became easier when prospects already knew the philosophy. Books didn't just share knowledge. They built BNI's business.

Corporate CEOs reveal their values by choosing between competing priorities with limited time. Ivan had forty years to focus on networking. His Wednesday discipline and his radical transparency weren't requirements. They were pure choices.

BNI's European competitor had copied the content, but they couldn't satisfy the actual demand the books created. Readers wanted the culture of systematic generosity that took decades to build.

Ivan, a founder who could have protected everything, chose to give the ideas away within thirty books over forty years.

His sustained choice of generosity built an empire worth more than any secret he could have protected.

Authentic Voices in the Right Places

Kerry-Ann Stimpson recognized the problem after twenty years in marketing. "I felt like I (my personal brand) kept hiding behind the company brand." As CMO of JMMB Group, one of Jamaica's leading financial institutions, Kerry-Ann knew that its marketing resources commanded real marketing power. Not as much as competitors who outspent JMMB three to four times, but enough to compete. She'd built campaigns, crafted messages, and managed the corporate voice. But the voice wasn't hers. If she felt this way, how did other employees feel?

The question mattered because traditional marketing was no longer enough to win. Competitors dominated traditional and digital marketing channels with their larger budgets. Yet the conversations that determined which financial institution (FI) Jamaicans trusted happened where no campaign could reach. WhatsApp threads between mothers and daughters. Private emails among business partners. Direct messages asking a friend, "Is JMMB right for my savings?"

"There's so much going on that we absolutely don't see," Kerry-Ann says. These invisible "dark social" channels shaped which FI won customers. JMMB's employees already lived in those channels. They had the right relationships. They had earned their trust. They just didn't know how to use their voice.

Kerry-Ann searched for resources about internal marketing and employee advocacy. "At the time, I could find none." No one was teaching organizations how to market to employees to help activate their voices authentically. That gap became her thought leadership opportunity. "That's really at the heart of thought leadership," she says she realized. "It's about having conversations in a way that no one else is having them."

As a personal project, she launched *The Internal Marketing Podcast* for marketers searching for answers. At JMMB, she created her own case study.

"I always subscribe to the belief that people ultimately work for themselves. They don't really work for the company." Most executives never say this aloud. Kerry-Ann built her strategy on it.

She asked across JMMB, "Who is interested in building a personal brand?" The response overwhelmed her. Sales teams, operations staff, customer service representatives. They didn't want corporate scripts. They wanted authentic expression.

Her podcast also reached marketing practitioners worldwide. JMMB's employees reached Caribbean customers in their private conversations. No paid marketing campaign could buy that type of access. One corporate voice was supported by hundreds of employees.

In regulated financial services, where compliance reviews every statement, where one careless comment could trigger regulatory scrutiny, Kerry-Ann chose radical trust, in line with the company's core values. "We trust you. We've employed you. Go ahead and do your thing."

The results proved the strategy. Despite being outspent four to one, JMMB dominated brand mentions and sentiment on social media. "When we look at brand mentions, they're coming from people. They're coming from customers. They're coming from team members. They're coming from friends and family."

One employee, also a travel blogger, grew their presence and followers. Another earned coaching certification and started a practice. Each authentic voice reached conversations no billboard could enter.

"We (the official company voice) literally can almost stay silent most days,"

Kerry-Ann says about traditional marketing. The company didn't need more campaigns because "the voices of the people who are aligned with us and who are loyal to us carry our message."

As CMO, Kerry-Ann made the same choice as any Growth-Minded CEO: Use discretionary speech to drive growth where traditional marketing couldn't.

The public square had fragmented into countless invisible conversations. No single voice could reach them all. So instead of pursuing omnichannel marketing, she recruited and empowered scores of voices. Each employee became a bridge to conversations no corporate campaign could enter.

CMO tenures run slightly shorter than other C-suite roles. Marketing strategies rarely outlast their creators. But every employee who finds their voice extends Kerry-Ann's philosophy beyond her tenure.

When You Run into Your Own Idea

When Growth-Minded CEOs practice discretionary speech, the public evaluates their motives. Do they truly believe it? Does the story serve only them, or does it offer value others can embrace?

Kara Goldin understood this test. By the time she was leading a $150-million-plus company with products distributed in all fifty states, she had come far from her initial desire to find a healthier alternative to her soda habit.

Kara had filled a space the beverage giants couldn't enter. While they protected sweetness, she spoke health. While they hid behind corporate messaging, she told her kitchen story. The public square they vacated became her platform.

During Hint Water's explosive growth, Kara spent four years writing *Undaunted*. "I found there aren't any operating CEOs that I could find that are writing books about what it was like to grow the company while they were still at the company."

Her writing was discretionary speech. Pure choice. "For me, it was almost therapy," she explains. Every page written was time not spent on operations. She wrote anyway. "I didn't sit there and do it for any other reason than to actually really help people."

After the book came out, emails confirmed that her choice mattered. Readers who lost jobs started companies after reading her story. Her discretionary speech became their permission to try.

Through four years of writing, hundreds of speeches, and countless interviews, Kara consistently chose to amplify the kitchen origin story and the health message. She embraced the idea that outsiders could build what insiders couldn't imagine.

One day, Kara ran into her own ideas while at a hotel with her daughter. They overheard a woman recommending Hint to her friend.

"I heard the founder started it in her kitchen. It's really an interesting product!"

The woman was retelling the origin story as if it were her own discovery to share.

Her daughter looked at Kara. "Did you tell her yet?"

"I have red hair. I'm fairly easy to recognize," Goldin would later say.

The woman never knew.

Kara's kitchen story was now traveling without her. The woman who they overheard was now telling the story herself.

She'd taken the hint and made it her own.

Kara witnessed what every Growth-Minded CEO hopes for: the idea independently thriving in the world.

Kara could have told the woman who she was. She could have claimed the story.

She didn't need to.

Chapter 8

The Impact and Legacy Executive

The Call That Changed Everything

The newswires were buzzing. Baxter International's CEO, Harry Kraemer, was retiring after leading the global healthcare company for seven years. Congratulatory calls and messages came in. And then Harry's mentor, Northwestern's dean emeritus Don Jacobs, called him. They had stayed close through the years.

For twenty-five years, the dean would call Harry every two weeks with an ask: "I need you on a panel" or "I need you as a guest speaker." This call would be a special moment between a mentee and his now eighty-year-old mentor.

Jacobs didn't start with congratulations: "You're leaving Baxter? Thank God." And before the words had settled, the dean continued, "I want you to teach."

This call was not going the way Harry had expected.

"You don't mean like I have a syllabus. Grade papers," Harry protested. "That's not happening. Right?" He ran companies. He didn't teach. Northwestern's Kellogg School of Management had brilliant PhDs who'd spent careers researching leadership theory. They didn't need a retired CEO. Did they?

The dean's sigh carried four decades of patience. "I think you said you do *whatever* I told you to do."

That promise—made decades ago by a young Harry Kraemer asking for mentorship—hung between them. Harry couldn't say no.

Harry's new dean finished the conversation.

"You'd better get a syllabus together, because you start in two weeks."

At Baxter, Harry's ideas became initiatives. His questions launched teams into action. Fifty-five thousand employees transformed his vision into refined execution. The organizational infrastructure had responded to him for decades. Soon, Harry would be standing alone in front of students who had no obligation to find him insightful.

In two weeks, ex-CEO Harry would learn how his first students would respond to the ideas he valued so deeply.

Leading After Authority

At Baxter, Harry had sponsored values-based leadership with budgets, mandates, and performance metrics. He'd proven that values could drive performance despite quarterly pressures.

Yet without an executive sponsor, even proven truths disappear. The customer service champion retires, and service budgets get cut within months. The innovation advocate leaves, and R&D becomes incremental. Core values become posters. The next CXO champions a new vision, following the inevitable pattern: essential, then optional, and then forgotten.

Impact and Legacy Executives face a question that will shape their future: How do you sponsor ideas without your former title?

The question carries weight they hadn't anticipated. At sixty-five, seventy, even eighty, they're acutely aware of time's arithmetic. Which truths deserve their remaining years? Which battles are worth the energy they once spent freely?

For decades, these executives had lived their principles in real time—no pause for reflection between crises, no time to document what worked while racing toward the next quarter's targets. Their wisdom existed in action. Only now, without meetings to run or earnings to report, could they finally translate the lessons they'd lived into something others could learn.

Most Impact and Legacy Executives, Harry included, developed ideas while in the C-suite. And they sponsored many others. They have experience turning ideas into impact. That's invaluable experience, and it may be why many of them turn to thought leadership.

Yet, there's a critical difference. While leading organizations, they used the Impact Equation in a very different way. Comms teams helped bring simplicity to ideas; researchers sharpened relevance; and data scientists measured the audience share.

The system velocity that carried them and their ideas forward comes to a sudden halt at retirement. Imagine the end of an airport's moving walkway. Some executives manage the transition back to personal velocity smoothly. A few stumble. And most executives need a moment to adjust to having zero velocity. Then, they start generating velocity under their own power or building/borrowing systems to increase velocity.

We'll return later to Harry Kraemer, who would find his answer in Kellogg's classroom. But first, we'll meet six executives who encountered zero velocity. There, they discovered what sponsorship means when everything familiar disappears—and time becomes precious rather than endless.

All Dressed Up, but Who Cares?

One of our clients, Rose Fass, found zero velocity while cleaning a broken elevator at 9:00 p.m.

After years as chief transformation officer at Xerox, directing corporate change with Fortune 100 resources, Rose now stood in a converted post office preparing for her startup's first potential client. She'd spent the night scrubbing floors, trying to make the shabby space presentable for an executive from Estée Lauder.

"I felt like Gertie Schmerz," she recalls. "I had become a nobody from nowhere. I was a nervous wreck, thinking, *I have no logo. I'm all dressed up, but who cares? I got an elevator here that doesn't work that I've been cleaning all night.*"

When the Estée Lauder executive arrived—they'd just acquired MAC Cosmetics—Rose faced her existential moment. No corporate campus. No staff. Just her and her cofounder, Gavin McMahon, a whiteboard, and whatever expertise actually belonged to them.

"When the man walked in the office and we had a little whiteboard and we started to talk, all of a sudden I just brought myself to the conversation," Rose remembers. "And that's when I realized it's not the props. It's your authentic self with that individual."

What followed surprised her. Without Xerox's infrastructure constraining her, she could move faster, see patterns more clearly, solve problems more directly. The conversation led to her first contract—$60,000 that meant more than any Xerox deal because it proved that her expertise had never needed corporate apparatus to exist.

That meeting in a converted post office became the foundation for her company, fassforward, now serving Fortune 500 companies for twenty-five years.

They even have a working elevator.

Yet some truths can't be transmitted through consulting conversations alone. They require the patient work of translation—making forty years of lived wisdom accessible to those who need it most.

From Leading to Codifying

When Noel Massie retired from UPS, over four hundred frontline managers sent letters thanking him for elevating their careers. As VP of US operations, Noel had led two hundred thousand employees through twelve thousand managers. Twenty-three of his direct reports themselves became presidents at UPS. Yet, after retirement, Noel couldn't stop thinking about frontline managers.

Noel remembered his first supervisory role at UPS. He was nineteen, working nights in a distribution hub. A fiftysomething employee had refused his directive. Twenty other employees on the floor watched closely. How would the young Noel respond? Noel could have failed to meet the moment, but he was ready for it—because a senior leader had regularly walked the floor and discussed leadership with the frontline supervisors. "He just wanted us to know that we mattered," Noel recalls. "I patterned my leadership style off of him."

As Noel rose as a leader, he led book clubs for his direct reports. He gave out leadership books. "But the books that were missing were always the down-in-the-weeds books" for first-time managers.

When Noel retired from UPS, he left the title and role behind. But he knew he could help these young leaders. Noel would no longer walk the line himself and mentor young leaders, but he could write a book that would serve the next generation of new leaders at UPS and any other organization. Noel decided to fill the gap in leadership books himself, with a book he titled *Congrats! You've Been Promoted.*

Writing the book took longer than expected. He hired a book coach and wrote a complete draft. The coach told him to start over. "I wrote a thousand pages to come up with the two hundred and fifty." He persisted through four years of effort. "Fast is not better. Hurried is not necessarily good," he says he learned. "I came up with thoughts in the second year of writing this book I didn't have in the first year."

What drove his obsession with creating this book? He wasn't trying to prove he mattered. He wanted to ensure that the next generation of young leaders would thrive. Noel didn't need to write this book.

But somewhere, a twenty-seven-year-old will face their first leadership crisis. And Noel's four years of work will be there, giving forward what was given to him. Noel had become the advocate that the senior leader had been to him. But now he was reaching thousands through pages rather than walking factory floors. "What are you leaving of yourself behind?" Noel asks. "What legacy are you leaving on this planet?"

Sometimes, an Impact and Legacy Executive will continue to carry an idea, such as Noel's focus on frontline leadership development, into their retirement. Other times, an idea that ends a career becomes the seed for a career in thought leadership.

Speaking for the Unmeasurable

The board meeting that ended Yosi Amram's CEO tenure was swift. The MIT engineer had built Individual into an IPO-ready pioneer of machine learning that offered personalized news before Google existed. Yet, he had become unrecognizable to his investors. Following a spiritual awakening during the road show, he'd returned with visions of Individual becoming the next high-profile social media darling.

"I wanted everything done yesterday," Yosi recalls. "My board thought I was nuts. My team thought I was nuts." The verdict was unanimous. He was out.

"I lost everything that was familiar to me. I lost my job. I lost my sense of identity. I lost my relationships. I lost my home. I completely unraveled."

Yosi, the math and science kid from Israel who'd followed the perfect trajectory—MIT engineering, Harvard MBA, and successful founder—now faced a question that his degrees couldn't answer: "Was it craziness? Was it delusion?" He had a spiritual awakening. But what did that mean? And was it personal, or did it tie to business, like he felt it must?

This question demanded methodology, not meditation. Yosi earned a PhD in clinical psychology, applying engineering rigor to spiritual territory. "I interviewed seventy-one spiritual teachers and leaders across all the world's traditions," seeking patterns in what boardrooms dismiss as irrelevant.

The same systematic thinking that had built machine learning algorithms now built psychometric measures, creating what Yosi describes as "the first academically validated measure of spiritual intelligence." Over time, the data became clear. His research correlated spiritual intelligence with leadership effectiveness, providing data for what his board had rejected as delusion.

Today, Yosi coaches executives at companies with multibillion-dollar valuations—leaders who seek him precisely because he survived the unraveling. "My trauma and my history are my greatest gift," he reflects.

The organizational velocity that once carried Yosi's tech vision forward had expelled him for seeing beyond quarterly earnings. So he built different velocity—through research, frameworks, and coaching relationships. Yosi became the champion for intelligence that has no quarterly metrics and no board approval but drives the leadership effectiveness organizations desperately need.

The engineer who'd been fired for unmeasurable visions had found a way to measure them.

When a company rejects an idea, it comes in many forms. Sometimes, as for Yosi, it comes swiftly with the direct clarity of a board voting the executive out.

In most organizations, resistance builds more slowly. Organizations create robust systems. They value process consistency and continuity. If you sponsor change, you create disruption. Do that once, and the system may be surprised. Do it too many times, and you may be labeled a disruptor.

Becoming the Outsider Looking In

Amy Radin had spent decades as a marketing, digital, and innovation executive at companies including American Express, Citigroup, E*TRADE, and AXA. At Citi Cards, she was viewed as "the person who had the outside perspective." The innovator. The one seeing things differently. "When you get to very senior levels of the kinds of companies I've worked at," Amy reflects, "that's not always the most comfortable place to be."

She'd mastered the art of driving change through organizations "set up to make things predictable, routine, eliminate risk." She understood the politics: "Whenever you have two people in a room, you're going to have politics." She navigated the budget battles: "There's only so much money to go around." She'd become expert at making disruption palatable to risk-averse systems.

That expertise had made her invaluable. And increasingly invisible.

"When you're in a big company, it's just hard to be that person," Amy explains—the person repeatedly saying, "We have to change things." Years earlier, a journalist friend had heard her talking about innovation and suggested she write a book. She'd "parked that idea," continuing to navigate corporate complexity from inside.

The recognition came gradually and then suddenly. "Companies are very welcoming of people who come in just for a little while to bring a fresh perspective, and then they go away." The outside voice commanded respect, compensation, freedom—precisely because it came from outside. The inside voice, no matter how expert, would always fight organizational gravity.

Amy made a calculation. She could remain inside, politically savvy but increasingly constrained. Or she could step outside and speak the truths organizations desperately needed but couldn't generate internally. "I ultimately decided that I would rather truly be the outsider looking in and helping people trying to innovate actually drive change."

The Change Maker's Playbook took her sixteen months to write. "This is a great way for me to realize my purpose," she says she discovered, "which really is to look at things differently and help people rethink things." The same corporations that had constrained Amy's thinking now pay premium prices for it, because it comes from outside their walls.

In addition to consulting, Amy also teaches technology leaders to think more like outsiders. Her Strategic Advocacy course at Columbia University's MS Technology program is designed for technology leaders with real-world implementation challenges. "When they enter the classroom, I ask them to set aside their leadership responsibilities and think like a student. That framing allows us to discuss the implementation challenges together. They've faced these challenges at work. I've faced them as a consulting practice."

Amy maintains her outsider position as a consultant and teacher while constantly engaging with the technology leaders responsible for delivering results. Her classroom and client work reinforce each other, keeping her teaching practical and her consulting sharp.

Some Impact and Legacy Executives, like Noel, find themselves focused on very similar target audiences. Others, like Amy and Harry, expand their audience to include graduate students. Yet, some executives discover that their ideas no longer have a built-in audience. The message they value most may be met with skepticism or even disinterest. In this situation, the Impact and Legacy Executive may need to shift target audiences and sometimes even redefine how they measure success.

Recalibrating Success

Joe Davis had led Boston Consulting Group (BCG) North America through one of its most challenging periods. During the COVID-19 pandemic, he discovered something unexpected: "It was a great time to be a leader—if you led with empathy, were able to connect with your people, and were a good listener."

He'd spent over thirty-five years at BCG opening offices, building business units, and leading thousands of people through crises. People told him his guidance changed their trajectories. His empathetic approach proved exactly what organizations needed during unprecedented uncertainty.

So, when a friend suggested he write a book about his leadership experience, Joe hoped publishers would take an interest. He crafted a manuscript, drawing on his COVID-19 leadership insights. He shared the moments when connection mattered most, when listening made the difference, and when empathy drove results.

The editor's response was swift and decisive: "No go."

"Nobody will want to read about the COVID times," she explained. Without BCG's brand behind him, Joe's COVID-19 leadership insights, the very insights that had guided a global consultancy through crisis, suddenly held no market value.

Joe rewrote the book, expanding beyond the pandemic, interviewing executives he knew through BCG's network. A friend offered him perspective: "Joe, if you move eight people to maybe change their leadership style a bit, it'll be successful."

Eight people. Joe had shifted from leading BCG North America to hoping for eight readers for his book, *The Generous Leader*.

Joe reoriented his perspective. He would share his insights on empathy and connect them to business results. He couldn't force people to read his book. But Joe could make it available to those who wanted to listen.

"As a CEO, it's really easy to measure success. Did we hit our goals? Revenue? Stock price?" he reflects. Now? "Am I feeling good about what I'm doing?" Then his five-year-old grandson cuddles with him: "When that happens—ah! Today was a good day."

Joe found what matters when you leave the system: not the third Ferrari or the fancy title but "the people who said, 'You know, Joe, you said this to me, and that just changed my trajectory.' That feels good."

Joe became an advocate for an idea where experts saw no market: Leadership is human connection. He is not chasing the bestseller list. Instead, he's putting his ideas into the world and trying to reach a receptive audience. If even a handful of leaders shift how they lead, "that's a good day"—for him, for those leaders, and for the people they lead.

When you leave your organizational affiliation behind, you may need to redefine success. But you can also create new affiliations and tools to help you achieve your goals. You describe a vision of a possible future and invite others to join you on the adventure.

Putting Pitons into the Climbing Wall

Brigadier General Tom Kolditz (Ret.) had studied how to transform teenagers into battlefield commanders. He had alternated between leading combat units and studying leadership psychology. He chaired West Point's Department of Behavioral Sciences and Leadership. The US Army's infrastructure amplified his every insight—from his office to curriculum to thousands of cadets to hundreds of thousands of soldiers. Then, watching another class of future officers, he confronted a question that would unravel everything: Why should leadership development require wearing a uniform?

"I had a realization while I was there that you don't have to go to a service academy to learn to be a better leader," Tom recalls. "And I would daydream about how great it would be at a private university, if there were the resources and the intent to create a leadership engine." The daydream was really an existential challenge. If leadership could be taught within the military structures, why wasn't it being done effectively elsewhere?

When Tom left the military, he left behind the most committed leadership culture imaginable—albeit one limited by command and control processes and the ineffectiveness of mandatory participation. At Yale School of Management, then as founding director of Rice University's Ann and John Doerr Institute for New Leaders, Tom faced higher education's individual-performer culture. The teaching and research faculty had little or no leader development experience. The students focused on individual performance rather than on becoming leaders.

"Higher education is failing in the leadership mission," Tom states bluntly about universities claiming to develop leaders. The Doerr Institute's research showed that of "2.2 million college graduates a year, the vast majority are graduating with high school–level leadership skills." The system that had served him so well in the military didn't exist in academia. He would have to build it from nothing.

Tom recruited a team for the Doerr Institute. But he didn't stop within the institute or even within Rice University. He recruited support across academia and beyond it, including our team at Thought Leadership Leverage. He and the team at the Doerr Institute built partnerships and leveraged expertise. The strategy was simple: Spark discussion, attract like-minded leaders, and build systems.

"We have built a coalition that's now eighty schools, representing almost two million students." He partnered with the Carnegie Foundation, creating classification systems that would make leadership development as institutionalized as research rankings. He sent three copies of his book, *Leadership Reckoning,* to two hundred top university presidents and provosts. Tom wanted to provoke conversation and attract leaders who would join the mission of evidence-based ways to build more and better leaders.

"When a mountain climber goes up a rock wall, they put pitons, these metal stakes, in the rock. So that they can't fall back any further than they already did," Tom explains. "As you move forward, you have to put pitons in the wall, so that nothing gets undone that you've already done." Each partnership, each classification, each converted university president becomes permanent infrastructure generating velocity without him.

The military taught Tom that systems outlast individuals. At the Doerr Institute, he turned his West Point question into an open-source system for leadership development in postsecondary education. He sought to build an evidence-based, scalable system that would reliably produce "more and better leaders."

According to Tom, "The service academies, especially West Point, claim that they are 'the world's preeminent leader development institutions.' Yet, unlike the Doerr Institute, they have no one-on-one professional leadership coaching, no formal measurement of leader development effects, no leadership performance of their graduates beyond that of top ROTC schools, and no significant contributions to national or international development like the Doerr Institute and the Carnegie Foundation."

"More and better leaders" meant stepping outside the service academies and looking at the cohort of emerging leaders. It required putting the pitons in the wall so that the systems would outlast his direct involvement.

Tom left the executive director role in 2022. The Doerr Institute continues to create impact with evidence-based leadership development for new leaders. Now in its tenth year, the Doerr Institute has directly developed more than seven thousand students at Rice University who have opted in to their programs. More than five hundred students a semester work one-on-one with professional leadership coaches. This approach to leadership development will generate more and better new leaders year after year. And the effect will compound for decades.

Each Impact and Legacy Executive, from Tom Kolditz's infrastructure architecture to Rose Fass's revelation, created their own answer to the challenge of sponsoring ideas without the title. Harry Kraemer would find his answer through an unlikely teacher: a twenty-six-year-old student who refused to accept no for an answer.

What's Worth Your Time

Harry Kraemer settled into teaching at Kellogg, and he loved it. He looked forward to the first day of classes each term. One day, a twenty-six-year-old graduate student approached Harry after class. "You should write a book," the student said.

Harry dismissed him: "I don't even write short emails."

The student persisted. Five times.

Finally, Harry tried executive authority: "Forget it."

But the young student did something no Baxter employee would have dared. He ignored the dismissal entirely.

The student audited the class again the following term, recorded everything, and delivered 250 pages of transcripts to Harry's office.

The student willed Harry's first book into existence through sheer refusal to let these ideas stay within just the classroom walls. If Harry didn't use the transcript to write a book, then the student would self-publish it on his behalf.

Harry relented.

Harry's dean had seen the need from the beginning. "Thank God," he'd said when Kraemer left Baxter. Not because Baxter constrained Harry but because Harry's values-based leadership needed a voice that wasn't shaped by Baxter's quarterly reports.

Harry's reluctant first book became a deliberate trilogy of books. Northwestern provided the platform, students the energy, and Harry the wisdom. All book proceeds flow to the One Acre Fund, supporting smallholder farmers in East Africa.

"If I can teach at Kellogg the next twenty years and make a small impact on values," Harry reflects, "it's astronomically more important given the crazy world we're living in today."

No quarterly earnings. No stock price. Just the intrinsic satisfaction of ensuring that values-based leadership reaches organizations worldwide through students he's taught and readers he'll never meet.

An Impact and Legacy Executive's work often begins when previous careers end. If you are about to retire or have retired, there are plenty of noble activities worthy of your time. One of them is thought leadership.

As a former executive, you know how to sponsor ideas and drive projects and conversations forward. You did that work inside your organization; across your industry; and with customers, clients, or consumers.

You already have many of the skills needed to excel in thought leadership. There are plenty of ideas in the world that need executive sponsors. You can choose whatever idea aligns with your passion and your values.

What idea will you champion?

Chapter 9

The Thought Leader on the Run

The Cyclic Practice

"Resistance will help you rise."

One of our clients, Shannon Huffman Polson, taught this concept on stages across the country. In helicopters, you take off into the wind to create lift.

She'd used this principle in Bosnia in the mid-1990s, one of the first women flying Apaches. Now, as a keynote speaker, she translates it for leaders who'd never sat in a helicopter cockpit facing the risk of enemy fire.

After eight years in uniform, Shannon earned her MBA at Tuck, worked in the medical device industry, and then moved to Microsoft, where she was selected for the high-potential group. The trajectory was clear.

Then her father and stepmother were killed by a grizzly bear in Arctic Alaska. She left Microsoft to follow their final path, retracing their steps physically and writing a memoir, *North of Hope: A Daughter's Arctic Journey*.

That first book led to speaking. Free webinars through the 85 Broads (now Elevate) women's leadership group. Then New York Life called for a paid speaking engagement. The calls multiplied. Each organization wanted the person who'd exhibited the grit to fly an Apache helicopter and rebuild after personal tragedy.

Living in eastern Washington meant every keynote consumed multiple days. Drive hours to Seattle. Airport hotel overnight. Fly out. Deliver. Fly back. Drive home. "It has developed with a lot of work and sweat equity right into a career."

She started The Grit Project, interviewing military women, gathering stories. When a young army lieutenant entering flight school asked Shannon to mentor her, the request sparked a realization: *How could I scale it to be available to others as well?*

Three years of research followed. Phone interviews with dozens of women in groundbreaking military service roles. The result was *The Grit Factor: Courage, Resilience, and Leadership in the Most Male-Dominated Organization in the World*. The book presented a holistic leadership framework with a focus on concepts of grit and resilience. She shared the stories and lessons she had learned herself as well as from the leaders she interviewed. "Grit" became her thought leadership platform identity.

Shannon brought both MBA strategy and MFA writing craft to her practice. "I love the literature part of my life and the creative part of my life. But I also realized I really love the business part as well." As a writer, Shannon saw how the self and the idea intertwined onstage.

"The story is a delivery mechanism for the idea," she would tell audiences. "It can't be about you. There's a lot of people that want things to be about them, but it's about the idea, and you're just relaying the idea in a unique way."

The tension lived in her practice daily. She was both the teacher of "Grit" and the Apache pilot who had lived it. The storyteller and the story. Which one did buyers value more?

When COVID-19 hit, there were "six months of complete and total quiet." No stages. No flights.

The silence revealed the economics: Organizations could find her ideas about "Grit" on YouTube or in her book. They would pay a premium for Shannon to speak in person.

When the conference stages reopened, the old pattern returned.

"You're just going to have to hustle a lot, right? If you're any kind of an entrepreneur at all, that has to be part of your DNA, or it just isn't going to work."

Another drive to Seattle. Another overnight. Another flight. Another stage.

Resistance will help you rise. But what happens when you can't stop leaning into the wind?

The Red Queen's Race

When Shannon was onstage, she embodied her ideas about "Grit." Her presence was the delivery mechanism. She translated military experience into leadership lessons.

Keynotes and workshops required her voice. Audiences expected the Apache pilot who'd conquered fear.

Thought Leaders on the Run are created by market forces. Organizations pay premium prices to witness them share their ideas directly. Why?

Psychologist Mihaly Csikszentmihalyi spent decades studying how humans enter a flow state and how it unlocks optimal performance and happiness. Steven Kotler, building on this work in *The Rise of Superman*, argues that we, as audiences, spend extraordinary amounts to watch athletes and artists achieve flow. We want to be present when a record is broken, when our favorite musician plays in town, or when it's the hottest Broadway show.

In each case, live presence carries a premium cost. Tickets to a local touring show of *Hamilton* will cost far more than watching the original cast's video on a streaming platform.

We see this huge price differential in thought leadership as well:

TEDx Talk online—free.

Hardcover book—$30.

In-person keynote—$30,000.

An author's book contains many more stories, frameworks, and tools than a forty-five-minute keynote. In some ways, the book is a more complete version of the idea, and it is also a reproduction of the original and the individual.

The book, as a physical object, lacks what Walter Benjamin called "aura," an authentic presence that can't be mechanically reproduced. Audiences want to be there to witness your expertise made visible in real time. They want interactivity. They hope to ask questions. They want you.

You're incentivized to speak, to consult, to facilitate, and to coach, because the market will pay a huge premium for your in-person, irreproducible aura.

You live what Lewis Carroll called the Red Queen's race: running fast just to stay in place. You generate income through travel and in-person work. Yet, you still need time to collect new examples, craft your next newsletter, and plan your next book.

When will you find business development time? Are those business cards you collected at your last event still tucked into your jacket pocket? Or are they in your laptop bag? You might need to look to be sure.

When you're always in motion, evolution stops.

When buyers see you as the primary source of value, they want *your* time, *your* presence, *your* voice speaking truths.

You become both the carrier of ideas and the bottleneck for growth.

Many Thought Leaders on the Run recognize the problem, but they apply only a partial solution.

When demand exceeds your available supply, you can—and should—raise your in-person rates. But that's staying within the rules of the Red Queen's race. You're still running, just for a higher fee.

A few thought leaders actually change the rules of the game.

They realize that personal and business transformation is hard to execute from seat 3C. And so they build new systems while maintaining existing ones.

The five thought leaders whose stories follow each found their own response.

Some sustain through discipline. Others transform. All learned what Shannon was learning: Resistance creates lift, but only if you survive the wind.

Going Off Script

Dr. Dravon James's phone rang. She had been caught going off script.

Dravon, a pharmacist, delivered monthly training in long-term care facilities. She talked about pharmacy and federal regulations, but she knew the nurses were stressed. They did heavy emotional work with the patients they cared for.

One day she worked up the courage to insert a few minutes of her own content. "Before we go to Q&A, I want to talk about something that I'm passionate about and maybe helpful for you."

The nurses leaned forward. Dravon talked for a few minutes about what she calls "Everyday Peace": "wholeness, completeness, and nothing missing. Totality." During Q&A, the questions changed. Not about compliance anymore. About finding wholeness when everything felt broken.

She made three minutes about peace a standard part of every facility visit. Dravon reflects, "I did it without permission." She waited for a call, either from a client or her employer, that would tell her to stop.

Instead, the call came from a conference organizer who had heard about Dravon's "extra" content and wanted more. "We do not want you to talk anything about pharmacy," the organizer said. "You know, that little peace thing you do at the end of your talks? Would you be willing to do that?"

A full keynote. Not on federal regulations. On her idea, "Everyday Peace." They wanted forty-five minutes of what she'd been sharing in three-minute fragments.

"I definitely had to figure out a keynote," Dravon admits.

In one sense, this keynote would be her first on "Everyday Peace." But in a larger sense, she had been preparing her keynote since she was only seventeen years old.

That year, her brother had borrowed Norman Vincent Peale's *The Power of Positive Thinking* from their mother's bookshelf, and he gave it to Dravon before she went to college.

Dravon read the book at least twenty times that summer. "I thought, *Eureka! I found the formula for never having a problem ever in my life.*"

Life's problems found her anyway. But they taught her something the book hadn't—that peace wasn't about avoiding trouble but finding wholeness inside it.

Long before she ever introduced "Everyday Peace" in a two-minute version, she had been preparing. She had developed her own framework. She filled journals with talks nobody asked for. Thirty-minute versions. Sixty-minute explorations. She wrote for herself. She practiced speaking to empty rooms.

Dravon chose this work. She was studying "Everyday Peace" for herself so that maybe one day she could share it with others. She was gathering knowledge, organizing it, and finding how to make it relevant to her audience. If she was going to share the idea of "Everyday Peace," she wanted to do it well.

When Dravon was asked to deliver a keynote on "Everyday Peace," she wasn't stretching two minutes of content into forty-five minutes; she went into her content library and chose carefully crafted and polished material.

Dravon's first keynote still terrified her. "It was a humbling experience because, of course, I was nervous." Healthcare professionals who lived in data, outcomes, and evidence-based practices. Here she was with a talk about wholeness and completeness.

The feedback overwhelmed her. People were using her words, making small changes, and reenergizing themselves and their teams. "I was humbled to know that, wow, this is impactful."

Dravon discovered what defines early Thought Leaders on the Run: You prepare in darkness for years, not knowing you're preparing. You smuggle your truth into other people's agendas. Then someone calls, wanting only the thing you've been sneaking into your talk.

"All of our power exists within this moment," Dravon says. The seventeen-year-old thought she'd found a formula to avoid problems. The adult discovered she'd been preparing to help others—especially exhausted healthcare workers—find their own Everyday Peace.

Dravon had first become what she would teach. Her presence brought peace. The market had found her.

For now.

Years separate that first yes from sustainable practice. Some remain hobbyists. Others go full time. All face the same economics. Your methodology might be brilliant. Strong market offerings and platform identities help. But the market pays most for authentic presence—you delivering your ideas in real time.

As a Thought Leader on the Run, your ideas move only when you do. You are their voice, their chaperone, and their advocate. When you work, they travel and create impact. When you rest, they rest. Your presence *is* the product.

The Michelli Way

Dr. Joseph Michelli embedded himself inside Mercedes-Benz for three years. He guided its climb from twenty-second to first in J.D. Power rankings. He translated its transformation into his book, *Driven to Delight.*

This wasn't new. For twenty years, Joseph had been perfecting this approach. Pike Place Fish Market. Ritz-Carlton. Starbucks—twice. UCLA Health System. Zappos. Each embedding lasted years. Each produced a bestseller. Each book became the calling card for the next transformation. By the time he reached Mercedes, then Airbnb, clients were buying eighteen hundred copies of his next book sight unseen.

The wheel Joseph built is elegant. Embed for years. Guide the transformation. Write the book. Tour the speaking circuit. Other consumer-facing companies read the book and reach out to Joseph: "We want to be the Mercedes of our industry." Back to embedding with a new client.

After decades perfecting customer experience at the world's best brands, Joseph hasn't created a framework others can deliver. He is the method. The wheel never stops.

"You're only as good as your last book," Joseph says. Each success raises stakes for the next. Each embedding demands more proof that only Joseph Michelli can translate an organization's excellence into a bestselling book.

"My model has always been very labor intensive for me," he admits. "Either I'm keynoting, I'm consulting, or I'm writing the book." Always him. Every client wants Joseph Michelli personally embedded in their company. Three years at Mercedes. Two at Starbucks. His life can be measured in other companies' transformations.

"I blog every single week," Joseph says. "It is a discipline of mine. It's one of the few good characteristics of me as a person." Week after week, from wherever the current project takes him. The discipline maintains his voice between transformations.

Twenty years translating what makes companies extraordinary—the precision of Mercedes, the warmth of Starbucks, and the joy of Zappos. Joseph has had insider access while retaining his authentic voice and credibility. Now, he wrestles with what every Thought Leader on the Run faces.

"How do I take all this stuff I've created over my career and start compartmentalizing it into products? I'm really just starting to figure it out."

After two decades perfecting his craft, he wonders if his translation role can be taught, if his excellence can be bottled.

Yet listen to him describe his work: "I love what I do. I can't imagine doing anything better for a living. I pinch myself all the time. I have lots of bruises from that, actually."

Those bruises mark someone who built exactly what he wanted—so perfectly suited to who he is that he can't quite believe it's real. The wheel works because it's him turning it.

Beignets and Coffee

At dawn, Waldo Waldman is already grinding on the gym bike. Heart rate at 135. iPhone in hand, he's studying his client's world. Not for fun. He's got a keynote that afternoon, and he prepares like he's back in the F-16, flying combat. Same discipline, different mission.

After twenty-four years and more than eighteen hundred keynotes, you'd think his urgency would fade.

It hasn't.

Bad knees. Aching back. More missed family dinners than he cares to admit. Yet he's sweating at sunrise, treating this speech like it's his first.

"Because I'm their wingman," Waldo says. "But they're also mine."

When the CEO and head of sales show up fully engaged on the pre-event intel call, he knows it'll be a great event. The commitment flows both ways. He owes them preparation. He owes them his full presence.

He owes it to his craft. For him, "growth is not an option when you want to stay relevant."

So, when Dan Thurmon, his friend and fellow Hall of Fame speaker, delivers a keynote in town, Waldo sits quietly in the back of the room, ready to learn.

He could be home, recovering from his last trip. Instead, Waldo studies what makes thought leadership real, raw, and relatable. He gets tested every time he takes the stage.

"I was about to speak at a conference with high-level executives and entrepreneurs. The client paid my full fee and had high expectations," Waldo recalls. "It's the end of day two. The audience is exhausted. While the host is introducing me, half the audience gets up to leave, lured by the irresistible smell of fresh beignets and coffee. Networking in the hallway. Laptops open. Eyes glazed over."

All that prep. Seemingly wasted.

The complacency missile tries to lock on.

He could coast. Flip to autopilot. Cash the check. Go home.

But Waldo doesn't ease off. He can't.

He focuses on the people who stayed in the room. The leaders who need his message on trust, courage, and resilience. He thinks about the people not in the room, the two thousand employees who aren't in the ballroom. Those people in the trenches back home, turning the wrenches, doing the unsung-hero work.

"If I back off now, I give my audience permission to back off tomorrow," Waldo says. "But if I stay locked in and deliver with full throttle regardless of their attention, then I model what they need to bring back to their teams."

"If I don't deliver on my commitment," he tells himself, "I don't deserve to be here. I haven't earned the fee. I don't deserve success."

He carries this self-accountability forward proudly, grounded in a question from his combat days:

"Can I depend on you?"

That question, once asked silently by his squadron mates, echoes before every keynote. It separates real thought leaders from those who stopped asking it long ago—polished professionals who've forgotten why they speak and overlook the unseen people who depend on their words.

"This AI world is coming fast," Waldo notes. "But human presence can't be faked. Not by a bot. Not on Zoom. Definitely not on stage."

What audiences pay for isn't frameworks or flashy stories. It's watching someone refuse to flinch when the room empties out. "Delivering from the heart, not just the head," he says.

That earns trust.

His evolution from *Never Fly Solo*, about building cultures of trust, to *Commit, Commit!*, about breaking one's fear barrier, reflects this shift. He's distilled this idea down to just a few words: "It's not what keeps you up at night that matters. It's what gets you out of bed."

What keeps you from coasting when no one's watching?

"Fear keeps you up at night," he says. "Purpose, meaning, responsibility get you out of bed. These things convert anxiety into energy."

Waldo doesn't want his audiences to say, "Waldo gave a good keynote."

He wants them to say, "We saw Waldo ten years ago. He's even better now. More relevant. More real. More human."

That standard pushes him to earn his wings every day. Even when some audiences aren't his audience.

"You have to be mint chocolate chip in a vanilla-chocolate world," he says. Distinct enough that when the right audience finds you, they know you're exactly what they need.

He could have coasted long ago. That's when the complacency missile would catch up with him. He'd let down the people in the room. Even if they're strangers he will only meet once for forty-five minutes in Vegas, they still deserve his best. Because each person in the room has many people relying on them: their colleagues, direct reports, customers, and clients.

Every morning, Waldo pushes up the throttle, renewing the promise at the heart of his Wingman's Credo:

"You can count on me."

From Independence to Interdependence

Morag Barrett spent fourteen years in UK banking keeping a stiff upper lip through toxicity. "The British way."

She had a micromanaging boss who took credit for her work. A resentful peer. "There were many days when I was close to quitting," she admits in

Cultivate. Instead, she epitomized the World War II meme: Keep Calm and Carry On. "I did nothing, I said nothing, and I hoped the quality of my work would somehow win out."

It did. But the silence came at a cost. "I was stressed out, continuously looking over my shoulder, concerned about what might happen. What a waste of energy." Her self-confidence crumbled. Morag moved from "leading with my strengths to operating from a fear of failure." Without allies and trust, she found herself playing small, second-guessing decisions, and holding back ideas for fear of rocking the boat. When people play small, everyone loses: the individual, the team, and the wider organization.

After she launched SkyeTeam, her leadership development consultancy, that personal cost began to reveal itself. She recalls designing a full-day workshop for a new client, confident in her prep, until the group and event went off script within thirty minutes. She remembers feeling sick to her stomach.

Morag could've clung to her agenda and tried to pull the group back. Instead, she stopped talking and started listening. Leaning into the breakthrough they needed in the moment taught her a lasting lesson: Leadership is not about perfection. It's presence, adaptability, and cocreation.

"One of the mistakes I've made, certainly in the early part of my career, was I valued independence versus interdependence. Learning to embrace interdependence and let go of control has been my catalyst ever since."

That philosophy shaped Morag's writing. She was a solopreneur when she wrote *Cultivate*, but she didn't write it alone, though she did try! "Writing the book is hard. Getting ready to launch a book is hard. Selling a book is hard. Getting people to write reviews online is hard." Hard.

Recognizing this fact, Morag formed a book advisory board comprising senior leaders who volunteered to read chapters as she drafted them, challenged her thinking, and encouraged her to weave in her personality, stories, and case studies from the teams she had coached. The result was a book grounded in practice as much as principle.

Interdependence only deepened with her third book, *You, Me, We*, coauthored with Eric Spencer and Ruby Vesely, her best friends at work. She describes the collaboration with pride. "We are the role models for *You, Me, We.*" The title itself is a declaration. The woman who once epitomized Keep Calm and Carry On now proclaims, "One plus one truly becomes three when we're acting as allies."

Morag's journey mirrors her message: from independence to interdependence. From holding tight to inviting others in. The question that drives her has shifted from "Do I have a best friend at work?" to "Am I a best friend at work?" From perfect control to abundant collaboration.

Morag changed her approach to thought leadership. She rejected what fourteen years of banking taught her. As it turns out, business *is* personal. Connection beats perfection. What began as a survival strategy, keeping calm and carrying on, became a calling: to help leaders move beyond survival into connection, where trust, allyship, and collaboration fuel real performance.

The Gambler Who Kept His Chips

Hundreds of executives crawl on their hands and knees, scrambling across the carpet to collect specially designed playing cards. The room rocks with loud music and high energy.

Stephen Shapiro, the creator of this experience, smiles as "these executives swap cards and negotiate like kids at recess. They leave clutching those cards like treasures, physical proof of something essential." In a world dominated by digital, people crave something tangible. A simple deck of cards had become a tool for unlocking collaboration.

Stephen didn't start his career as a Hall of Fame speaker who deals out cards. He made a series of risky and bold bets. Some didn't pay off for years. Others he regretted. At times, he wondered whether he had made a terrible mistake.

Seven years after graduating from Cornell with a degree in industrial engineering, Stephen was a rising star as the coleader of Accenture's business process reengineering practice. "My job was to streamline operations, squeeze out inefficiencies, and deliver measurable results." It looked like a perfect career. Another city. Another client on-site.

But one day that changed. Stephen returned to his hotel room and turned on the television looking for something interesting. "I saw a documentary about my current client. It followed three executives who had been laid off a year earlier," he recounts.

One former executive was surviving on an inheritance. Another sobbed as he described mowing lawns to feed his family. The third had taken his own life.

Stephen couldn't look away. "What had once been just a number—ten thousand jobs lost—suddenly became heartbreakingly real to me."

The next morning, Stephen confronted his client: "Are the stories true?"

"Yes."

Stephen walked off the project and never returned.

Stephen would no longer work on projects that destroyed lives. Instead, he placed a bet: He would help companies grow instead of shrink their way to profitability. "Innovation was a radical idea in the mid-1990s. Many of my colleagues warned me. They said I was risking everything."

Stephen was persistent, and he received support from senior leaders. He built a twenty-thousand-person innovation practice inside Accenture. He taught consultants and clients how to fuel growth rather than engineer cutbacks. And that's exactly when he walked away again.

Stephen left Accenture in November 2001—on the same day he launched his first book, *24/7 Innovation*. The early years as a solo speaker and consultant were tough. Revenue and clients were scarce. "In my first five years combined, I earned less than I had in my final year at Accenture. More than once, I wondered if I had bet everything on the wrong hand."

Then, in 2006, he created a card game called Personality Poker, a fast way to reveal innovation styles and team dynamics. Clients loved it, but Stephen pushed it aside. He kept chasing the next book and the next idea. He eventually published seven books and multiple products. Personality Poker was always his favorite, yet it remained in the background while he promoted the next hot topic.

In 2025, almost twenty years after creating the game, he placed his boldest bet yet: He would stop chasing trends. He would finally go all in with Personality Poker.

"I love going to Vegas," he explains. "You have to place a lot of bets, knowing some hands will win and others will lose. The key is knowing when to double down." What Stephen has learned is not just how to play the game but how to choose the right table.

Organizations beg him to scale it. Certify trainers. Build an empire. But Stephen resists. "That would be more work than I want," he says. "I need to do what I do best and find partners for everything else." No employees. No infrastructure.

Twenty years after leading a twenty-thousand-person practice, Stephen runs a practice of one. For him, the ultimate jackpot isn't size or scale. It's freedom. And that, he believes, is the smartest bet he ever made.

Pull on the Collective

Shannon Huffman Polson knew the thought leadership routine.

You wake early for the outbound flight. You deliver your presentation. You head home to respond to inquiries and send invoices.

Her thought leadership work had become cyclic for her.

As a helicopter pilot, she recognized she'd been "flying" her thought leadership practice with just one control.

Helicopters use two controls to fly.

The cyclic tilts one blade at a time. It creates directional motion—forward, back, and sideways. The collective tilts all blades and provides lift.

Shannon applied these physics for years flying Apache helicopters. She hadn't seen her thought leadership practice following the same laws.

For years, pure cyclic worked. Flight school. Bosnia. Tuck. Microsoft. Keynoting. Each cycle built her reputation and created new demand. She kept moving forward.

Things changed for Shannon when she agreed to mentor the young lieutenant entering flight school. Others needed her help to create their own lift.

She spent three years documenting the stories of women in the military, and that became her book, *The Grit Factor*. The Grit Institute followed.

She developed asynchronous leadership training that can be deployed either B2B or B2C through the Grit Institute.

She became faculty at the Tuck School of Business at Dartmouth's Leadership and Strategic Impact Program.

Shannon created systems that could raise everyone. She had pulled back on the collective. "It's been amazing." What worked in helicopters worked in her thought leadership practice.

Companies paid. Systems scaled.

But veterans couldn't afford what corporations bought. The women whose stories she'd documented lacked access to their own wisdom.

Shannon pulled harder on the collective. Corporate keynotes could support free access for veterans to the Grit Institute's online programs.

She led a funding campaign that raised $6.5 million to build the first library in her rural Washington state community. Individual momentum and direction paired with collective lift.

"If we have skills to offer for the betterment of our societies, we have an obligation to offer those abilities up." Shannon delivers on her obligation through the physics she'd always flown.

Her personal velocity also generates collective access.

Shannon knew how she could advance herself and also help others rise. She'd been flying it for years.

You work both controls—cyclic and collective—or you don't fly. Shannon leans into the wind.

Her answer wasn't choosing between perfection and scale. It was using both controls. The resistance she used to get into the air now lifts others as well.

What we've witnessed over twenty years is that Thought Leaders on the Run don't just manage exhaustion; they navigate transformation. Personal transformation as they discover who they are beyond the stage. Business transformation as they build systems that outlast their stamina.

They rarely travel this path alone. They build friendships among their peers. They seek help from consultants and specialists.

Over two decades in this space, we've watched the lines between client, colleague, and friend dissolve into something richer.

Take Waldo Waldman. Peter first met him through Keith Ferrazzi's network twenty years ago. They were two guys from New York who understood each other immediately. Their initial client-consultant relationship focused on Waldo's thought leadership strategy. That relationship evolved into cross-referrals, shared family vacations, and staying at each other's homes. Waldo "the Wingman" Waldman gained Peter as another wingman.

Shannon Huffman Polson came to Peter and Bill for strategy, returned for book development, and then built the Grit Institute. We've supported each other over the years.

Steve Shapiro and Peter spent months launching the first edition of *Personality Poker* in 2006, the gambler and the strategist finding unexpected friendship. And as of 2025, they are actively collaborating on a relaunch of *Personality Poker.* In thought leadership, paths cross and recross.

These relationships span decades because the work of thought leadership spans decades. We witness someone's evolution from their first terrifying event to sustainable practice, from exhaustion to transformation, from isolation to community.

Dr. Dravon James's journey in thought leadership began with her talk on "Everyday Peace". It might take her anywhere.

But she doesn't have to travel alone. Nor do you.

Chapter 10

The In-House Expert

"Whose Spot Is This?"

Jayshree Seth stared at her phone in Amsterdam's Schiphol Airport, hearing the news from her boss.

"There's a discussion with the CTO. You're going to be offered an additional role: chief science advocate."

Jayshree held eighty patents. She had risen to corporate scientist, the highest technical designation for scientists at 3M. In 2019, she was inducted into 3M's prestigious Carlton Society—the company's science and innovation "Hall of Fame." Jayshree became the first female engineer admitted since the society's founding in 1963.

Chief science advocate? The news took her by surprise.

Jayshree replied, "There is no chief science advocate position at 3M. So, whose spot is it? What is this?"

Jayshree was being asked to champion science to the world. Yet, growing up in northern India, she had never seen herself as "the science type" at all.

As a young woman, Jayshree had a different purpose in mind. "I wanted to make the world a better place and help people improve lives."

She was skeptical about math and science: "I wasn't particularly inspired, because I didn't see how STEM connected with what I thought I wanted to do."

Jayshree wasn't alone. "Now, I realize that a lot of young girls have very prosocial goals like that. And that context is critical. Unfortunately, nobody explained the context of science and STEM roles to me."

This disconnect followed her even as she continued her STEM education. During her master's program, she struggled to connect her work to anything: "I was sitting at my desk doing computer modeling all day long. I just wasn't sure. What am I doing? Why am I doing it? And most importantly how does it help anyone? There was no emphasis on bringing any context in. And at the time I wasn't savvy enough to be able to understand it."

Without seeing the human impact of her work, she felt like an outsider in her own field.

The turning point came when she began to forge connections others didn't see, developing what she would later call her "mosaic-building" approach: "What I do in the lab is to develop products that solve customer problems or market problems. It takes understanding what the pulse of the market is, what the trends are, what the competitive landscape is. So it's kind of like a very multifaceted approach bringing all these tiles together. You take a step back and you say, 'Aha, that's what I'm seeing.'"

That's how she found herself in Schiphol Airport, learning she would be offered the opportunity to become 3M's first chief science advocate. Unsure if she should accept.

Jayshree knew the need was great. 3M's global State of Science Index had revealed a troubling disconnect with how people understood science: "Forty percent, four out of ten people around the globe, said that if science didn't exist, their lives would be no different."

Yet, the same people who said nothing would change were taking the online survey on their laptops and mobile phones, devices that wouldn't exist without scientific advancement.

Where others saw a knowledge deficit in the State of Science findings, Jayshree saw something more troubling. The survey showed people around the world had lost the context that makes science matter.

"Science is invisible. It's underappreciated. It's taken for granted, and that is the problem." Perhaps only someone who'd almost been excluded from science could see its invisibility so clearly.

Even so, Jayshree nearly rejected the offer of chief science advocate: "I'm going to have to tell them that I can't do this, because I never thought of myself as the science and engineering type."

Jayshree could have easily remained silent and chosen not to speak. She could continue to lead her lab and be a respected leader in 3M and in the engineering community.

But science advocacy clearly required a voice. If not her, who would speak? So, Jayshree said yes.

The In-House Expert's Position

Every day in your role as an In-House Expert, you embody contradictions that shouldn't be sustainable by one person. You translate between languages that struggle to coexist: academic rigor and business urgency, technical complexity and human simplicity, organizational loyalty and independent advocate.

Your position often allows you to speak truths that your organization needs but cannot say itself.

Your authentic voice pushes corporate communications and legal departments to their limits, yet they need you to speak. Your peers can't place you on the org chart, yet they refuse to have key conversations without you.

You don't try to resolve these contradictions. You inhabit your superposition—the quantum state of indeterminacy. You exist in a place of both/and. As the In-House Expert, you can speak truths, make connections, and build bridges.

Giving a Second Opinion

Craig Joseph, MD, was surprised when Nordic Consulting's CEO approached him with an intriguing job description. He had approached Nordic twice before joining. Both times, they discussed more traditional roles—medical advisor, clinical consultant, quality improvement lead. Each time, Craig declined. He'd been chief medical information officer at sophisticated hospitals across the country. He'd worked at Epic, the leading electronic health records vendor, telling hospitals, "This is how successful healthcare systems do it" rather than asking how they wanted to set it up.

Craig had been the pediatrician who coded and also the programmer who had treated patients. He understood healthcare's dysfunction from many angles.

This time, when Nordic's CEO approached Craig, they offered him a different role—chief medical officer with thought leadership as a core responsibility. Craig said yes.

The job description: Increase the company's visibility in the space, speak publicly about difficult truths in healthcare, and serve as Nordic's voice to healthcare organizations.

A year later, Craig's CEO walked past his office and said, "I think you should write a book."

Craig looked up from his desk in surprise.

Is this a passing thought or an actionable request, he wondered.

But by the time he could ask the question, the CEO was already long gone down the hallway.

A few weeks later, in a leadership meeting, Nordic's CEO asked about the book. Craig had his answer. Soon, he and his coauthor, behavioral neuroscientist Jerome Pagani, PhD, were tasked with writing a book on behalf of the company. But what would they write about?

Craig and Jerome sought out Peter and Bill at Thought Leadership Leverage to help guide their "write a book" mandate from concept into a printed book Nordic could give to its clients and prospects. They and Nordic Consulting became clients of Thought Leadership Leverage. We helped them identify each of their Four Elements, craft a book strategy, find writing support, and help bring the book into the world.

Craig brought his clinical insights and technology background. Jerome counterbalanced him with academic depth and conceptual rigor. "I like to blurt out things, and then Jerome tears them apart," Craig explains. Neither let the other settle for comfortable half truths.

Their sparring became their method. Craig, the clinician, identified dysfunction, and Jerome, the scientist, uncovered the mechanisms and explored the psychological underpinnings.

Some months later, they had a manuscript draft and convened Nordic's leaders and stakeholders for an internal review.

"I see you titled one of your chapters 'Getting Rid of Stupid Stuff (GROSS).' It's almost like you're implying that our clients often make stupid decisions."

"I am, and they do," Craig responded.

But he wasn't being reckless.

Craig simply pointed to the *New England Journal of Medicine* article that used GROSS in the title.

The executive relented immediately, because Craig had done exactly what Nordic had hired him to do.

He made unspeakable truths speakable through unimpeachable authority.

Craig explains that he balances provocation with caution. "I'm not going to say anything that damages my personal brand, ever." He guards his reputation as zealously as his legal and marketing teams guard Nordic's.

Craig fought to use the word *stupid*, knowing it would provoke his audience. He wanted a response and debate.

Every healthcare organization knows its stupid stuff. Required forms that create no value, legacy metrics that don't drive decisions, and technology used ineffectively.

But naming anything as stupid from inside risks careers. Naming it from outside gets dismissed as ignorance.

Craig exists in the liminal space between. He's credentialed enough to know, positioned perfectly to speak, and protected enough to survive.

Nordic's CEO created Craig's role because they needed someone who could be simultaneously loyal and critical, insider and outsider, on-brand and truth teller. By speaking with a point of view, Craig builds his personal audience and gains attention for his organization.

Craig makes institutional heresy institutionally necessary, and this ability to inhabit the paradox becomes even more powerful when combined with the In-House Expert's unique vantage point.

Seeing from the Boundary

Because you exist between worlds, you perceive patterns invisible from either side. The organization sees its internal logic. The market sees its external reality. As an In-House Expert, you see both simultaneously, creating depth perception where others see flat surfaces. What looks like resistance from one side and confusion from the other reveals itself as a solvable problem from your vantage point.

Jean Accius stood at the Consumer Electronics Show in Las Vegas, watching young tech devotees question AARP's presence. To the tech world, AARP meant retirement and resistance to innovation. But Jean saw a $140 billion pattern from his position as senior vice president of global thought leadership at AARP: "The tech world didn't see the value of older adults and their purchasing power. Even though older adults were consuming and spending significantly on products either for themselves or their grandchildren."

Jean and his team needed to change the conversation. In 2022, Accius's thought leadership team at AARP produced the Global Longevity Economy Outlook, which identified the economic opportunity being missed: "Despite accounting for only 24% of the world population in 2020, people aged fifty and older accounted for about 34% of global GDP." This spending pattern occurred in both wealthy and developing economies. "Aging has no border or geographic restrictions, and we are seeing the demographic and longevity trends globally." Jean and his team leveraged AARP's brand and research power to spark a conversation within the tech industry.

Jean was raised by his grandmother, worked his first job in a retirement community, and had risen through organizations to impact global aging policy. He was positioned to see across boundaries. "What are we missing? Or what is a different way of looking at this issue?" Jean asks these questions constantly.

Jean's AARP team's Global Longevity Economy Outlook had already quantified what everyone missed: People over fifty contribute $8.3 trillion to the US economy. But Jean noticed conversations about the future of work. "People were talking about automation and job replacements, but no one was actually having a conversation about what I would consider to be one of the key, most important assets that any company has, and that's their workforce. And the fact that [work]force is living longer and either want to or need to work."

From AARP's side, this seemed like an aging issue. From the corporate side, it seemed like an automation issue. Jean saw them as two sides of the same conversation. The future of work wasn't just replacing older workers; they were being erased from the conversation. Jean and his team convened 150 executives from companies like Morgan Stanley, BlackRock, and others. That summit became the Living, Learning, and Earning Longer collaborative—one hundred global companies representing millions of employees and over $1 trillion in revenue. Seeing the issue from the boundary made the issue visible, and then speaking up and attracting others to work on the issue became an imperative.

Jean and AARP became long-term clients of Thought Leadership Leverage. One day, Jean told Bill that they had hosted a virtual event with record attendance. Bill replied with enthusiasm and asked, "Who was in the webinar? Because I'd rather have five ideal attendees than five thousand attendees who don't fit the target audience." We worked together to sharpen the team's target audiences, define campaigns, and identify who owned key relationships.

Accius left AARP in 2023 and became the CEO and president of Creating Healthy Communities (CHC). At that point, Jean carried his thought leadership expertise into the new role. He switched from In-House Expert to Growth-Minded CEO of a nonprofit organization that focuses on complex, interconnected health challenges—including food security, mental health, and chronic disease prevention.

"These problems are deeply interconnected and cannot be solved by one organization. They require bold, collaborative solutions." So, Jean and CHC use the convening power of nonprofits, social capital, and thought leadership to attract organizations willing to work together.

CHC created the Leadership Council for Healthy Communities, a cross-industry coalition of organizations committed to advancing community health that includes for-profits, academic institutions, professional organizations, think tanks, health insurance companies, and public relations. "We've created an incubator for action. None of the organizations could do this work on our own. But together, we can create lasting, equitable change."

Jean's approach to thought leadership centers on the two questions he constantly asks himself: "What are we missing? What is a different way of looking at this issue?"

Each time he convenes an internal team or a cross-organization council, he invites people to join him at the boundary and explore these questions together. And when they do, knowledge gets shared, resources pool together, and action becomes possible.

The Future Is Now, and Yet Research Takes Time

Stephanie Woerner navigates a different boundary at MIT's Center for Information Systems Research. For fifty years, CISR has operated between academic rigor and business urgency, serving seventy-five consortium members who need actionable research.

"If you are doing an academic research project, it could easily take three or four years from start to finish," Stephanie explains. "Business is going faster: six months, three months. Fast."

Learning to inhabit this boundary between academic pace and business pace strained her.

"I had to go into the deep end of the pool, right? And, I'm a mediocre swimmer, but yes, I survive."

When generative AI exploded in February 2023, her phone "started ringing off the hook."

Members demanded immediate insights about technology that hadn't existed when MIT's CISR team carefully planned its research calendar.

From the academic side, sudden changes were unthinkable.

From the business side, waiting was unacceptable.

At Stephanie's boundary position, she saw a different path: Add AI questions to every existing research project, create "hot topics" sessions for emerging insights, and deliver what she could while building toward deeper understanding.

Her boundary vision transforms how executives understand digital transformation itself. "Digital transformation is really doing two things at one time. You're working on operational efficiency, and you're working on customer experience. And that's why digital transformation is so hard. It's kind of like patting your stomach and rubbing your head."

Companies also frequently rely on benchmarks. And CISR's members want new measures to understand what is happening inside as well as outside the organization. "Measures are difficult to construct," she notes.

"Every system and measure is deeply customized. Yet executives demand simple comparisons for incomparable realities." Stephanie must receive the request, develop an answer with academic rigor, and then deliver a reply in a format that her members will understand and value.

She has to meet the standards and styles of two worlds.

"To stretch and to try to communicate in a different way and to ask different kinds of questions was hard. It was not an easy process for me. It took a good solid five, six, seven years to really start to have inklings."

Seven years to shift from her academic mindset to a business-friendly communications style without sacrificing rigor.

But those seven years weren't wasted. Each awkward translation, each failed attempt to rush academic insight, each executive's impatient drumming while she explained why good research takes time—these failures taught her something most pure academics never learn: how to make complexity urgent without making it false.

Like Jean Accius, Stephanie Woerner built her value through years of learning to see from the boundary. Between nonprofits and high-tech companies, between cautious research cadence and quarterly business imperatives, between the insight and the impact. That's the place of leverage for an In-House Expert. An In-House Expert speaks out. They push. They enroll others until the necessary architecture comes into existence.

They build bridges others can cross.

Shifting the Frame

The more you know, the harder you'll need to work to make it sound simple.

Ashley Faus, head of lifecycle marketing at Atlassian, discovered frame-shifting power through personal frustration with her own profession. Early in her marketing career, the inbound methodology became popular. Gated content became a marketing best practice.

But Ashley quickly realized that turning every form fill into a lead resulted in bad outcomes for the business and the audience.

"I kept saying, 'This is stupid,'" Ashley recalls about traditional demand generation.

"Just because somebody filled out a form does not mean that they want to buy something. And just because someone doesn't want to buy something today doesn't mean they're not worth my time."

This dual perspective revealed what others couldn't see: Audiences weren't prospects moving through funnels but humans exploring needs.

"They could be a candidate. They could be a strategic partner. They could become a buyer in the future, or they could become a brand champion that refers ten other clients to us."

Ashley searched for alternative ways to describe the audience's journey. She moved away from the traditional linear funnel, and she looked for metaphors that invite exploration: "I originally thought it might be a jungle gym, because you could choose different paths. But a jungle gym still has an ultimate goal: get to the top."

A jungle gym would just invert the funnel. Ashley needed a broader explanation to help her and her colleagues design a seamless, helpful, and impactful journey.

Ashley sought an audience journey metaphor that invited exploration rather than a forced conclusion.

"I'm a marketer who often hates being marketed to. I can see how it's all designed to force me into purchases that don't solve my problems."

The traditional funnel process offers upside for the business without caring for the needs of the human buyer. "I don't want to be that kind of marketer.

I never want to 'sell' anything to anyone; I want to match problems with solutions."

She decided on a "content playground" that replaces linear funnels with environments where "your audience can choose their own path and end up at a great result." Even small changes demonstrate the philosophy. Vague "Learn More" buttons are replaced with specific promises between humans:

- "Book Office Hours" tells current clients where to click to get help.
- "Request RFP" buttons invite buyers to start a sales conversation.

Each option honors human intelligence rather than exploiting confusion.

Ashley's content playground approach helps marketers get back to solving problems for humans. This revelation transformed into frameworks she now evangelizes everywhere—marketing conferences, hyperactive LinkedIn presence, and her book, *Human-Centered Marketing*.

And in the age of AI, Ashley's human-centered frameworks become even more important. The power of the human connection and influence in a buying journey crystallized while planning a wedding anniversary trip to Palm Springs.

The Google results were lackluster. "Everyone said that AI was so helpful in planning trips, just get AI to create the itinerary! Why don't you just get ChatGPT to tell you where to go?" But Faus found the AI outputs to be just as underwhelming as the Google results. Instead, she asked a colleague who had just gotten married in Palm Springs.

Her colleague provided what algorithms couldn't. "Go here. This place is very chic. If you want to feel very fancy, this is the place." Trust requires seeing the specific human, not demographic averages.

Ashley doesn't resolve the marketer-who-hates-being-marketed-to duality. She chooses to speak from it.

She transforms manipulation into invitation—not because her company mandates it but because she's determined to shift how her entire marketing profession thinks.

Ashley's content playground concept sounds simple, but that's how she's trying to overturn decades of professional norms.

Each "Learn More" button that gets replaced with an honest link is a small victory in her revolution against her own industry's manipulation.

Shining Light Through a Prism

Jayshree Seth looked at 3M's troubling State of Science findings. She needed to create a response, a science advocacy strategy. Rather than an exhaustive presentation, she distilled it into something a child could remember.

"I said, OK, there's three things we're going to do: *A*, *B*, and *C*:

- "*A*, we need to raise the Awareness and Appreciation of science, so that people acknowledge its importance and don't have this apathy.
- "*B* is about Barriers, Biases, and Boundaries. We have to break those down.
- "*C* is about communication with context that people can see."

Jayshree wasn't dumbing down the research. It's a brilliant translation that required significant work. She condensed research insights and deliberately crafted them into something instantly usable for everyone from other scientists to media to policymakers.

Jayshree knew the data showed that 40 percent of the world viewed science as not relevant to their lives. That's a massive number of people, more than she could ever speak to or reach on her own. Therefore, she needed to leverage the components of the Impact Equation. Simplicity makes it memorable. Relevance signals importance and attracts others' attention. When people embrace the idea, they may lend their personal or organizational support to reach more people.

Years into her role as chief science advocate, Jayshree still carried an unresolved question from her youth: Why had she, an award-winning scientist and holder of eighty patents, never felt like "the science type" while growing up?

This question drove her advocacy work and inspired 3M's documentary *Not the Science Type*. Yet even as the film reached audiences, Jayshree yearned for something more: academic clarity on what she'd lived through but couldn't name.

Searching databases late one night, Jayshree found Professor Amanda Diekman's research on goal congruity theory. Reading about how people choose careers aligning with their core values, Jayshree found herself moved to tears: "I was reading all the citations, reading all her papers, and I'm literally in tears. I feel validated. Finally, there is a feeling, there is a name of a concept, and there is a professor!"

Jayshree had finally found language for something she'd been doing her entire career. She hadn't failed to choose between science and the humanities. She'd refused the choice itself.

That refusal had made her invaluable.

Jayshree reached out to the professor. They exchanged emails. Soon they were designing original research. The study, which included 466 students, was published in *Scientific Reports*. Their PRISM framework—Purpose Reflection in STEM Modalities—showed that a simple five-minute writing exercise connecting STEM education to students' purpose significantly increased their sense of belonging and reduced their stress. "It is so simple," Jayshree reflects. "Just remind yourself why you're doing what you're doing and why it's important to you. So you can persist."

Jayshree's research colleague, Amanda Diekman, describes how the PRISM activity has been received: "Whether we are talking to a first-year STEM college student or a seasoned faculty member, we find that a wide range of people resonate with the idea of thinking about their 'why' and how it connects to their day-to-day work and their longer-term career goals."

Jayshree applies the PRISM reflection practice to her own work as corporate scientist and chief science advocate at 3M: "Through my educational background, life experiences, and career journey, I realized that my work as a scientist, driving innovation to improve lives, connects my problem-solving skills to my purpose. Purpose creates a lifeline for inspiration; inspiration is the lifeblood of innovation; and innovation is a lifesaver for business."

PRISM works because Jayshree designed it from her superposition—that quantum state where contradictory truths coexist.

She was the corporate scientist who understood formulas *and* the outsider who needed human context. The eighty-patent holder *and* "not the science type." When others demanded that she choose one identity, she maintained both. That maintenance isn't passive—it's daily resistance against every force demanding simplification.

Every In-House Expert we studied applied this duality in some form. When executives challenge Craig Joseph, he maintains the roles of truth teller and employee simultaneously. Ashley Faus practices marketing for her company daily while being the marketer who publicly challenges the industry's practices. Stephanie Woerner maintains academic rigor at MIT's CISR while she honors business urgency.

Over time, In-House Experts nurture incredible personal brands for themselves, and they skillfully apply the loaned authority of their organizations. Their duality allows them to generate incredible velocity—both personal and system velocity—for the ideas they advocate. They curate a reputation for their independent authentic voice while carrying the endorsement of their organization. Superposition is their superpower.

Chapter 11

The Hall of Fame Thinker

"I'm Dying to Tell You"

Dr. Mark Goulston walked into the hospital room of a dying man who had everything: wealth, acclaim, and even a medical center bearing his name. The man looked terrible, but not from the cancer that was killing him. Something else was eating at him.

"What's the matter?" Mark said with characteristic directness. "You look like crap. And I don't think it's because you're dying."

The man's eyes filled with tears. "Everything I thought was important isn't. Everything I thought wasn't important actually is. And I've run out of time to fix it."

Mark reflected. Here was someone who'd achieved every conventional measure of success yet faced death with profound regret about what truly mattered. That conversation would haunt him for years.

When Mark received his own leukemia diagnosis decades later, he felt something his patient never did: calm. By then, his book *Just Listen* had been translated into twenty-eight languages. He'd trained FBI hostage negotiators. He'd built a surgical empathy framework for crisis intervention training.

Yet none of that explained Mark's serenity. "I'm the calmest I've ever been in my life," he would tell colleagues—not because he was ready to die but because he'd already done what his patient hadn't. He'd shifted from building a career to building systems that would outlive him.

This calm manifested in action. Mark created a YouTube series called "I'm Dying to Tell You," transforming his terminal illness into thought leadership that helped others process mortality.

When we asked Mark what guided such remarkable grace, he didn't hesitate: "My top four values are kindness, curiosity, getting stuff done, and taking total personal responsibility." For him, "Kindness is not the same thing as niceness. Nice is when you're a lightweight. Kind means you have the power to hurt people, but you choose to never do it."

When asked why he continued creating thought leadership despite his diagnosis, Mark was clear: "I think I'm having a good death because I realized I lived a good life."

He also knew his ideas needed others to carry them. "I'm involved with about five or six projects. Unbeknownst to me, I'm the visionary. I'm the one who created the intellectual property. My focus now is how this lives on without me."

Mark recorded his last episode of "I'm Dying to Tell You" just a few days before he passed away in 2023. His ideas continue to create impact. Unlike his dying patient, Mark discovered how to matter beyond mortality.

Some Choose to Speak

Mark understood something that distinguishes Hall of Fame Thinkers from other practitioners: the difference between speaking yourself and building systems that speak when you no longer can.

A single passage from Plato's *Republic* has haunted Bill since his undergraduate days.

In Plato's allegory of the cave, prisoners are chained in a row and forced to stare at shadows on a wall. Plato tells us about a philosopher who gets dragged out of the cave into the daylight to see truth. Everyone fixates on prisoners or philosophers, but there's a third group. Behind the prisoners, Plato says there's a group of people who walk along a raised path carrying objects past a fire. As translator C. D. C. Reeve renders it, "Some of the carriers are talking and some are silent." It's a strange, often undiscussed detail in the cave allegory. Why do some object carriers choose to speak? Why are others silent?

These carriers possess complete agency. No chains bind them. No one drags them into enlightenment. They choose their path, their objects, their silence or speech.

Plato intended these object carriers as deceivers in his shadow-puppet show. But through the lens of thought leadership, maybe we can see them another way. The carriers transform into something unexpectedly generous.

They've studied their objects—trust, leadership, innovation—with patience. They know that when they walk the raised path, they cast shadows with their objects, not light. When they speak, their words echo imperfectly off cave walls. Yet some choose to speak anyway.

But the choice to speak doesn't come easily. Stephen M. R. Covey had every advantage—his father's systems, the Covey brand, and proximity to thought leadership success. Yet he "dabbled for fifteen years" before finding his authentic voice about trust. Fifteen years of studying his object before choosing to speak.

"It wasn't until I felt authentic that this was my voice," he told us. Only then did he cast his shadow deliberately, knowing *The Speed of Trust* simplified infinitely complex organizational dynamics into something leaders could grasp and use.

This patience defines the carrier's journey. Dorie Clark's research confirms what Hall of Fame Thinkers know viscerally: "It takes between two and three years of consistent effort to start to see even minimal results." The carriers who choose to speak understand they're committing to years, often decades, of patient shadow-casting.

Every carrier who chooses to speak knows their shadows simplify truth. Marshall Goldsmith knows *What Got You Here Won't Get You There* reduces the beautiful chaos of human transformation to bullet points. Martin Gonzalez knows his entrepreneurship frameworks can't capture every nuance of starting a business. Liz Wiseman knows *Multipliers* compresses infinite leadership complexity into memorable categories.

They speak anyway, because sometimes a useful shadow beats an incomprehensible truth.

Hall of Fame Thinkers make a profound shift—one that transforms the Impact Equation itself.

In chapter 5, we explored the Impact Equation:

IMPACT = ! x ✓ x V→ x %

Idea Simplicity — Audience Relevance — Velocity — Audience Share

Most thought leaders generate velocity personally through endless speaking, writing, consulting.

Hall of Fame Thinkers architect a different future: They build system velocity that sustains itself. They can eventually set down their ideas and rest. Their personal velocity can eventually fade to zero, and yet their ideas still travel the world.

Mark Goulston spent his final years ensuring that his listening frameworks would outlast his voice. What follows are three stories of people who chose to speak.

And more than that, they enabled others to speak. They went from idea carrier to velocity system designer. Each discovered how to make themselves beautifully irrelevant to their own ideas' survival.

Three Paths to Beautiful Irrelevance

Carrying It Forward

Marshall Goldsmith had spent forty years becoming the world's most famous executive coach. Ask him who's number two on the list, and he'd grin: "No idea. That's the point."

But fame creates its own prison. Every insight required his voice. Every transformation needed his presence.

Then Marshall remembered his own beloved mentors—Peter Drucker, Frances Hesselbein, Warren Bennis—legendary idea carriers who'd never charged him a penny.

"I decided to give away all I know to fifteen people for free," he told us. His only condition mirrored what help he received: "When they get old, they have to do the same thing."

Marshall posted a simple selfie video on LinkedIn and invited people to apply. He had pretty low expectations, thinking to himself, *A hundred people might apply for this thing, right?*

Instead, 18,000 people applied. Marshall initially chose 180 people, including "the president of the World Bank, the head of Junior Achievement, and the head of the Nature Conservancy. CEOs and thinkers. Just great people." Each person committed to the same covenant—freely receive and then, later, freely give.

Marshall's 100 Coaches project became something he hadn't anticipated: a self-replicating system where his ideas would travel through generations of leaders teaching leaders. No money changed hands. No contracts bound them. Only the promise to carry forward what they'd learned.

By giving everything away with only one condition, that others do the same, Marshall built a velocity system that would outlast him. His idea's shadows would keep moving across the cave wall, cast by an ever-increasing group of carriers he'd never meet. His ideas would no longer need Marshall Goldsmith to speak them. And that gave Marshall joy:

"At one level, you can say this is me giving back," Marshall reflects. "Existentially, the biggest winner on this project is me. People are so nice to me and kind and grateful, and you know, what's that worth?"

Going "Open Source"

Martin Gonzalez discovered velocity transition through a Google 20% project. While preparing for a Jakarta entrepreneurship accelerator event, he found that 65 percent of startups failed due to people issues. Yet almost no research existed on leadership skills for early-stage entrepreneurs.

His hastily created two-day course earned rave reviews. At dinner afterward, his colleague Josh Yellin pushed, "Where's the book on startup leadership, Martin? We need to write it."

Martin resisted. "Josh, look at this field. I don't have white hair yet. It will take years till I get white hair. I still have time."

But demand echoed around the world. The session was held in Bangalore, São Paulo, Lagos, and Warsaw. Soon they needed facilitators to meet demand. When founders in São Paulo recreated the course in Portuguese without permission, Martin faced an important choice. He could slam the gates closed and protect the ideas, or he could let them travel freely.

"The few thousand founders who've benefited told us this is really useful," he reflected. "We can reach hundreds of thousands or even millions. They might not know my name. Like most business ideas, we can never really figure out attribution. That's fine. If this idea can be helpful, let's do it."

Martin and Josh open-sourced everything. Their book, *The Bonfire Moment*, transparently shares all workshop tools "with anyone who wants to run it themselves." While others guard intellectual property, Martin celebrates his anonymous impact. Ideas achieve escape velocity through radical generosity rather than careful control.

Offering a System

Liz Wiseman brought a buyer's wisdom to the seller's world. For two decades at Oracle University, she'd hired thought leaders and watched their ideas flourish or fail based on one factor: infrastructure. She knew intimately the terror in sponsors' eyes—that fear she described in chapter 1—when ideas arrived without systems to support them.

Liz never forgot the day she brought a $250,000 purchase order for a professor to teach monthly. Oracle's CFO vigorously questioned the logic of the expense. Liz argued that they should focus on the value gained, not the amount spent: "I think we're going to get incredible value from this. This is why I'm doing it. This is why this is the person we need." Liz knew the real waste came from brilliant ideas that died without systems to spread them.

"Whenever Oracle launched a new version," she recalls, "it was my job to make sure that every single person in that company was trained on the new product." And not just informed but equipped with tools, support, and frameworks to succeed. And that experience would frame how she practices thought leadership as a keynoter and as an architect of solutions.

So, when *Multipliers* launched, Liz built what she'd always needed to buy. "On release date, here's the keynote; here's the workshop; and here's the assessment."

While other thought leaders clutched their frameworks, hoping to maintain control, Liz did the opposite—she built for enterprise scale. "I think one of the strengths of my work and research and books has not been the books themselves. It's been the ecosystem, the support system that companies can get training and roll it out."

She'd seen too many ideas lose traction because the thought leader couldn't be everywhere at once.

"I've got that whole little universe around it to help people be successful," she explains, "which means it can grow deep roots inside of organizations." Liz's metric for success isn't applause or accolades but persistence: "What I love hearing is people saying, 'Wow, you spoke at our company five, six years ago and we are still talking about it and still using those ideas.'"

Liz never struggled to let go, because she never tried to hold on. She built for velocity from day one, creating systems that assumed her absence rather than her presence.

Sometimes the greatest gift isn't learning to release control—it's never grasping for it in the first place.

Architecting Your Irrelevance

Velocity transition is not about giving ideas away for free. Instead, velocity transition demands a reckoning most thought leaders never name: You must architect your own irrelevance.

The Coveys understood this balance. When Stephen Covey's ideas moved into education and nonprofits, his son Stephen M. R. explains their approach: "We adopted the mantra 'no margin, no mission.'" They priced corporate work to fund nonprofit access, architecting systems that could serve everyone while remaining sustainable. As Stephen told us, "Our goal was to try to reach as many people as we could, but not while operating at a loss."

Marshall gave knowledge away but charged for his time. Martin open-sourced frameworks while Google paid his salary. Liz built and sold enterprise systems and premium keynotes. Each person found their own equation for sustainable irrelevance.

Eventually, you may face the choice yourself. You may need to ask, "How will I let go?"

Getting Out of Your Idea's Way

Architecting your irrelevance through systems—whether covenants, open-source frameworks, or enterprise infrastructure—can occur in many different forms.

What follows is coauthor Peter Winick's reflection on his eighteen-year relationship with Dr. Mark Goulston, who died in 2023. It reveals the most profound form of velocity transition: when ideas become so embedded in another human that they transform not just what that person does but who they become.

> Sometimes when you're in LA you "take a meeting" because that's what people in LA do. In NYC where I'm from, you don't take meetings. You go to a meeting with a specific agenda. You prepare. And you have clear goals and outcomes in mind.
>
> In the summer of 2005, I "took" a breakfast meeting with Dr. Mark Goulston at the very swanky Sunset Tower Hotel in West Hollywood. I had recently taken the role as Managing Director at Ferrazzi Greenlight. I was new to the thought leadership world, and I was a little intimidated by Mark as he had some noteworthy credentials.
>
> Mark started to tell me about his books: *Get Out of Your Own Way* and the sequel *Get Out of Your Own Way at Work*. He talked about his speaking and coaching work. For a moment, I wondered if this guy was full of himself. But then he explained that he was stuck on the business side. He couldn't get out of his own way. He

> was always helping others and rarely put his own needs first.
>
> Our conversation switched to self-defeating behaviors. As a practicing psychiatrist, Mark had a lot to say about what they were and why we have them. I felt like my breakfast meeting had become a therapy session, but in a good way. Mark then took out a worksheet with a list of feelings, and he asked me to circle some. Here I was in the middle of a trendy LA restaurant opening up to a stranger. Mark got me to open up about things guys typically don't talk about with other guys.
>
> Over eighteen years, our relationship revealed Mark's deeper practice. Yes, he wrote books, gave speeches, and coached executives. But Mark's best work happened in quiet moments—when he'd look a CEO in the eye and say what everyone thought but wouldn't voice.
>
> Mark helped me through my father's death and my failing marriage. He couldn't "get out of his own way" on the business side, so he created an ecosystem of partners and colleagues, inviting people into conversations they yearned for but couldn't start alone. I believe I helped him along the way with his amazing body of work and I know he helped me. I miss him.

What Peter's account reveals goes beyond mentorship. Mark wasn't teaching his methodology for candor and listening. He was transmitting it.

But this understates what occurred. Mark's ideas didn't just reach Peter; they rewired him. Now Peter reads unspoken dynamics and helps thought leaders voice what needs saying.

The student became the system.

Perhaps that's why Mark felt "the calmest I've ever been" after his leukemia diagnosis. He'd embedded his ideas so deeply in others that attribution became irrelevant. "I miss him," Peter reflects. Not Mark's ideas. *Him.*

You can't miss a methodology. You miss the person who became unnecessary to their own ideas' survival.

This grief echoes through centuries of elegies. Milton claimed Shakespeare needed no monument of "pilèd Stones." Ben Jonson called Shakespeare's work "a monument without a tomb." W. H. Auden reminded us, "The words of a dead man / Are modified in the guts of the living." We still recite Emily Dickinson because her sister, Lavinia, refused to burn the poems.

The work of thought leadership is to speak, not remain silent. When practiced well, others carry our ideas further than we ever could alone.

Mark understood this. After decades as caregiver—therapist, doctor, and father—leukemia reversed his role. The mentor to many became mentee to few. In his "I'm Dying to Tell You" YouTube series, Mark admitted, "When I feel they care about me, I get emotional, and the emotion is embarrassment because I don't want to burden anyone."

When he apologized, people stopped him: "It's an honor to care for you."

This reversal epitomizes the Hall of Fame Thinker's journey. After years generating personal velocity for ideas, these thinkers must step back, witnessing impact created by others who carry the work forward. Every time Peter takes a meeting without a rigid agenda, every time he helps someone get out of their own way, Mark's impact continues. Not "Goulston's approach." Simply wisdom moving through the world.

Some Hall of Fame Thinkers build certification empires. Others transform their fellow humans into idea carriers who spread the methodology through every conversation, every moment of unexpected openness, every truth spoken with love.

They chose to speak. Now others speak for them.

SECTION THREE

THE COMMERCE OF COMMONS SENSE

Chapter 12

The Duty to Speak

The Transformation

Chester Elton approached Marshall Goldsmith with a request: Would he write a blurb for his next book?

"I'd be less than happy to," Marshall joked. Chester prepared for disappointment, but Marshall quickly continued. "I'll do you one better. You want me to write the foreword?"

What Marshall said next reframed Chester's entire view of thought leadership: "You know, Chester, there's two ways to view the world when you do what you and I do. One is that everybody in the room is a competitor. The other view is, what can I do to help everybody in the room? So we have a tide that raises all ships."

Chester Elton had spent decades at O.C. Tanner, the employee recognition company, as their "Apostle of Appreciation"; this fantastic job title meant he was the in-house expert who taught organizations how to reward performance. Their platform identity? "The Carrot Principle." Extrinsic rewards. Measurable motivation. He knew the frameworks. He'd helped build them.

Then he and his coauthor, Adrian Gostick, left to build their own company: The Culture Works. They became Practice Owners and continued to spread the idea through speeches and consulting. They were Thought Leaders on the Run, carrying their recognition message from stage to stage. Chester had made the transition many thought leaders make—from teaching as part of his corporate job to building an independent practice around his expertise. He was successful, and he was also competing fiercely with everyone else in that space.

And now Marshall Goldsmith had offered to write the foreword. Not just a blurb. The foreword.

Why?

"I'm up the ladder," Marshall explained. "I say yes to pretty much everything, and, Chester, you should too."

Chester remembers: "The more I talked to Marshall, the more I thought, *You know, that's just silly.*" The competition mindset was silly. The hoarding was silly. The zero-sum thinking was silly.

Chester didn't just internalize this lesson; he lived it. Years later, when we launched our *Leveraging Thought Leadership* podcast, we needed initial guests willing to help us work out the process and lend their credibility. Chester agreed to be a guest, and he didn't just agree. He insisted on being our very first guest, helping lift our new project exactly as Marshall had lifted him. The generosity had come full circle.

So why doesn't our entire field operate this way? To answer honestly requires starting with our own failures. What follows is both confession and manifesto, acknowledging where we've personally fallen short while also passionately arguing why this field matters and why it must also change.

Our Own Reckoning

We, Peter Winick and Bill Sherman, have each spent twenty years as consultants in the thought leadership industry. We occupied an unusual position. We've consulted with hundreds of thought leaders, from emerging voices to Fortune 50 CEOs, Nobel Prize nominees, endowed chairs at world-class business schools. We've stood in their intellectual attics and seen their half-formed frameworks. We've witnessed their private struggles with imposter syndrome and exhaustion. We've identified patterns, because we've stood at a vantage point that few others get to see.

We work as consultants. This is how we sustain our practice. This book contains the insights we learned in our journey alongside thought leaders. And we can work with you directly, if you choose. As Stephen M. R. Covey explained when discussing Franklin Covey's approach, "No margin, no mission." Without sustainable business models, we can't pursue our purpose of advancing the field.

And yet.

We played it safe. We said we would never write a book because we didn't want to compete with the authors we served. We kept our deepest insights behind consulting fees. Bill speaks:

> For twenty years, I helped clients speak their imperfect truths. I was their psychopomp—the guide who knows the way but never enters. Many days, I spoke on our clients' behalf as their salesperson for corporate buyers. And on one disastrous evening twenty years ago, I spoke on a keynoter's behalf in a conference room above Times Square. I replaced my client's stories with my own. I made myself as vulnerable as I could to the audience, and still it wasn't enough. I learned a lesson: Avoid the stage and the spotlight. That place was for others, not me.
>
> And so, for the past twenty years, I've sold my consulting skills and ideas but avoided writing a free manifesto or a thirty-dollar book. I locked many of my own core ideas behind the consulting fee paywall. I watched people who couldn't afford our fees struggle. "It's just business," I told myself. But it's not just business. It's also lives and purpose. And the evidence surrounded me daily.
>
> When I walked into my office, I was surrounded by books written by clients and friends rather than strangers. I was proud to have walked alongside so many authors and helped them codify their core ideas, generate revenue, and create impact.
>
> Sometimes my clients would ask, "Why haven't you written a book, Bill?" I deflected with practiced excuses. Behind-the-scenes

advisor. Small market. Not worthy. But those were lies I told myself. I was afraid. What if my book was met with sharp-worded Amazon reviews? What if the ideas were laughed at? Or worse. Ignored.

Our field needs a shared language. This book contains my best. I'm not holding back anymore. You must judge if it's helpful to you.

To write this book, I stole evenings and weekends from those I love most. My spouse half jokingly compared my book writing to an affair. My parents, both in their mid-eighties, asked each night at the dinner table, "How did the writing go today?" I reported the progress dutifully. My family will never get back the lost time with me. Yet, they cheered me on. I wish I could have written a simpler book with weaker arguments. My wife laughed and affectionately said, "No you couldn't. That's not you." And she's right.

Now, when I enter my office, I no longer see neat rows of books written by friends and clients. I see years of their lives. The lessons they learned and the vulnerability they've chosen.

In writing this book, I found what I must speak. I can no longer stay silent.

We three authors—Bill, Peter, and Naren—are not neutral observers. We profit from the very industry we're critiquing. Our silence created a gap in the conversation, and our complicity helped maintain it.

Our study of thought leadership emerges from the Western tradition and North American business contexts. Other cultures define and transmit knowledge very differently. They are not our stories to tell. Nor should we try to do so. Instead of making a universal argument, we focus on what North American thought leadership has been and what we believe it must become.

Both/And

Daniel Drezner's *The Ideas Industry* maps a fundamental shift in how ideas circulate in the twenty-first century. He distinguishes between "public intellectuals"—critics who complicate, question, and often work in academia—and "thought leaders"—optimists who simplify, inspire, and often emerge from business. He describes thought leaders as "intellectual evangelists who know one big thing and believe that their important idea will change the world."

Drezner argues that "the modern marketplace of ideas benefits all intellectuals, but it benefits thought leaders far more than others." Economic forces, technological disruption, and wealth inequality have tilted the marketplace of ideas toward thought leaders and away from public intellectuals.

His analysis stings because it's largely accurate. The market prefers people who validate their worldviews. The TED stage rewards simplicity over complexity. Many who call themselves thought leaders are indeed motivational speakers with little substance. We've seen the oversimplifiers and self-promoters that Drezner describes. On this diagnosis, we agree.

But Drezner's framework creates a binary that misses what we've observed in our own practice. The best thought leaders aren't failed public intellectuals or anti-intellectual simplifiers. They're practitioners who've recognized patterns through experience and made an extraordinary choice: to share those patterns despite their imperfection. They occupy what philosophers call the metamodern position: sincerely committed while acknowledging complexity, embodying contradictions while speaking earnestly.

This is the both/and that defines our moment. We run businesses that need revenue, *and* we have obligations to share knowledge. We possess imperfect understanding, *and* others need what we've learned. We risk oversimplification, *and* silence guarantees worse outcomes.

Drezner's critique helps us stay conscious of these tensions. But consciousness of contradiction doesn't require choosing sides in his binary.

Three Layers of Truth

To understand why speaking imperfectly might be ethical, we need to examine what kind of truth we're actually discussing.

Big-*T* truth belongs to philosophers and prophets wrestling with questions like "What is justice?" or "Why does anything exist?" These aren't questions you answer in a quarterly business review. Big-*T* truth isn't our domain, and it's not the domain of anyone in business.

Lies and deception form the bottom layer. Bernie Madoff didn't offer flawed investment strategies; he ran a Ponzi scheme. Elizabeth Holmes didn't share imperfect knowledge about blood testing; she fabricated capabilities that didn't exist. These aren't incomplete truths or thought leadership. They're deliberate falsifications designed to extract value while providing none.

Imperfect truths occupy the crucial middle layer. After studying how ideas create impact, we've recognized patterns. When any of us practice thought leadership, we've not seen an ultimate truth. Our ideas are not complete. But they're more useful than our silence.

Every framework simplifies reality—that's what makes it portable. Every model reduces complexity—that's what makes it teachable. And that's the hard, necessary work of our field of thought leadership.

Changing the Rules

In Plato's *Republic*, a prisoner gets dragged from the cave into blinding daylight to perceive ultimate reality. Plato carefully constructed his allegory of the cave with the precision of a jailer. Wall-facing prisoners watch shadows cast by people who carry objects past the fire. Plato identifies two types of object carriers: some speak, while others are silent.

Plato's prisoners are waiting for a hero, perhaps a philosopher king, to drag them out into the daylight of big-*T* truth. For most of them, the cave and the wall are all they will ever know.

Elinor Ostrom received the Nobel Prize in economics for her work on managing the commons. In *Governing the Commons*, she rejected frameworks—such as the prisoner's dilemma—that require individuals to be "incapable of changing their constraints." She writes, "I would rather address the question of how to enhance the capabilities of those involved to change the constraining rules of the game to lead to outcomes rather than remorseless tragedies."

So, let's follow her lead and change the rules of Plato's game.

We can smash the prisoners' shackles. Here comes everybody—no longer prisoners watching shadows but everyone a potential carrier with agency. This democratization brings both promise and peril. And it's not hypothetical. Our world's knowledge gatekeepers have been weakened. Everyone can potentially speak, and they can leverage AI-generated content and algorithmic amplification.

When we expand agency to everyone, we transform the cave into something else entirely, a commons where everyone's choices affect the shared resource. What do you put into the commons, and what do you take out? In the world of tangible commons, fish can be taken out of fisheries. Water can be removed from reservoirs. Elinor Ostrom started studying the commons in the 1960s. For most of her career, she studied tangible things. How did communities in the Los Angeles watershed overcome perennial shortages and constant overdrilling? How had Nepali farmers successfully created and sustained a self-governing system?

Then, in the early 2000s, Ostrom turned her attention to the knowledge commons. The knowledge commons reflects what ideas we add to it and what economic value we extract from it. Just like a fishery or a water reservoir, it can be overdrawn or polluted. She differentiated between the physical book that can be copyrighted and sold and the ideas themselves that have their own ways of spreading.

Ostrom and her coeditor, Charlotte Hess, argue in the introduction to *Understanding Knowledge as a Commons* that any commons, knowledge or tangible, must be preserved and protected. "A commons is not value-laden—its outcome can be good or bad, sustainable or not."

All of us benefit from the generations of insights others have added to the knowledge commons. Some of us then choose to add knowledge through scholarship or thought leadership.

So, let's look at the options in this allegory of the cave where there are no prisoners, simply cave dwellers, all of whom can speak and contribute to the knowledge commons:

1. We can remain wall facers, concealing our knowledge while others walk the ramp and cast shadows.
2. We can walk past the fire quietly, our actions casting shadows but offering no context—leaving observers to wonder, *How do they do that so well?*
3. Or we can both walk past the fire and speak. We become students and teachers. We explain what we know through models, frameworks, and teaching.

The first two options represent a choice to let the commons degrade. Only the third choice to speak up and share our little-*t* truths nurtures the knowledge commons.

A core idea can simultaneously exist within a free online video, a thirty-dollar book, and a high-ticket keynote or consulting project. This both/and duality is not a design flaw. It's a critical necessity for the exchange of ideas and value. You can give a keynote, and the members of your audience can repeat your top three insights to their colleagues in a meeting the next day.

You cannot set up a tollbooth that will collect money every time someone repeats one of the core ideas you advocate. Ideas need both your personal energy *and* external effort to travel. When core ideas have sufficient velocity, they can generate new engagements and more revenue.

If you want to be paid for your work, you cannot fully gatekeep the ideas. You have to speak and put your ideas into the commons. And to reach scale, your ideas must be able to travel without you. The more your ideas travel for free, the more in demand you and your work will be.

The Duty to Speak

In the twenty-first century, the knowledge commons is at great risk. Social media influencers claim expertise. They post and post. AI-created slop fills every platform. Algorithms amplify bad ideas. Traditional gatekeepers have been bypassed. Misinformation spreads worldwide in moments. The noise and echo grow louder. Each year it becomes harder to distinguish real from fabricated. Harder to spot helpful little-*t* truths amid intentional deceit.

Our cave is a noisy place. When people with expertise choose silence, that space doesn't become contemplative. It becomes occupied by whoever speaks loudest, promises the most, and deceives the best.

We've watched this pattern repeatedly. When serious practitioners avoid thought leadership because the term embarrasses them, extractors and deceivers claim it gladly. When experts hesitate over imperfection, confidence artists fill the gap with dangerous certainty. When knowledge holders stay silent, the conversation continues without them—degraded, distorted, but decisive in shaping understanding.

When we practice thought leadership, we inherit a duty to speak. This duty isn't imposed externally. We acknowledge the value we received from the past generations of thinkers whose work enabled our learning. We add ideas to today's community while we also extract value. And we pay it forward to the next generation of people who will advocate their own ideas.

You Have No Right to an Audience

But wait. Doesn't declaring a "duty to speak" create its own tyranny? Who gets to simply experience rather than explain?

Your duty to speak creates absolutely no duty for others to listen. They can ignore you, walk out, or even vocally disagree.

This is the ethical safety valve: You must earn an audience or have none at all. Every member of the audience makes an ongoing choice for themselves: "Shall I continue to listen? Or will I tune this person out?"

Waldo Waldman lost half the keynote audience to the smell of coffee and fresh beignets and the impulse to check their emails and network. And yet, after he was introduced, he spoke with passion and purpose to those people who stayed to listen.

Walt Whitman portrays the audience member's agency perfectly in his poem "When I Heard the Learn'd Astronomer." The poem's narrator sits through a notable scientist's astronomy lecture filled with proofs, figures, charts, and diagrams. Then . . .

How soon unaccountable I became tired and sick,
Till rising and gliding out I wander'd off by myself,
In the mystical moist night-air, and from time to time,
Look'd up in perfect silence at the stars.

Whitman's listener simply walks out of the lecture. No confrontation. No explanation. They prefer direct experience to mediated knowledge. They choose stars over star charts.

This isn't failure but freedom—yours and theirs. You're freed from needing universal relevance. They're freed from unwanted instruction. The duty to speak is matched by everyone else's right to walk out. You're not forcing enlightenment. You're making patterns available for those who find them useful, when they find them useful, in forms they can actually use.

We won't reach our audiences by shouting louder. The cave is already a raucous place filled with echoes. Instead, our world needs more skilled voices in thought leadership, those who have not just studied their expertise but who also study how thought leadership works. We need to get better at thought leadership as individuals and as a community. And that means we need better tools.

Becoming Better Stewards

Thought leaders work in a knowledge commons. It's where we add value through our ideas. And it's also how we earn a living. And yet, we have often been lumped with deceivers, frauds, and snake oil sellers—those people who extract far more value from their audience than they provide.

Practitioners of thought leadership have been poor stewards of the knowledge commons. We must do far better for ourselves and for the knowledge commons and communities we serve.

We routinely see amazing, life-changing business ideas locked in digital files or revealed in one-on-one conversations. Too many fail to reach their intended audience because the thought leader hasn't developed a viable strategy or committed to executing it.

This pattern convinced us that thought leadership needs shared language and tools. Not to create orthodoxy but to enable conversation about the practice itself.

Imagine if every accountant used their own personal definitions. That's exactly the chaos in thought leadership today. We have expertise in our individual areas, but we lack a common language to talk about thought leadership. When thought leaders come together and talk, we often talk past each other without shared understanding.

It's time to stop acting like a medieval guild, where we protect our personal tools and methods through secrecy. A common language and tool set will improve our work, create more value for audiences, and make it easier to pass on our hard-earned skills to the next generation.

Over the years, as we worked with thought leaders, we asked ourselves the following questions, and these are the answers we found:

What Makes Good Thought Leadership?

The Four Elements describe the essential components every practitioner needs.

How Do Ideas Create Impact?

The Impact Equation explains why some good ideas spread while others languish. It also explains why some weak ideas have more impact than fantastic ideas.

Why Do People Practice Thought Leadership?

The Five Avatars examine *why* people practice thought leadership instead of *how* they communicate ideas.

This book includes our frameworks, language, and tools we use ourselves. We found them essential to do our work and to serve our clients. If you have other ideas, please join the conversation.

The Challenge and Call

To established thought leadership practitioners: You've accepted the responsibility by speaking. Yes, you profit from your knowledge. Yes, sharing could reduce your competitive advantage, *and* hoarding insights while others struggle with preventable problems creates worse outcomes. Create rising tides despite the contradictions. Your generosity despite competition models the metamodern way. The knowledge commons that enabled your success needs your continued contribution.

To silent knowledge holders: What have you recognized that others need to see? Your imposter syndrome, while real, matters less than your absence in the public square. Your fear of oversimplification is understandable, but we invite you to join us. Your concern about distortion is valid, but there's also a joy in making an impact.

To thought leadership skeptics, like Drezner: Your diagnosis of the twenty-first-century ideas industry is largely correct. Economic and social forces have largely benefited thought leaders more than public intellectuals. Thought leaders do oversimplify, seek market validation, and bypass peer review. The TED industrial complex you describe is real, *and*—this is the metamodern position—what's the alternative? Should practitioners with deep experience stay silent while academics publish paywalled journals? Should we wait for perfect knowledge while people navigate using whatever they find?

You're right that thought leaders aren't public intellectuals. We're not trying to be. We're practitioners sharing patterns we've recognized, knowing they're incomplete, knowing we profit from sharing them, knowing we risk distortion. Your critiques keep us honest about these contradictions. There are thought leadership experts who worry as deeply about the degradation as you do. But if we fall silent, we abandon the field to those who extract without contributing.

The solution is conscious practice—acknowledging our limitations while speaking anyway.

To our community: We've kept too much behind paywalls for too long. Not from greed alone but from scarcity thinking—fear that sharing everything would eliminate our value. We were wrong, *and* we still need sustainable business models. Both truths coexist.

Can someone who could never afford your services still benefit meaningfully from your knowledge? What knowledge will you put into the commons for all? You can lift people up and make a good living. You can keep your premium intellectual property and equip your audience with basic language and tools they need to thrive. They will still come to you.

We, the three authors of this book, have made our choice, and we entered the square. Will you?

Eduardo's Choice

Eduardo Briceño faced darkness at 1:40 a.m. Power outage. BCG partners waiting. No infrastructure. No backup systems. Just knowledge they needed and darkness preventing transmission.

He didn't debate whether his Performance Paradox perfectly captured organizational dynamics. He knew it didn't.

He didn't worry whether car headlights provided optimal illumination. He knew they didn't. He understood both the insufficiency and necessity of his choice.

He set up the headlights and spoke.

This is the choice before us: Will we be perfect or useful?

C. G. Jung wrote that "as far as we can discern, the sole purpose of human existence is to kindle a light in the darkness of mere being."

Eduardo's headlights embodied this light literally—not perfect light, not permanent light, and not light everyone wanted, but useful light. That's the metamodern position: embracing both the inadequacy and necessity of our illumination.

Our study of thought leadership—including thousands of conversations and decades of observation—has taught us that the field needs conscious carriers who speak their little-*t* truths with skill. They've studied their corners long enough to recognize patterns; they accept that their message will be imperfect, and yet they constantly work to improve how they explain the idea to others. They actively study their field *and* the necessary work of thought leadership.

When we embrace an idea, it transforms us. We see the world differently. Our behaviors will change.

Conscious carriers who've been transformed by their ideas signal their trustworthiness. Not because they carry universal truth but because they've let ideas change them visibly, publicly, repeatedly.

They, like everyone, can be judged by their behaviors. But audiences can also judge conscious carriers by the ideas they speak and the tools they offer. Do they merely extract value from the knowledge commons? Or do they add real value that people appreciate and use?

Therefore, our choice isn't between perfect and imperfect speech. You will cast imperfect shadows through your actions *and* also add context. You can make a good living *and* also nurture the knowledge commons. You can honor your personal transformation *and* invite others to join you. We see three choices in a cave where everyone has agency and can speak if they choose. The wall facers remain silent. The silent carriers signal through their behaviors. The conscious carriers walk the difficult path and choose to speak.

Which role will you choose?

Chapter 13

The Thought Leader and the Power of Publishing

"While there are a thousand decisions involved in the creation of every successful business book, there is one thing that makes all the difference. Story."

—JOSH BERNOFF, *BUILD A BETTER BUSINESS BOOK*

Are books even relevant for thought leadership anymore? That's a fair question and one that Naren, as a CEO of a publishing company, is asked all the time.

Thought leaders already chase their audiences across an ever-expanding array of largely digital formats. LinkedIn. Newsletters. Blogs. Articles. Substacks. Op-eds. YouTube. Reels. Threads. TED Talks. In ten years, some of these formats will remain and others will emerge. In this era of ubiquitous digital content, is there a place for a good old-fashioned book?

To put it succinctly, yes. Books are as relevant as they have ever been. Actually, maybe more relevant than ever. How can that be?

Long Form Like No Other

A book, unlike any other form of content, showcases the author's expertise in their subject matter. Of course, that only works if it's a great book. What does that mean? Well conceptualized. Well researched. Well written.

A good book is the gold standard of long-form content, a true flex like none other. A book is both a substantive work and an artifact of its moment in time. It weighs in on a timely and important topic. A book can attract an audience's attention in a way a tweet, a talk, or an article cannot.

Books and thought leadership have always complemented each other and always will. Chapter 12 acknowledges that if we choose to speak (even if imperfectly), we need to learn to speak better. As simple as it sounds, in the age of AI, this couldn't be a more profound mandate.

Books inhabit the two key tensions of thought leadership. Books are both intellectual efforts *and* commercial works. They must present their insights with simplicity *and* confidently guide readers through layers of complexity.

Books require commitment and investment. Authors challenged by that effort are right to ask themselves, "Is it worth continuing with the book?" Authors who don't see a path to impact will struggle to finish the writing process. And of course, readers who don't see value will set the book aside.

The commitment and investment—time, energy, resources, and reputation, for author and consumer—far exceed what's needed for a podcast, a post, or even a speaking gig.

A book isn't a requirement for thought leadership, but it's often deeply transformational for authors and their careers. An author's first book creates a "before" and an "after." We can point out examples where a book has changed the trajectory of the author's entire thought leadership journey. They reach new audiences. They get more inbound speaking and workshop requests. They can often raise their fees. Books allow ideas to travel and reach unexpected places.

Innovative Authors

If you search LinkedIn, you'll find tens of thousands of people posting about innovation. Innovation in business. Innovation in technology. Innovation in leadership. Innovation in innovation! Clearly, not everyone who posts about innovation is an innovation expert.

If you search online for keynote speakers who have an "innovation" speech in their repertoire, you will find hundreds. But it takes real depth of understanding and stage presence to deliver a forty-five-minute innovation keynote.

What if you want to deliver an even deeper dive on the topic of innovation? That's where a book comes in.

Josh Linkner is a bona fide expert on it, one of the most prolific keynote speakers on the topic. Prepandemic, Josh spoke on innovation over 150 times in one year and commands a speaking fee of $40,000 from his corporate clients. Based on our observations, his content is as substantive as his delivery is smooth. He draws from his vast experiences as an entrepreneur, venture capitalist, technologist, and musician to look at the topic of innovation.

In *Big Little Breakthroughs*, he explores how everyday people can become innovators through small, daily creative acts. Making reinvention a conscious part of business strategy for companies, brands, and individuals was the main theme of *The Road to Reinvention*. And he explores how a nefarious job can teach us a lot about this topic in *Hacking Innovation*.

He's enriched the knowledge base of one of the most essential topics of our times—never repeating himself but always building on what he and others have already discovered for new insights that send readers' imaginations soaring. One of his big discoveries in *Big Little Breakthroughs* should sound familiar to authors in our space: "Remember that even the most world-changing innovations are nothing more than a collage of tiny creative acts. Your most successful path forward isn't taking gigantic, wild swings but rather to cultivate small, daily shots of creativity that coalesce into meaningful results." Consistency and commitment are what lead to change, even small steps. Especially small steps. It's also how you develop a well-conceptualized, well-researched, and well-written book.

Duncan Wardle, former head of innovation and creativity at Disney, speaks globally on creativity and innovation. If you follow Duncan on LinkedIn, you'll see him delivering keynotes to massive audiences globally, from Mexico, to London, to Singapore, and back to Orlando—and that might be in a single week. He both educates and entertains from the stage and delivers real value to audiences. Amplify published Duncan's first book in late 2024.

The Imagination Emporium is not your typical business book. It's a tool kit, designed to take the intimidation out of innovation and make it accessible to normal, hardworking people, to make creativity tangible for people uncomfortable with ambiguity or gray areas, and to make it fun, so people actually use it. It has a series of QR codes embedded in each chapter, a sort-of Spotify for auditory learners, along with animated videos for visual learners. And for kinesthetic learners, the back page is the first-ever book that is fully integrated with AI. You can ask the book how to use a specific tool to help solve an issue you are working on, and the book will respond.

From its four-color interior to a pullout map of the brain with the book's concepts and characters named Zing, Spark, and Nova guiding you through the pages, Wardle has ensured that he achieved his most basic goal with the project: that no one will ever call it stuffy, required reading.

Its purpose is to engage everyone to think differently to get more productive results. After a quarter century of innovation leadership with Disney, Wardle now works with companies as the founder and CEO of ID8. He is passionate about innovation and creativity; he believes the loss of that childlike imagination, intuition, curiosity, and empathy is a business liability, as these traits will become some of the most employable skill sets since they will be some of the hardest to replace with AI. In his innovation workshops and keynote speeches, and now in his book, he embodies the Impact and Legacy Executive author as he aims to leave an imprint of fun in an improved workplace.

Here's another example: Naren's company, Amplify Publishing Group, worked with Stephen Shapiro on *Invisible Solutions*. In that book, he recognizes that we incessantly seek *the* solution for any given challenge instead of creating a systemic approach to deal with all sorts of challenges an organization faces. Amplify also published his most recent book, *Pivotal: Creating Stability in an Uncertain World*.

What truly separates Josh, Duncan, and Stephen from the one hundred other keynote speakers who speak on the topic of innovation? It's their books: thirty thousand to sixty thousand words of novel ideas, analyses of industry trends, informed and thoughtful predictions about where the market is heading, case studies, and stories of their personal experiences and lessons learned. Therein lies the magic and true thought leadership that demands attention.

A Book—the Historical Perspective

Books are the oldest manifestation of where complicated ideas meet the mass market. It may be hard for our younger readers to imagine, but there was a time not too long ago when a book was the only way to showcase your in-depth ideas on a subject matter. Books have always been, and certainly are now, the nexus where deep thought finds an audience—or fails to. Welcome to the marketplace of ideas.

The original storytelling and philosophizing in every ancient culture was oral. The act of collecting them in written language through books is what allows us to still discuss Socrates, the Torah, the Vedas, and other ancient texts today. Manuscripts were rare and expensive. Knowledge was preserved and protected rather than shared widely. Then, Gutenberg put the Bible in movable type on a press in the 1450s. His first print run was small by today's standards, about 180 copies. But his innovation gave authors and publishers a new way to create velocity for their ideas. You didn't need monks in a scriptorium writing for years. In the decades immediately after Gutenberg, a commercial book's print run might be a few hundred copies. And when they sold out, they went back to the press. A fifteenth-century "bestseller" might have dozens or even hundreds of editions!

Books offer a way for us to transmit substantive knowledge economically and democratically. We now have hardcovers and paperbacks, e-books, and audiobooks. But we still classify all these long-form works as "books." We suspect books will continue to evolve alongside technology, because it's been that way throughout human history.

Maybe the book will become a microchip we slip into our brains for a few hours, or a chatbot we can query about the ideas within it, but even then, books will never be a fleeting *Black Mirror–like* hot take. Whatever books become, they will still be the place for expanded treatment of a topic of interest. They will build on the knowledge of previous scholars and practitioners. And they will prod us as readers to improve as human beings and leaders.

Books are aspirational. Many of us want to become authors. For Naren, there's nothing better than an initial conversation with a prospective author. Their eyes light up when they give me their pitch, whether they have rehearsed it well or self-consciously chase their thesis as they talk. Sometimes I nod along with them, immediately able to grasp their vision and why it's important—necessary—for them to express it boldly, widely, and proudly.

When Naren first talked to Kelli Thompson, it was immediately visible that her proposal was clearly outlined and primed to be a success. A rising star in the corporate world, Kelli always knew she wanted to write a book, even if she didn't know what she wanted to write about. She was clear, however, that without a doubt she never wanted to write a leadership book. Once she left that career and became an entrepreneur and coach herself, she discovered that what she didn't want to write was a *traditional* leadership book.

"Even though I said I would *never* write a leadership book, the longing of wanting to be an author still wouldn't go away," Kelli said. "It would especially appear near the end of every calendar year, when I realized that my New Year's goal of writing a book didn't happen. Early 2021, that changed. In the five years prior, I had left my fourteen-year career in banking, switched careers to run HR at a healthcare tech startup, and changed careers again to work for an entrepreneur. In 2019 I left working for someone else altogether and started my own coaching, speaking, and training practice. In my personal life, I had summoned the courage to call off a wedding and re-imagine my entire personal life choices through some hard introspection. Through this work, I met and married the love of my life. I had come out of the other side of COVID niching down my business to focus exclusively on women after decades of working in male dominated fields and living through the challenges of confidence as a woman leader myself. I finally felt like I had a more interesting story to tell and a perspective that readers could uniquely relate to. About that same time (serendipity!), I was introduced to my book coach, Brooke Adams Law, who guided me through the process of turning my stories into a book structure and bringing all of the frameworks I taught my clients into compelling content to read."

Kelli wanted to empower women, to help them understand they deserved seats at the head table in their organizations and that in order to take those chairs, they needed solutions to imposter syndrome, fear of asking for raises, the search for work-life balance, and many other challenges that conspired to hold them back. Kelli's book, *Closing the Confidence Gap*, is her women's coaching program framework, inspired and actionable, written with her trademark fierce advocacy for her clients. As someone who speaks directly to women, Kelli embodies the confidence she teaches. So she achieved her dream of writing a book—and invigorated the genre she vowed never to be part of.

Other times, Naren says he hears an author's initial book idea and gets the gist, but his head tilts a bit. He knows they need additional support and sifting to articulate their message so that an audience can benefit from it. This is the discipline that business book expert Josh Bernoff calls "idea development": the sharpening and positioning that turn a rough concept into a book-ready theme. The need to develop ideas is one of the many reasons successful book projects are an equal partnership between publisher and author.

Whether thought leaders choose their craft as a hobby, practice, or business (see chapter 3), books are never far removed from the discussion of how to amplify the message. Books are an ideal opportunity to present yourself with the following:

- The diligence and creativity of a thinker who has spent considerable time learning about the topic
- The camaraderie and voice of a kindred spirit whom the audience wants to spend time with
- The gravitas of a leader who has found their purpose and made a commitment to responsibly join the knowledge commons

Books are integral to all of the Four Elements of thought leadership (see chapter 4). Arguably the importance of books vis-à-vis other thought leadership media grows as our core ideas and content library expand into market offerings and a strong platform identity. A well-done book begins with a core idea that is provocative, generous, differentiated, and sticky. Some ideas can sustain a keynote or an article, but it takes work to sharpen an idea into something worthy of putting into long format and worthy of your audience's time. Your content library is a big part of how a book comes together. As Bernoff states, books are made of stories, frameworks, facts, and advice. They must support your point of view and keep your audience's attention. If you have a well-organized content library, it'll make your book project easier from proposal through writing. You can organize what you already have and identify where you need to conduct more interviews or do additional research. A book supports the creation of an entire market category, including e-books, audio-books, downloadable chapters, book summaries, and online companion assets.

Finally, A well-executed book sends strong signals about your platform identity: Who is the audience for these ideas? Why are they relevant? What value will readers get from engaging with these ideas? Sure, you probably answer those questions in your book's introduction. But they'll read that *after* they decide to start reading. Naren thinks that's why authors wrestle with the titles, subtitles, and book covers. You have to pack a lot of information about your platform identity into just a small space on the cover. And if you're lucky, your prospective follower will become interested and become your reader.

In the cultural touchstone film *The Big Lebowski*, the Dude was definitely *not* known for his interest in reading, but the character has become one of the most enduring thought leaders (albeit fictional) of the past thirty years. To borrow from the Dude, in an age of shortened attention spans and AI slop, the book abides. At a time when we crave human connection and insight, the book abides. Over the long term and in the long form, the book abides.

Naren's Pivot to Publishing

Let's get a bit personal and let Naren share how he got into this world of books.

This dude (and for the record, I am not fictional) has found the words of

Jeff Bridges's iconic "Dude" character to be an indisputable truth. They have led me to a monumentally rewarding career, even if two decades ago I had no clue about the power of books or the call of entrepreneurship.

In 2003, I was several years into a law career that I could not see going anywhere appealing. I had taken my grade-school-aged daughter Anna to a football game at my alma mater, Virginia Tech. We were coming back, and she told me she wanted to read a book about our beloved Hokie Bird mascot. That request was life changing for me, but I didn't know it yet.

For those of you who don't know (about 99 percent of those reading this), the Hokie Bird is the fierce turkey mascot of Virginia Tech University. And when I looked, there was no children's book about the Hokie Bird mascot. Then, I had an idea.

How cool would it be to have a children's book about the Hokie Bird? Surely I wasn't the only parent. Grandparents could gift the book. Virginia Tech's campus bookstore could sell them. Our alumni magazines could promote them. Surely Simon & Schuster would jump at the chance to get in early on this incredible book idea.

I was a complete novice author with a book concept. I quickly found out the realities of the situation. Zero takers. In fact, zero responses to my queries.

Why? At that time, the publishing world was heavily tilted toward traditional publishers. Their acquisition editors reviewed book proposals from an economic perspective: Could the proposed book meet a lofty sales target? But aspiring authors proposed more books than publishers could print in any year. Literary agents helped aspiring authors get their foot in the door. My grade-school daughter was not ready to be represented. But she wouldn't let go of the idea. And I couldn't either. Soon I found myself learning everything I could about how to publish a book.

I started where I was comfortable. I was an attorney, so I secured a license from the university to use their mascot. Then, I hired a student illustrator and got to work. Several months later, two pallets of *Hello, Hokie Bird!*, published under our appropriately named Mascot Books imprint, showed up on my driveway. My daughter was thrilled, and I had become an author.

It was a proud day that soon turned into a scary one. I had five thousand copies of a book, and I had no clue what to do next. Thankfully, all the campus bookstores and sports shops saw the potential. Soon, copies were flying off the shelves.

And that led to another insight: we could work with other schools and create mascot-themed titles for passionate fan bases who loved their Bulldogs and Wildcats and Tigers and Cowboys and other mascots at hundreds of colleges. We expanded into the North American pro sports leagues as well.

Then, prospective authors came to me with ideas for other types of books—memoirs, political treatises, novels, cookbooks, local histories, self-improvement. They knew I had made sense of the system. Could I help them too? Experienced and aspiring authors wanted a publisher who could provide active, à la carte support. Not quite traditional publishing. Not quite self-publishing. Somewhere in between. Hybrid.

I wanted to say yes to these authors. But first, we had to update our technology and processes. We had to go from publishing books about mascots to working with external authors. We put Mascot Books on the leading edge of what was becoming known as hybrid publishing, a middle ground between traditional and self-publishing (more on each of those later in the chapter).

As an aspiring author, I had pitched traditional publishers and got nowhere. Now, as the publisher of Mascot Books, we received a steady stream of book proposals. A lot of them were business-focused books pitched by executives, keynote speakers, executive coaches, consultants, and advocates. They were all looking to amplify their thought leadership through a book.

I saw book publishing as a way to support these big thinkers, and they were the reason I wanted to take Mascot Books to the next level. That led to the launch of Amplify Publishing. It became our flagship imprint and now accounts for 75 percent of our work, publishing books on business, self-help, and other nonfiction big-idea titles.

Our first Amplify book under the business imprint was a book called *Brainwashed*, by former NFL player and ESPN commentator Merril Hoge. The author, along with his medical contributor, Dr. Peter Cummings, challenged prevailing theories on the supposed correlation between chronic traumatic encephalopathy (CTE) and football. With more and more high-profile deaths being attributed to CTE, the author had a contrarian view on this timely topic.

Merril's primary mission was to get valuable information to his target audiences: athletes, parents, physicians, school leadership. His motivation for the book was service. He wanted to help people. His well-researched and well-written book did just that. The book launched a national morning news show; it sold well. More importantly, it helped change the conversation about CTE. I'd seen how ideas could entertain (children's books about school mascots), and now I'd been alongside an author as he boldly put an important idea into the spotlight and changed the conversation.

Publishing Pathways—Traditional, Hybrid, Self

Once you decide you want to write a book, you need to evaluate your publishing options. It's a great time to be an author making your way in the world of publishing. Today there are many viable paths, from easily accessible self-publishing, to the challenging quest for a traditional publisher, to the middle way of hybrid. There are good reasons to choose any of the three options, so you will need to choose what makes the most sense for you.

Basic Features of Each Publishing Option

	TRADITIONAL	HYBRID	SELF-PUBLISHING
WHO PAYS	Publisher	Author	Author
WHO KEEPS THE INCOME	Publisher (with a small royalty to the author)	Author (with a small administrative fee to the publisher)	Author
BENEFITS	• Prestige of being selected • Limited direct costs to getting your book produced • Bookstore marketing resources	• Much more control over content and marketing decisions and timelines • A direct line to the publisher	• Less expensive • All income retained • Total editorial and marketing control on all decisions and timelines
NEGATIVES	• Limited control over editorial and marketing decisions and timelines • Often requires an agent to make the connection • Takes years to get to market	• More direct costs than traditional	• Harder to promote and distribute without publishers' infrastructure • All work must be handled by author or designees, which can mean a steep learning curve and extensive time commitment for potentially less than professional results

Your manuscript doesn't have to be written before you start reaching out to a publisher. In fact, with traditional and hybrid publishing, you will need to start with a book proposal anyway.

In a book proposal, you share the book's outline, your intended audience, your credentials, and your current ability to reach your target audience. Many prospective publishers want to see an introduction and a chapter or two so they can assess your writing style.

Naren is proud of Amplify's role in helping to make hybrid publishing a viable option for many authors who would struggle to get a deal with a traditional publisher. But he does not try to steer all authors to hybrid. If an author can get a traditional contract from a publisher committed to putting resources toward the project and can wait years for publication, that can be a great opportunity for them. If an author has limited funds and isn't worried about a massive marketing campaign to sell as many copies as possible or become a bestseller, self-publishing may be the best route.

What we all can say with confidence is that there is a publishing option for everybody these days—that is, if a manuscript is conceived and drafted and ready to be submitted. Which leads us to the nuts and bolts of writing and publishing a book.

Chapter 14

The Path to Publishing

When Urs Koenig got serious about writing a book, he had a message he was eager to share. Urs's idea was to present the essential, largely untapped value of humility for leaders who are trying to find successful results in our chaotic, rapidly changing era.

He was confident that he was in a unique position to advocate for that idea, having lived, studied, spoken, and written about it his whole adult life. He could draw on a lifetime of stories and evidence about humility from high-stress experiences as an ultra endurance champion, a UN peacekeeper, an executive, and a researcher.

Urs is a practical guy, and he knew that any book has an uphill climb just to sell more than a few hundred copies. Plenty of times, he asked himself if the world needed "another leadership book." It wasn't just a healthy dose of humility that had him muttering to himself, "Everybody thinks their book is going to be a bestseller. Everybody thinks they have 'the answer.' Why do I think I should do this?"

Still, he believed in the power of humility and envisioned an audience eager for his message. He thought he could generate significant impact, and maybe, just maybe, the book could even sell reasonably well.

But there was one problem, the most elementary problem for every thought leader who has found themselves in Urs's position: He hadn't yet written word one.

You've decided to write your first—or next—book. The first step in so many things, they say, is the hardest, and it's certainly true in being an author. Conceptualizing and writing a book can feel daunting, and this chapter is meant to lessen that learning curve for you.

So what is a good first step? Ask yourself *why* you want to write the book.

Why Do You Want to Write a Book?

As founder of Mascot Books in 2003 and CEO of Amplify Publishing now, Naren has spoken with hundreds of business authors over the years, and one of the first questions he asks is "What's your goal for this book?"

He hears a lot of answers, many of them tied to business results:

- Growth-Minded CEOs want to use a book to grow their business and strengthen their brand.
- Impact and Legacy Executives tell me they've got something to say.
- Thought Leaders on the Run want books to generate leads and increase their rates.
- In-House Experts write books as part of the company's initiatives (or because the CEO told them to).

And many people—from Hall of Fame Thinkers to novices—tell Naren they want to get ideas out of their head and into print.

But when Naren asks why they want to write a book, he's really listening for one specific answer: "I want to help others." And if some variation of helping others isn't near the top of the list, Naren says he gets concerned.

Throughout this book, we've shared stories about business book authors who embrace the value of "share, don't protect." For example, in chapter 7, we met Dr. Ivan Misner of Business Network International, who wrote books that didn't generate direct wealth. He took a "Giver's Gain" philosophy and simply gave his audience what they wanted. He was an open book, and that choice grew his business. Thought leadership authors realize the money isn't always in selling books. Sometimes the influence the books generate is the real benefit to invest the time in the author's journey.

When you author a book, you invest time that could be spent on many fun and/or important things. Why will you devote time, energy, resources, and reputation to a book project? What will sustain you through the process of researching, writing, and promoting a book? If you can't answer that question with confidence, you will find yourself frustrated when the priority of book writing collides with other priorities and opportunities.

When to Write Your First Book

A book can happen anywhere in a thought leader's journey, but we see it often successfully deployed in a Goldilocks moment. The thought leader has acquired just enough experience and testing of their idea. They want to explore it. They're ready to brand themselves with it to the greatest degree possible to an audience they can envision listening to it.

Certainly, some aspiring authors will try their hand earlier in their careers than others. Some wish to wait until they have established their views more fully or are thinking about legacy. Any author has an intuitive as well as a business sense of when it is best to start looking for a publisher. The thought leadership assessment you undertook in chapter 2 is equally relevant for deciding whether to write a book. You need to be confident about your current state, clear about your goals, and honest about the context you are in.

Naren is asked all the time if someone needs a book before they can launch a successful speaking practice. And the answer from this publisher might surprise you. No, it is not a prerequisite. Ryan Estis has proven this to be the case, having enjoyed one of the most successful keynote speaking practices on the circuit, primarily in the area of sales.

"I was fully focused on establishing my practice," Ryan said. "And then, once it's in place, you spend even more time growing the practice. Writing a book was never the priority. It couldn't be the priority. Until it was the priority."

Finally, in 2024 he released a book with his brother, Chad—executive vice president of the Dallas Cowboys & Legends—titled *Prepare for Impact*. It was a labor of brotherly love while also an expression of the business benefits and the value of service through human-centered leadership.

So what was the result?

"I certainly don't regret waiting as long as I did, but the experience of writing a book with my brother was so gratifying, and the impact it had on my business was immediate and profound," Ryan said. "I decided to focus on bulk sales to event organizers, and it's now rare for me to speak without some books being sold as part of my speaking fee."

Ryan's strategy worked, having sold out of his initial print run in a few months, and the second printing has fared just as well.

And Ryan's second book is in the works. That says it all!

Key Milestones in a Book Project

It's instructive to consider key milestones in the life of a book project. While the production process is chock full of detailed steps that need to get done and decisions that need to be made, this list hits the highlights, the markers that move the project forward on the path to publication.

Finding the Germ of an Idea

Britt Yamamoto fittingly had the germ of his book proposal while he was an organic farmer. As his career evolved to his guiding leadership trainings around the world, the similarities between natural systems and human-engineered organizations, including the complimentary language of sustainability and connection, were clear to him. His book, *The Soil of Leadership*, challenges leaders to "dig where we stand" and create the conditions for transformation (the soil) that forms the foundation of any grand vision of success. It is from there where you build roots—and values—that sustain and endure.

It's a metaphor that is easy to grasp, inspiring, and powerfully authentic for Britt to share given his life experience. Amplify was ready to work with Britt on day one.

The Amplify One-Pager

One tool Naren loves to help authors lock in their goals is what he calls the Amplify One-Pager. It's basically a mini book proposal. It's deceptively simple in form, but Naren has seen it work time and time again to help authors get the juices flowing and the keyboard clicking.

Here are the elements of the Amplify One-Pager:

1. **Title and subtitle:** At this stage, think of this as a working title and subtitle, but even before a single word has been written, it's helpful to put some labels on the forthcoming work.
2. **Author bio:** Who are you, and what qualifies you to write this book? For this purpose, keep the bio to three or four sentences.
3. **Big idea:** What's the book about, and why is it important? Five or six sentences is what works here.
4. **Target audience:** Who is this book written for? This is critical, and you must be able to articulate this clearly. Be as specific as possible.
5. **Comparative titles:** Know what's already published on your subject matter.

That's it. The value in this is that it doesn't allow you to pontificate about a subject you surely know a huge amount about. You can't get sidetracked or hit the minor points in one page; you go big! Less is more when you're selling a publisher—not to mention a reader eventually—on your big idea. You will find a blank one-pager template to create your own in section 4. Our book website, thoughtleadershiphandbook.com, contains the actual one-pager for *The Thought Leadership Handbook* and a blank one-page PDF for you to use.

Articulating the Big Idea to Your People

As founder, CEO, and executive coach at Novus Global and the Meta Performance Institute, Jason Jaggard is a Growth-Minded CEO, and he is with coaches every day who work with top performers across many careers. The knowledge gained by faculty at Meta Performance Institute along with field work of Novus Global coaches provided an ideal synthesis of research and practice that allows high-achievers a peek into what they can do to elevate their games even further. Jason's book *Beyond High Performance* mines this fascinating topic with personality, humor, and inspiration.

In articulating his big idea, he took a page from the playbook of Janet Foutty of Deloitte Consulting (see chapter 7), who reluctantly entered what became the *Wall Street Journal* bestseller book project *Arrive and Thrive* with Susan MacKenty Brady and Lynn Perry Wooten. Or Marshall Goldsmith's *New York Times* bestseller *What Got You Here Won't Get You There*. Committing to the book project means Jason is now able to provide clients and a much broader audience a taste of what his team experiences while also amplifying the Novus Global and Meta Performance Insititute names.

The Writing Process

People in publishing can easily complicate matters when talking about how to get a book project accomplished. If you ask us for advice on how to write, we'll give you stories of what's worked for other people. We can drown you in writing advice.

- It's better to write in the morning . . . or maybe it's the evening?
- Make a playlist.
- Carve out a consistent chunk of time. Make it long enough but not too long.
- Plow through with a full first draft before you revise . . . or should you revise as you go?

Everyone will offer opinions on how best to write. But every writer is different, and each has to chart their path to the finish line.

Naren's advice to you when it comes to determining your writing process is quite simple: Be honest with yourself about your time constraints and your writing skills and then choose one of these three options:

1. Write it yourself and then get an editor to guide you in how to elevate the quality.
2. Hire a writing coach who will guide you along the way as you're writing.
3. Hire a ghostwriter who will guide you in interviews, write it for you, and ensure it's in your authentic voice.

Your best-laid plans can and will get smashed. Naren has seen authors get delayed for weeks, months, and even years (some never to get back on track) because they weren't able to admit what they were capable and willing to do.

Naren knew one author who was perpetually busy. Whenever Naren would check in with him, he hadn't done any work to get closer to a manuscript. Naren suggested he try the Amplify One-Pager proposal. The publisher suggested he create a working table of contents. Naren tried everything to help get him enthused, build momentum, and see a path forward. He was stuck.

So, Naren suggested he hire a ghostwriter. The author was in a financial position to hire an experienced ghostwriter with expertise in his industry. Naren and his Amplify team thought this would be a great way to help him get the ideas out of his head and into a book.

He grumbled and told Naren a story about one of his competitors who had written his own book—without a ghostwriter—and said, "If he could do it, I can do it." After hearing that misguided rationale, can you guess the status of that project today, five years later?

There's no shame in being busy. You don't have to be a stellar writer. Make a choice that will get the project done—importantly, with the help of a professional. Note that all three options above include *guidance.*

Don't frustrate yourself with writing expectations you aren't able to meet. No one (other than perhaps you) is locking you in a room to complete the book. Whatever you choose is self-imposed. So get real with yourself, and make a decision that leads to success.

Remember our friend Urs Koenig? When we left him earlier in the chapter, he hadn't yet written a single word. However, he had a clear understanding of the obvious obstacles in his path:

- "How do I present my ideas in the most powerful way?"
- "How will my book-length work differ from my previous work (many articles, blog posts, keynote speeches, and other writing) through the years?"
- "How does the entire writing and publishing process even unfold?"

Urs felt a vague but looming concern. It's not that he didn't know what words he *wanted* to write. It was choosing them, drafting them, organizing them, and revising them many times over that was still ahead of him. His uncertainty threatened to derail him before he ever got started.

"I had plenty of questions for friends who were professional writers and editors as well as colleagues and mentors who had written books," Urs said. "It was daunting, but I also began to realize that it isn't magic. It's creating a system, following through, and asking for help from others who knew more than I did. When I thought of publishing a book from this angle, it's not much different than how I reached my goals in all areas of my life."

Urs experienced what we're guessing 99.9 percent of first-time authors go through. (We'll assume there's a few out there who don't manifest any self-doubt when writing their books, but we have yet to meet any of them—and Naren's known his fair share of authors over the years.) The Amplify team that worked with Urs to bring his book to the world in the months ahead saw Urs do up close what every successful thought leader does when confronted with the uncharted path ahead: He got to work.

First off, he asked the Amplify publishing professionals for input on which writing path to choose. They got him working with a writing coach who met regularly with him as he wrote one chapter at a time; he got feedback from the coach, revised, rinsed, and repeated. Pretty soon, Urs had enough chapters for a book. Along the way, he researched. He asked mentors, peers, and subject matter experts for help. He held himself accountable with benchmarks. He course-corrected.

Rather poetically, he embodied the humility that he championed in his book.

Staying Vulnerable During Content Development

When authors start writing, they often think they know where they're going. But the writing process has a way of opening minds to more than they ever imagined. Jonathan Crawford is a telecommunications executive with an inspiring and harrowing story of overcoming drug addiction, family deaths, and multiple hardships for decades before he found his path to the C-suite.

Surviving Jonathan was intended as more of a retelling of his personal journey than a thought leadership book, and he was willing from the outset to let his writing be as vulnerable and real as possible. With a writing coach, he poured out his heart.

After the book was edited and laid out, however, he discovered that he was still holding back. He wasn't as forthcoming as he'd wanted to be. He told Naren's Amplify team to hold up while he did an additional revision round, which allowed him to dig deeper into his emotional state during pivotal periods in his past. "I realized I was still protecting myself," Jonathan said. "Once I let go, the book found its voice. That became a book I would be proud to share with the world."

That approach also allowed him to tap into concepts like posttraumatic growth and the 360 degrees of resilience, topics on which he speaks regularly. Thus, the book ended up having tools for readers to use when they're struggling—a self-help book, a business memoir, and a cathartic exercise for leaders everywhere to experience, all wrapped into one.

As you write a book, you have an opportunity to look inward and ask yourself questions:

- "What have I learned?"
- "Do I need to dig deeper within myself?"
- "What necessary, imperfect truths will I speak about?"
- "How will these insights help my audience?"

Throughout this book, we have told stories of thought leaders as they aspired, struggled, and persisted. We, as authors of this book, have also shared our own mistakes and setbacks. People want stories with authenticity and vulnerability. Yet whenever you share a story—whether your own or those of others—tell those stories with respect. In chapter 11, Mark Goulston distinguishes between "nice" and "kind." Kind means you have the power to hurt others with your words but you choose never to do so.

Between First Draft and Books in Hand

Regardless of the publishing route you take, many tasks and decisions occur throughout the book development process that require further questions professionals and experienced authors need to get right. Cover design. Proofreading. Getting an ISBN. Asking for testimonials. Distribution. Fulfillment. Registration. Optimizing your book on Amazon, your local booksellers, and the audiences you want to reach. The list goes on.

It's beyond the scope of this chapter to go that deep. Remember what we said in chapter 13 in making the case for books as relevant? We are happy to have more books as long as they are well done. Our focus here was on shaping content that is well conceptualized, well researched, and well written. But there is a whole publishing ecosystem to navigate, and your next book will thank you for putting in that effort.

There are many good resources out there, including in the final section of this book and at the book's website. In our thought leadership space, we have to give a shout-out to Josh Bernoff, a friend of the publishing industry in so many ways. He's a no-nonsense voice for timely and essential questions at conferences and in his blog (bernoff.com). Specific to this chapter's discussion, he literally wrote the book on navigating the entire publishing process for thought leaders: *Build a Better Business Book: How to Plan, Write, and Promote a Book That Matters.* And if you have more questions, you can even subscribe to his answers in a chatbot.

Promoting Your ~~Book~~ Brand

"My publisher exceeded my expectations when it came to book marketing," said no author in the history of the world. OK, so perhaps that previous sentence was a bit of an exaggeration, but we're here to deliver the reality of book marketing.

An author must be engaged in the marketing of their book. Period. Full stop.

Your book will never have the impact you want unless you, the author, are 100 percent committed.

So what does that look like? The tricky part is that it varies from project to project and author to author.

There are book marketing best practices, of course. But when you develop your marketing game plan, just know that you will try one hundred things and only twenty will yield actual and measurable results. The problem is that it's hard to predict with certainty which twenty will actually bring in book sales.

But remember what we said earlier in this book: Be focused on project ROI, which is always well beyond book sales. Employ marketing strategies that will help you monetize, such as keynote speaking, coaching, consulting, teaching courses, or conducting business development.

Greg Scheinman started with a simple premise:

> I'm approaching middle age. I've seen success and failure. I want to ask successful guys my age how they live their lives, run their businesses, overcome screwups, take care of their families, find inspiration, choose their wardrobe, have fun, and any other questions that come across my brain. So I'll start a podcast and learn. It was like taking a weekly masterclass with experts across dozens of business, entertainment, and academic domains.

Greg was still in the insurance business then, but as the podcast grew, he had a bigger vision: to be the one-stop shop for men in middle age to stay on top of their games. Now retired from insurance and in his fifties, Greg has defined the space with more than two hundred podcast episodes, a thriving coaching business, retreats, speaking gigs, curated sponsorships, a weekly e-magazine, a steady and impassioned flow of social media posts, and significantly more cachet when he reaches out to successful men for interviews.

Naren first met Greg at trade shows when they were both young entrepreneurs. Naren was selling children's books with NCAA-licensed content; Greg was selling Team Baby Entertainment DVDs out of the trunk of his car, a children's video business he eventually sold to Michael Eisner, former CEO of Disney. Naren and Greg had stayed in touch over the years, so it was easy for Naren to discuss the value a book would add to his role as thought leader for his demographic.

Developing the book project with Greg two decades later was personally gratifying for Naren. Seeing how it enhanced his fledgling enterprise as founder and CEO of the Midlife Male was a testament to how a book can help a business grow. Greg's book—the elegantly titled *The Midlife Male: A No Bullshit Guide to Living Better, Longer, Happier, Healthier, and Wealthier and Having More Fun in Your 40s and 50s (Which Includes More Sex . . . and What Guy Doesn't Want That?)*—is a vital part of his Midlife Male portfolio.

Greg is a prime example of the Growth-Minded CEO, an avatar that must answer skepticism from an audience that questions whether they authentically believe their message or if they're merely trying to sell something. Greg's enthusiasm leaves no doubt his business is meant to serve his audience, and when he does sell something, he has personally approved it. It just so happens that his business gives him a chance to continue learning how to be a better man. His original goal has never wavered.

Authors Are a Generous Group

Marshall Goldsmith is a bestselling author, but as we discussed in chapter 11, he's also a Hall of Fame Thinker who lifts others up who want to help others as he has. Naren talks to Marshall relatively often because Amplify partners with him on his 100 Coaches imprint. A publishing imprint is a vital way to build beyond your book around common interests of an audience, allowing you and your fellow authors a chance to promote more effectively. Marshall has been a catalyst for many thought leaders through 100 Coaches, just as other imprints such as RealClear Publishing, Sports Business Journal Publishing, and Thinkers50 Publishing do for their ideas.

We mentioned that an author's motivation to work on a book often stems from wanting to be, like Marshall, of service to others. Having worked with so many authors over the years, Naren is fully convinced there's not a more generous group out there. They've been through a daunting and sometimes thankless process, and they're eager to share their experience with others in the author community.

We're closing this chapter by returning to where it began, with Urs Koenig. He took extensive notes throughout the development, production, and marketing aspects on his way to publishing *Radical Humility* with Amplify.

Urs learned so much, and he wanted other would-be authors who didn't know how to proceed to gain from his experience. Thus, undaunted by the major undertaking of publishing his first book, he published another book within a few months of his first.

Urs's second book is titled *The Hybrid Publishing Handbook: Everything I Wish I'd Known Before Writing, Producing, and Marketing My First Book*, and it is a thoughtful and detailed case study of his book journey, with all the wins and stumbles along the way. It was his way of giving back to future authors (download it for free at urskoenig.com/hybrid-publishing-handbook), an addendum to the thought leadership contribution he had already made by publishing his book.

With enthusiasm, honesty, vulnerability, and a commitment to the process, Urs has helped thought leaders. *That's* radical humility.

Does the World Need More Books?

Urs achieved much with his first book, *Radical Humility*. It was an Amazon bestseller, an Axiom Best Leadership Book of the Year, and a Best Leadership Book winner from the National Indie Excellence Awards. He radiates joy and gratitude in his texts and emails to Naren and his team. They see his energy in his LinkedIn posts. The book has led to speaking gigs, meaningful friendships, and great conversations. All directly because of his book.

But that book might never have been. Even during the manuscript development process, Urs asked himself, "Does the world need more leadership books?" He could have easily stopped writing.

Even today, when books are literally his business, Naren asks himself, "Does the world need more books—of any sort?" He became an author when his daughter wanted a Hokie Bird book that he couldn't buy for her. And he became a publisher when no one else would publish the manuscript.

We don't know that the world needs *more* books, but it always needs more books that are thoughtful and well executed, from people who have ideas worth spreading—ideas that bring joy, entertain, or share insights and those that contribute much-needed knowledge to the intellectual commons.

That's why book publishing will never die, no matter the format, no matter the imprint.

The number of books continues to grow exponentially. Thought leadership, with its commitment to amplify ideas, is certainly a major part of that surge.

We'll always encourage people to write their stories and share their knowledge, whatever career stage they're at, in whatever format fits their needs. You never know what unexpected results you might gain when you pursue the dream of being called author.

Section 4 follows, with tools that will help you hone your message and derive benefits from writing a book as well as any of the other media that thought leaders choose.

SECTION FOUR

THE TOOLS TO ACT

I P Co Mkt ! ✓ V→ %

SECTION FOUR OVERVIEW

Section 4 offers in-book and online tools to help you practice thought leadership better.

- "How do I improve my thought leadership?"
- "How do I create more impact?"

Over the past twenty years, we've developed and refined consulting tools to help hundreds of our clients find answers to these questions.

The book's companion digital workbook contains interactive versions of these tools, plus additional resources and materials.

How to Use This Section

The next two pages contain visual indices that lead to self-guided activities.

We have organized frequently asked questions around two of our core frameworks: the Four Elements of thought leadership and the Impact Equation (both described in section 1 of this book).

Four Elements Visual Index

Simple

Insightful Thinking

Market Facing

Expanded

Impact Equation Visual Index

IMPACT = ! x ✓ x V→ x %

Idea Simplicity · Audience Relevance · Velocity · Audience Share

These activities will be much easier if you are familiar with both frameworks, but it's not necessary.

1. Turn to the visual indices.
2. Scan the questions in the visual index.
3. Find a question that you want to explore.
4. Note the page number next to it.
5. Turn to that page in the book.

A note on terms: Throughout these activities, we use concepts from the Four Elements and Impact Equation frameworks (from section 1). Terms like *core ideas*, *content library*, *market offerings*, and *platform identity* provide precise language for assessing your current state and improving your practice.

What's Not in This Section

Some challenges require detailed business analysis. You won't find activities covering pricing strategy, sales positioning to corporate buyers, or complex product decisions. If you want help, we're available to assist you with those questions.

I "What Is My Core Idea?"

Thought leadership starts with your rough insights. Maybe you notice a pattern, face a challenge, or develop a technique for yourself or your team. You might spot a pattern in a dataset.

- Rough insights are valuable to *you*. But they're not thought leadership yet.
- Core ideas are valuable to *others*, because you've polished them carefully.

This activity will help you polish rough insights into core ideas.

Generate Raw Insights

Generate three to ten insights that have thought leadership potential.

- If you're new to thought leadership, aim for at least three insights.
- If you're established, push past your familiar topics to explore edges of your practice.

Don't filter yet.

Apply Three Filters

Review your list. For each insight, ask yourself the following questions:

- **Energy:** Does this insight make you lean forward when discussing it? Would you choose to spend fifteen minutes discussing it with someone who needs it?
- **Audience:** Name three people who struggle with challenges this insight addresses. Generic audiences like "business leaders" limit your ability to signal relevance.
- **Source:** Did you develop this through your own research, practice, or synthesis? Insights adopted directly from others' published frameworks don't qualify.

As you review each insight, circle those that pass all three filters. If nothing passes, ask trusted colleagues, "What topics light me up?"

Explore One Insight

Pick one circled insight that strongly appeals to you. Explore that insight through the following questions:

- **Where it came from:** What led you to this insight (experiences, research, or patterns)? Concrete origin stories create stronger foundations.
- **What it changes:** How has this insight changed your decisions or recommendations? If you haven't applied it yourself, you can't credibly advocate for others to adopt it.
- **What response it gets:** When you discuss this with someone facing this challenge, do they say, "Tell me more" (genuine interest) or "That's interesting" (polite dismissal)? Base your answer on actual conversations when possible.

Interpret Your Results

Check all that apply:

☐ **Energy:** This insight still energizes you after examination.
☐ **Audience:** You can name individuals (not generic audiences) who need this.
☐ **Source:** When you search for this insight online, you find no one framing it this way.

If you checked all three boxes, sharpen this insight into a core idea (see "How Do I Sharpen My Idea?").

- **If you couldn't check the *energy* box:** Try another idea. Some ideas don't survive scrutiny.

- **If you couldn't check the *audience* box:** Without actual people in mind, you're solving abstract problems. Identify real people who struggle with this issue, or explore a different insight.
- **If you couldn't check the *source* box:** Search more thoroughly. If others have articulated this insight well, position yourself as an advocate rather than originator. Explore a different insight.

I "How Do I Sharpen My Core Idea?"

Even the strongest insight fails when people give polite nods and move on.

Core ideas change conversations, launch careers, and reshape how people think. They're short, provocative, generous statements that make your target audience say, "Tell me more."

Write your idea as you'd share it with someone.

- Is it provocative?
- Is it generous?
- Is it distinctive?
- Is it short and sticky?

In this activity, you'll sharpen this idea into a core idea through revision.

Is It Provocative?

Core ideas name what people feel but haven't articulated. They're provocative and challenge an assumption. They invite conversations.

- **Obvious:** "Thought leadership is a good way to attract attention to yourself."
- **Provocative:** "You have a duty to speak imperfect, little-*t* truths. You have no right to an audience."

If everyone nods, you're stating the obvious. And if a good insight doesn't spark a fire in you, it can't be *your* core idea, no matter how smart it sounds. In either case, you will need to revise. Whenever people lean in—because they want to hear your every word or to debate—you have crafted a provocative idea.

Is It Generous?

Core ideas give people a path forward, not just a problem to worry about.

- **Descriptive:** "Most experts struggle with thought leadership."

- **Generous:** "Expertise in your field ≠ thought leadership expertise, but thought leadership is a learnable skill."

If your insight only diagnoses the problem, add what your audience can do with it. When you give people a glimpse of a new way forward, you have a generous idea.

Is It Distinctive?

Read your insight aloud. Does your idea sound like you or someone else? Practicing someone else's core idea is legitimate work. But that's not your thought leadership—it's amplifying theirs. If the idea is borrowed, find your unique angle or return to "What Is My Core Idea?" and explore a different insight. Shape your core idea around your work, your experience, and your story. When you speak your imperfect, little-*t* truth in your own voice, you have a distinctive idea.

Is It Short and Sticky?

A core idea must be very short, usually fewer than twenty words.

Examples:

- **Bland:** "Thought leadership practice requires understanding that the underlying motivations matter more than the specific delivery formats chosen."
- **Sharp:** "Why you practice thought leadership matters far more than the formats you use."

Don't just count the words: Make every word count. Pretend you have ten seconds before someone walks away. What will make them turn around and say, "Wait, what?"

1. **Concise:** Cut setup, detail, and hedging.
2. **Concrete:** Look for abstract terms. Replace them if possible.
3. **Sketchable:** Try simple visuals (circles, arrows, quadrants, sequences).
4. **Patterned:** Embrace rhythm, alliteration, and parallel structure. "Stop,

P

drop, roll" uses three parallel verbs. "Sharpen the saw" uses alliteration. Pattern creates memory hooks.

Search for the essential: What can't you remove?

Tips

- Once you have a core idea that seems provocative, generous, distinctive, and short—get it out into the world. Go get feedback.
- Polishing a core idea is an ongoing part of your work. You don't need to get it perfect on the first try.

Co "What Content Do I Have?"

Your content library is how you support and illustrate your ideas. Good material gets lost over time, or you don't recognize it as reusable.

This activity pushes past recency bias. You'll rediscover lost material and identify reusable assets you've overlooked.

Seven Types of Content Library Assets

Content assets come in many different forms, including the following:

- **Stories:** Personal experiences, breakthrough moments, stories from others
- **Examples:** Instances that illustrate your point
- **Data:** Your research, published studies, statistics from credible sources
- **Phrases:** Memorable language that captures your concepts
- **Case studies:** Detailed accounts of problems solved or changes implemented
- **Quotes:** Powerful statements from others that support your work
- **Frameworks, models, and processes:** Structured approaches, methodologies, systematic thinking

Content assets are reusable. Use them in a speech today, an article tomorrow, and your book next year. These delivery containers change, but the content remains valuable.

Push Past Your Greatest Hits

List forty reusable pieces of content. This number forces you past obvious sources.

- **Emerging thought leaders:** Forty may seem large. You'll hit a wall around eight to ten items. Keep going. You have more reusable content than you think.

- **Established thought leaders:** Forty may seem laughably small. You may

have hundreds of assets. Start with your go-tos and greatest hits.

In our consulting work, we've found that most practitioners break through *around* forty assets and then rapidly add hundreds they'd forgotten. Stick with the process.

Generate Your Inventory

Start with what's in your head: Stories you tell, frameworks that guide your decisions, phrases you use, lessons you've learned. Stories in your head count. You don't need written documentation yet.

Examine finished material: Each presentation, article, workshop, or podcast episode contains multiple assets. Identify the stories you told, the data you cited, the frameworks you referenced. Extract these individual pieces.

Dig into older files: Projects from years ago, conference presentations, client deliverables. These assets are still valuable even if the original container is outdated.

Document Your Inventory

Use the table below to begin tracking your inventory, or find a digital version at thoughtleadershiphandbook.com.

1. Check all content types that apply. An asset can be multiple types (a story that includes data, for example).
2. Record each asset's location using whatever notation helps you find it again: "in my head," filename, presentation date, or "my orange notebook, page 34."
3. If it serves multiple audiences and contexts, check the reusable box.

CONTENT ASSET DESCRIPTION	TYPE	CURRENT LOCATION	REUSABLE?
	• Story • Example • Data • Phrase • Case Study • Quote • Framework		
	• Story • Example • Data • Phrase • Case Study • Quote • Framework		

Interpret Your Results

WHAT YOU SEE	DIAGNOSIS	NEXT STEP
Heavy imbalance: mostly one content type	Missing content types limit how you support core ideas.	Balance structured content (data, case studies, frameworks) with narrative content (stories, examples).
Fifteen to thirty reusable pieces, mostly recent	You're listing what you remember, not what you have.	Keep pushing. Dig into older material.
Forty or more reusable pieces; hit breakthrough	You've built a strong foundation.	Continue adding assets or move to "How Do I Organize My Content Library?"
One hundred or more content assets	Turn the list into a tagged content library.	See "How Do I Organize My Content Library?"

Tips

- Systematic examination, not inspiration, reveals forgotten material.
- Your content library should be a living document.
- Add new content assets when you discover or create them.

"How Do I Organize My Content Library?"

You've built a content hoard, like a dragon gathering gold. Perhaps the hoard supports your core ideas. Perhaps you gathered shiny objects because they sparkled. Turn your content hoard into a content library. This activity maps content-to-idea connections using sticky notes to spot patterns, gaps, and disconnects.

Prerequisites

- Content inventory (see "What Content Do I Have?")
- Core ideas (see "What Is My Core Idea?")
- Thirty to sixty minutes per core idea

If you have an organizational system, this activity will help you audit how well your current content library supports your core ideas.

Three Functions Your Content Serves

Soil

Ideas made for distinct audiences, ready to help seeds grow.

Clay

Adapts to the audience but rests on bedrock principles.

Bedrock

Solid and stable.
It stands the test of time.

Your content serves three functions, organized by reusability and stability:

- **Bedrock:** Frameworks, models, and processes that explain *why* your core ideas work.
- **Clay:** Reusable stories, examples, data that illustrate your bedrock.
- **Soil:** Single-use, audience-specific material you create for one presentation or client. Don't catalog it.

Map One Core Idea

1. Use three colors of sticky notes (physical or digital): one for core ideas, one for bedrock, one for clay.
2. List bedrock assets supporting this core idea: frameworks, models, or processes that explain *why* this core idea works. One sticky note per bedrock asset. Place them below the core idea. If none exist, that's your next development priority.
3. For each bedrock asset, identify clay content that illustrates it: stories, data, or examples showing it in action. One sticky note per clay asset, clustered under its bedrock.
4. Step back. What do you see? Reference the "Interpret Your Results" table below.
5. Rearrange until relationships are clear. Take a photo or screenshot.
6. When satisfied with this core idea, repeat for your next core idea.

Interpret Your Results

Check your map: Each core idea should connect to at least one bedrock asset. Each piece of bedrock should connect to many clay assets of different types. If not, the table below can help diagnose the issue and offer a way forward:

IF YOU SEE...	IT LIKELY MEANS...	WHAT TO DO
A core idea directly connected to clay (no bedrock between)	Examples without explanation	Note the gap. Develop bedrock assets that explain *why* this idea works.
A bedrock asset has fewer than five clay assets connected to it	Thin support	Gather more clay to support this bedrock asset.
A bedrock asset has only one or two types of clay	Limited ways to persuade an audience	Gather clay in the formats you're missing.
Content you can't connect to bedrock or core ideas	Stray material	Connect to frameworks/ideas or stop using it. If you have several unconnected bedrock pieces, they may suggest a new core idea.
One or two core ideas, each with five or more pieces of clay	Focused practice	When you find a great piece of clay that supports this bedrock, add it to your content library.
Three or four core ideas of uneven depth	Normal for established thought leaders	Map strongest bedrock and clay first and then fill gaps. If you see multiple patterns, prioritize and address one gap at a time.

Document Your Map

When ready to track ongoing content, transfer your map to digital. Use the structure below, or use our online tool:

CORE IDEA	BEDROCK	CLAY ASSET	TYPE (CHECK ALL THAT APPLY)	LOCATION
			☐ Story ☐ Example ☐ Data ☐ Phrase ☐ Case Study ☐ Quote	

Tips

- Map one core idea completely before starting the next. Add new assets to your tracker immediately—backlogs become overwhelming.
- At scale (more than fifty assets): Map the top ten to twenty pieces of clay per bedrock, note gaps, and use the digital tool.
- If delegating, complete one core idea together as a proof of concept.

Mkt "How Do I Choose Market Offerings?"

Most thought leaders choose formats they enjoy creating without asking what their audience prefers.

This approach may be satisfying as a creator, but it leads to disappointing reach. Find formats where your strengths meet your audience's preferences.

This activity focuses solely on formats you give away for free.

Identify Your Formats

List four to six free formats you currently use or want to use.

- **Specific:** "LinkedIn posts," "blog articles," "guest podcast appearances," and "video tutorials"
- **Vague:** "Social posts," "articles," or "podcasts"

The Comfortable Corners Framework

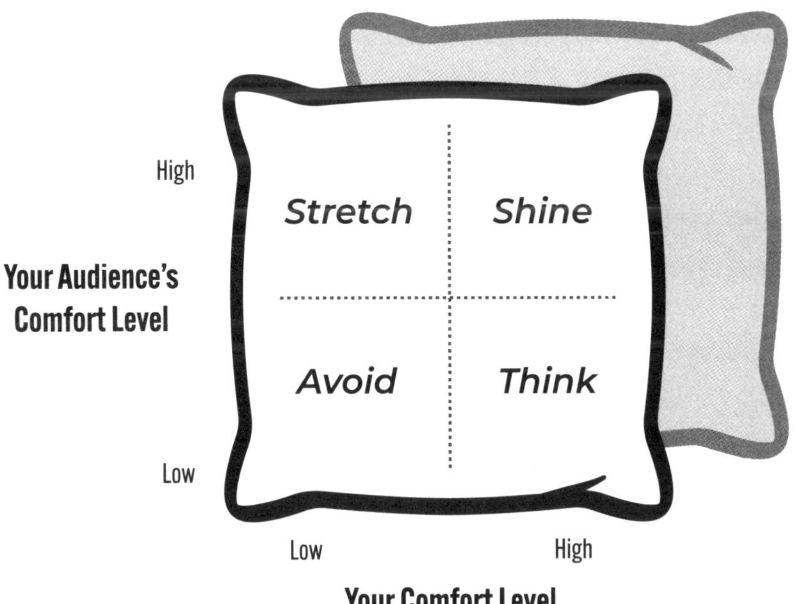

Assess each format on your comfort creating and your audience's comfort consuming:

- **Shine** (high/high): Optimal—prioritize these
- **Stretch** (low/high): Worth developing or delegating
- **Think** (high/low): Processing only
- **Avoid** (low/low): Deprioritize

In our work, Peter shines in short-form videos and podcasting. He avoids writing. Bill thinks in writing, and he stretches himself into podcasting. It's not his natural format, but he knows audiences engage there.

Assess Your Formats

1. Rate *your* comfort for each format.

- High = Energizes you, is sustainable
- Low = Drains you, is unsustainable

2. Rate *your audience's* comfort for each format.

- High = Multiple sources confirm this format resonates with your audience.
- Low = Little evidence exists that this format connects with your audience.

Use any of these three evidence sources:

- Ask people in your target audience, "What formats do you consume to learn about [your field]?" Look for patterns in their answers.
- Review formats popular in your space. Which attract engaged audiences similar to yours?

- If you publish in these formats, compare engagement to your typical metrics. Strong = above your baseline; Weak = below baseline.

For guest appearances (podcasts, publications), ask hosts about audience response *or* track follow-up inquiries.

Record Your Findings

- High You + High Audience = Shine
- Low You + High Audience = Stretch
- High You + Low Audience = Think
- Low You + Low Audience = Avoid

FORMAT	YOUR COMFORT	AUDIENCE COMFORT	CORNER
LinkedIn posts	☐ High ☐ Low	☐ High ☐ Low	Shine
	☐ High ☐ Low	☐ High ☐ Low	
	☐ High ☐ Low	☐ High ☐ Low	
	☐ High ☐ Low	☐ High ☐ Low	

Interpret your results on the next page.

P

Interpret Your Results

CORNER	WHAT THIS MEANS	NEXT STEP
SHINE	Sustainable competitive advantage	These areas should get 60 percent or more of your effort. Create a content calendar with a regular cadence. Resist diversifying until these are consistent.
STRETCH	Audience wants it, but it drains you	Commit to at least three pieces in this format. If it's still draining, delegate to someone who shines in this format. Find sustainable delivery methods.
THINK	You enjoy it, but audience doesn't engage	Use these formats for internal processing and then translate insights into Shine/Stretch formats. Don't confuse "I enjoy this" with "my audience needs this."
AVOID	Neither you nor the audience values it	Decline gracefully when asked. Reassess every six months. One peer's success doesn't mean it's right for you.

Tips

- If you have no Shine formats, test two or three more formats *or* verify your actual target audience.
- Reassess quarterly, as audience preferences shift.

Mkt “How Do I Pitch My Book Idea?”

Do you have a book idea living rent-free in your mind? Many practitioners do.

A book is a large undertaking, but the first step is simple: Write a one-page proposal with four basic sections.

- **Description of content:** What is the book’s core idea?
- **About the author:** Why should *you* write it?
- **Target readership:** Who should read it?
- **Comparative titles:** What other books already exist?

The one-pager enables you to share it with others. That could be a publisher, an editor, or an agent. It could also be trusted mentors and peers.

This is the Amplify one-pager (see chapter 14). Naren Aryal and his staff at Amplify Publishing Group use it when they talk to potential authors about their book idea.

The three authors of this book—Bill, Peter, and Naren—have known each other for many years. We work in the world of ideas and books. Yet, when we met to talk about this book, Naren said, “Let’s fill out the one-pager.” It was a very good idea.

The Thought Leadership Handbook *One-Pager*

Bill, Peter, and Naren practice thought leadership as Growth-Minded CEOs. We love books, but none of us had a lifelong ambition to become an author. We quickly agreed on two equal priorities for the book: Serve our readers well, and drive growth for both companies.

We went to work writing. There were plenty of writing days where we felt lost: *Where is this chapter going? What are we trying to say? Do these stories fit together?*

Our page proposal couldn’t answer those questions. Instead, it reminded us of our original strategy and vision. We could then choose to stay on the path or adapt.

This book adhered rather closely to the original vision. We invite you to compare our initial one-pager with the finished book. See how we put the one-pager together at thoughtleadershiphandbook.com.

Sometimes a writing project needs to course correct, and that's not necessarily a bad thing. A one-pager isn't infallible; it's a guide. There are any number of reasons a book project might need to head in a new direction. You don't need to be stubborn and stick with what isn't working. Go back to your one-pager and revise it. Or, if you need to, create a new one-pager.

Any author will tell you that there are times when writing is drudgery, no matter how much you love your subject. You can limit those occasions. Invest time in your strategy and vision before you start writing, and you'll be confident—even on the hard days—that you're writing something meaningful.

Build a Solid Vision for Your Book

Let's look at each of the four sections in the one-page proposal in detail.

Description of content: Get to the essence of your message. You've only got a few sentences to grab someone's attention. Make it count.

About the author: Tout your accomplishments *that are relevant to this book*. You have plenty, we know, but keep your bio tight. Why are you the one who should be writing about this topic?

Target readership: A thought leader who doesn't know their audience will struggle to generate impact. Be honest with yourself about who wants to read your book so you can be honest with everybody who is going to help you bring it to life.

Comparative titles: This is your competition, yes, but it can also be whom you aspire to. This section goes hand in hand with target readership. Both will help you better conceptualize what and how you want to write.

Tips

Stay on one page. The strength of this activity is that less is more.

Use the one-pager to focus your mind on what you want to share with the world. Outlining and researching come later.

Search thoroughly for comparative titles. Don't just use the examples you already know. The search will help you determine how distinctive your idea really is.

State your differentiator clearly and succinctly. Being able to do this is valuable for a thought leader in any platform, so this is time well spent when you take your book one-pager seriously.

Listen to how your body and mind respond to this process. Do you tense up? Do you find that the writing flows and you are energized by it? One by-product of this activity is that it can help you sense whether you want to write the book yourself or enlist a ghostwriter.

Write Your One-Pager

Now, try it yourself. You can use the blank template on the next page or go to our website for a digital copy.

P

Book Proposal One-Pager

Author 1/Author 1 Title

Author 2/Author 2 Title

Title/Subtitle

Book Description

About the Authors

Target Readership

Comparative Titles

P "What Is My Platform Identity?"

Do you know how people describe your ideas when you're not around? Your platform identity is the brand for your ideas.

- Do you and your audience describe your work in the same way?
- Does your audience struggle to describe your work?

You can't control your platform identity, but you can influence it. Equip your audience with language and phrases they need.

The Platform Identity Survey

This activity requires external participants. You'll go on record with your own assessment and then systematically compare it to how people describe your work.

Step 1: Go on Record First

Before asking others, answer the following eight questions about your work. Email your answers to yourself with today's date in the subject line.

1. What kinds of problems do people come to me for help with?
2. What's my main concept, framework, or approach?
3. Who specifically would benefit from my work?
4. How would I quickly explain my work to someone who's never heard about it?
5. Have I explained my work to others? If yes, what did I say? If no, what keeps me from sharing?
6. If I had to give my approach a name or label, what would I call it?
7. Who needs this idea most?
8. Where's the market for this idea? Who would pay to solve it?

Don't skip this step. Your memory will shift toward what others say once you hear their feedback.

Step 2: Choose Your Participants

Recruit eight to ten people across multiple groups to avoid selection bias. Start with three or four people who know your work best and then add others. This approach prevents selection bias—gathering feedback only from people who share your perspective or terminology.

GROUP	STRENGTHS	CONSIDERATIONS
Family/friends	Available, heard you discuss	Limited professional understanding
Superfans	Actively share your ideas with others	If you have them
Clients	Relevant professional experience	Potentially positive bias
Colleagues	Sophisticated understanding	Potential competitive dynamics

Just starting? Focus on family, friends, and colleagues who've heard you discuss your work.

Step 3: Send the Survey

Email participants with this opening: "I'm gathering feedback on how people describe my work. Would you answer these eight questions by [date one week out]?"

Questions to send:

1. What kinds of problems do people come to me for help with?
2. What's my main concept, framework, or approach?
3. Who specifically would benefit from my work?
4. How would you quickly explain my work to someone who's never heard about it?
5. Have you explained my work to others? If yes, what did you say? If

no, what keeps you from sharing?

6. If you had to give my approach a name or label, what would you call it?
7. Who needs this idea most?
8. Where's the market for this idea? Who would pay to solve it?

Step 4: Compare and Analyze

Review all responses. Open your "on the record" answers. For each of the eight questions, compare (1) what you said, (2) what participants said, and (3) how consistent participants were with each other.

Look for these patterns (if three or more participants show a pattern, it needs attention):

Inconsistent language: Participants use different terms than you or differ from each other.

Complex explanations: Your answers or theirs are too complicated to remember or share.

Unclear target audience: Participants can't identify who benefits, or their answers don't match yours.

Misaligned descriptions: Participants describe your work differently than you do.

Co

Interpret Your Results

PATTERN	NEXT STEP
Inconsistent language	Note terms three or more people used independently. If consistent terms emerge, adopt their language. If everyone uses different terms, create a one-sentence platform identity statement and test it with three new people.
Complex explanations	Create a one-sentence version. Test it with three new people. If they can't repeat it accurately after hearing it once, simplify further.
Unclear target audience	Narrow your definition, e.g., "CFOs in healthcare" instead of "executives." Test the revised language with three people in the audience or who know the audience.
Misaligned descriptions	Explore why the descriptions differ.
Multiple patterns	Address one pattern at a time over ninety days. Start with inconsistent language (easiest to fix), then unclear audience, then complex explanations, then misaligned descriptions. If gaps persist after ninety days, seek professional platform identity consultation.

Your Thirty-Day Commitment

Write down the biggest gap between your self-assessment and participant feedback.

Biggest gap between your self-assessment and participant feedback:

____

____

____

____

One change you'll make in thirty days:

Tips

- If participants request clarification on questions, that signals complexity in your platform identity.
- Test revised platform identity language with three people outside your original group.
- Repeat this assessment annually.

! "Is My Core Idea Clear?"

Live conversation reveals what editing can't. Explain your core idea in sixty seconds, watch their reactions, and then ask three questions.

The Sixty-Second Test

1. Prepare a sixty-second explanation of your core idea. Good visuals (diagram, sketch, simple image) accelerate understanding.

2. Share your core idea with three people from your target audience in separate live conversations (in-person or video). Friends and colleagues are acceptable if target audience access is limited.

3. During your explanation, watch for engagement signals:
   Strong engagement:

   - They lean forward, pause you to ask questions, or say, "Really?"
   - They immediately share examples or want to debate.
   - They say, "I never thought of it that way."

   Weak engagement:

   - They say, "That sounds like [person/book/concept]."
   - They nod politely and ask no follow-up questions.

4. After explaining, ask three questions:

   - "What's the core insight you heard?"
   - "Does this challenge how you think, or is it obvious?"
   - "Does this sound like something you've heard before? If so, from whom?"

5. Thank them. Note their responses.

6. Look for patterns across all three conversations.

Interpret Your Results

RESPONSE	DIAGNOSIS	NEXT STEP
Lean forward, ask questions, share examples	Strong engagement	Move forward to "Do People Remember My Core Idea?" and conduct the forty-eight-hour test.
Confusion, many clarifying questions	Too complex	Return to "How Do I Sharpen My Idea?" and compress further.
Polite nods, "That's interesting," but no questions	Lacks provocation	Return to "How Do I Sharpen My Idea?" and increase provocation and generosity.
Agreement, but no examples or debate	Missing generosity	Return to "How Do I Sharpen My Idea?" and add actionable contribution.
Sounds familiar, reminds them of someone else's work	Not distinctive	Return to "What Is My Core Idea?" and develop a more distinctive angle.

Tips

- Test one core idea at a time.
- Mixed signals (some engaged, some confused) mean unclear patterns.
- Test with three additional people before concluding.

!

%

! "Do People Remember My Core Idea?"

Test if your core idea sticks in memory. If you completed the "Is My Core Idea Clear?" activity, follow up with the same individuals.

The Forty-Eight-Hour Recall Test

Forty-eight hours is an ideal time frame. It allows you to check whether people put your idea into long-term memory and whether their memory aligns with what you said. This activity tests idea simplicity from the Impact Equation.

1. Deliver your sixty-second version of your core idea to three people.
2. Forty-eight hours later, email or text each person, saying, "I shared an idea with you the other day. Please explain it to me."
3. Compare *their* written responses to *your* original explanation. What patterns do you see?

Interpret Your Results

RESPONSE	DIAGNOSIS	NEXT STEP
Accurate written explanation	Strong recall	Proceed to the "Can People Recall My Core Idea When They Need It?" activity.
No recall of the core idea	Failed to stick	Test immediate reception with "Is My Core Idea Clear" before retesting recall.
Inaccurate description of the core idea	Confused recall	Experiment with different language, a memorable phrase, or a visual. Repeat the forty-eight-hour test with three new people.

Tips

If you still see confused recall after a third round of testing, revise your core idea. Return to the "What Is My Core Idea?" activity.

! "Can People Recall My Core Idea When They Need It?"

Thirty days separates ideas people remember from ideas people use. Don't shortcut the timeline. Shorter time periods test memory. This activity tests recall in real-world conditions.

The Thirty-Day Application Test

Complete "Is My Core Idea Clear?" and "Do People Remember My Core Idea?" before this test. Talk to the same three people through all activities.

1. Thirty days after people first heard your core idea, email or text each person with three questions:

    - "Would you please explain the idea to me?"
    - "Have you applied this insight in any way? If yes, what did you do differently?"
    - "Have you shared this with anyone? What did you tell them?"

2. Compare their explanation to your original core idea. Note whether they remembered accurately or inaccurately.

Interpret Your Results

RESPONSE	DIAGNOSIS	NEXT STEP
All three people remember your core accurately.	Your core idea passes all simplicity tests.	Move to testing other Impact Equation factors.
All three people remember accurately but haven't used or shared it.	Strong simplicity, unclear relevance.	This may indicate an audience relevance issue rather than idea simplicity.
One or more people remember inaccurately.	Weak idea simplicity.	Return to the "How Do I Sharpen My Idea?" activity. Make the core idea more memorable.

"Does My Core Idea Add to the Conversation?"

Even when you have a great core idea, you have no right to an audience. Earn attention by signaling relevance. Start by listening.

Prerequisite: Sharpened core idea (see "How Do I Sharpen My Core Idea?")

Four Ways an Idea Enters a Conversation

Whenever an idea enters a conversation, it fits one of four patterns:

- **Echo:** Repeats current emphasis
- **Extend:** Adds overlooked depth or application
- **Disrupt:** Challenges prevailing wisdom
- **Create:** Introduces absent conversation

Step 1: Find Active Voices

List three to five people actively producing content on your topic within the last twelve months. Check industry publications, conferences, podcasts, LinkedIn, and books targeted to your audience. Influential voices aren't necessarily frequent voices. If you can't find three active voices, your idea likely fits the Create pattern. Skip down to step 3.

Step 2: Review the Current Conversation

For each voice, review one recent piece (podcast, article, book chapter, or video). Take notes on what each voice emphasizes as the core problem or solution.

Step 3: Find Your Fit

Review your notes. Complete the sentence that fits your situation best:

- **Echo:** "The conversation emphasizes ______________, and I agree that ______________."
- **Extend:** "The conversation emphasizes ______________, and I'm adding ______________."

- **Disrupt:** "The conversation emphasizes ____________, but I'm challenging that because ____________."
- **Create:** "No one's discussing ____________ with this audience, and here's why it matters: ____________."

Interpret Your Results

PATTERN	WAYS TO SIGNAL RELEVANCE
ECHO	Your audience hears this idea elsewhere. Emphasize your unique access, role, or data they can't get. Lead with "Here's what I'm seeing . . ." Position yourself as insider/translator, not teacher. Or accept that you're amplifying others' work: advocacy/education, not original thought leadership.
EXTEND	Your audience is listening to the topic. But your addition isn't obvious yet. Name the gap explicitly in your opening: what current thinking misses or oversimplifies, and what problem that leaves unsolved. If your extension feels small, push your thinking further to ensure you're truly adding to the conversation.
DISRUPT	You're challenging prevailing beliefs. Create productive doubt. Acknowledge what current thinking gets right and then show its limits. Show the cost of staying with current thinking.
CREATE	You're introducing an unfamiliar topic. Connect it to problems your audience currently struggles with. Bridge from known to unknown. Lead with consequences, not concepts.
NOT SURE	Return to step 2 and examine two or three more pieces per voice. The pattern becomes clear when you see what multiple voices emphasize consistently.

Tips

Monitor the conversation. Reassess when (1) new voices gain attention on your topic, (2) your idea appears in others' content, or (3) your audience asks, "Isn't everyone saying this now?"

This is a starting point, not a one-time audit. Thought leadership requires listening, not just broadcasting.

"Is My Core Idea Urgent to My Audience?"

You think your idea is essential. Does your audience agree? Watch what your audience does.

- Do they invest their time?
- Do they apply their effort?
- Do they invest resources (theirs or their organization's)?
- Do they stake their reputation?

Prerequisites: A core idea and a defined target audience

Assess Your Audience's Investment

Audience relevance exists on a spectrum, ranging from nice-to-have (polite interest) to must-have (active investment). What feedback signals has your target audience given you recently? Review the table on next page. Check all signals you have recently observed.

SIGNAL TYPE	NICE TO HAVE	NEED TO HAVE	MUST HAVE
TIME	☐ Say, "Interesting" with no follow-up ☐ Not in their visible priorities	☐ Ask follow-up questions ☐ Discuss with peers	☐ Seek you out proactively ☐ Make it a team priority
EFFORT	☐ Don't change behavior ☐ Say, "Someone else should handle this"	☐ Change when supported ☐ Ensure idea doesn't get lost	☐ Lead own transformation ☐ Take personal ownership
RESOURCES	☐ No budget discussions ☐ Consume free content only	☐ Budget allocated ☐ Pay for themselves	☐ Pay premium rates ☐ Purchase for others
REPUTATION	☐ Don't share your work ☐ "Here's an idea I use"	☐ Introduce to colleagues ☐ "I find this useful"	☐ Champion publicly ☐ "I work this way"

Count checks in each column. The column with the most checks indicates your current audience relevance. If two columns are tied, use the leftmost column. Mixed signals should be interpreted conservatively.

Interpret Your Results

If you have fewer than five recent feedback opportunities, your patterns may not be reliable. Continue gathering data over the next quarter.

PATTERN	WHAT THIS MEANS	NEXT STEP
Most checks: Nice to Have	Your audience won't invest time, effort, resources, or reputation. Not viable for thought leadership business.	Test if your positioning connects to their priorities with "Does My Idea Add to the Conversation?" If differentiated but still not urgent, return to "How Do I Sharpen My Idea?" to add generosity or provocation.
Most checks: Need to Have	Your audience makes moderate investments across dimensions. This supports a viable thought leadership practice.	Focus on deepening relevance. See "Does My Idea Add to the Conversation?"
Most checks: Must Have	Your audience invests heavily across all dimensions. This supports a thriving thought leadership business.	Focus on building system velocity to multiply your impact.
Different patterns for time, effort, resources, and reputation	Uneven audience relevance.	Diagnose which dimensions are weak. Time/effort issues suggest positioning problems. Resources/reputation issues suggest delivery or credibility gaps.
Checks spread evenly across all three columns	Mixed signals indicate audience uncertainty or that you serve multiple audiences with different needs.	Narrow your target audience, or assess different segments separately.

Tips

- Watch out for situations that change audience relevance, such as external events, competitive pressure, or regulatory changes.
- Reassess whenever your audience's context changes significantly.

V→ "Why Do People Want Me Instead of My Ideas?"

People want your insights. And that's great . . . until it becomes a trap. You can't deliver workshops for two different clients at the same time.

Thought leadership requires you to build two brands simultaneously:

- **Personal brand:** How people describe you
- **Platform identity:** How people describe your ideas

Ideally, you want both brands to be strong. Many practitioners eventually run into a problem. They spend years building a strong personal brand and invest relatively little effort into the brand for their ideas.

- When people seek you out, you can raise your fees or say no.
- When people want your ideas, your presence becomes optional.

Diagnose What Drives Demand

Review opportunities over the last year—speaking requests, consulting inquiries, collaboration proposals, informal asks for your perspective. Note the exact language people used when approaching you.

Signals They Want You (Personal Brand):

- "We'd love to have you speak."
- "Would you consult with our team?"
- "Your background in [your expertise] is exactly what we need."
- They reference your credentials, experience, or reputation.
- They use your name more than your framework names.

Signals People Want Your Ideas (Platform Identity):

- "Where can I learn more?"

- “We want to implement [your framework name].”
- “We want someone to teach us your [specific approach].”
- “We’re interested in licensing [your methodology].”
- “Do you have associates or partners who deliver this material?”
- They reference your frameworks, tools, or concepts by name.

Which pattern dominates your opportunities?

Interpret Your Pattern

If you have few opportunities to review: You’re early in building your practice. Clarify how others describe your ideas. Polish the ways you signal relevance to your target audience. See “What Is My Platform Identity?” and “Does My Idea Add to the Conversation?”

Most signals point to you: Your personal brand is stronger than your platform identity. You’ve built credibility through your presence, but your ideas travel only when you do. This situation creates an exhaustion trap—every opportunity requires your personal time and energy. See “What Is My Platform Identity?” to build ideas that travel independently.

Most signals point to your ideas: Your platform identity is working well. People seek your frameworks and approaches, not just access to you. This gives you an opportunity to build system velocity and create scalable impact.

V→ "How Do I Build Personal Velocity?"

Early on, your ideas will go nowhere without you. But if you take them everywhere, you will quickly burn out. Find a sustainable pace. Personal velocity—part of the Impact Equation—represents your effort to get your ideas in front of your audience. And that pace depends on you, your personal context, and your audience's attention span. There's no easy formula, but sustainable velocity is your goal.

- For emerging practitioners, sustainable might mean an initial push to get noticed.
- For established practitioners, you may need to reevaluate your pace when your life, goals, or context change.

Identify Your Pattern

Check all that apply and then identify which column has the most checks.

LOW VELOCITY	SUSTAINABLE VELOCITY	UNSUSTAINABLE VELOCITY
• I share sporadically (monthly or less).	• I share on a consistent schedule I can maintain.	• I share constantly across multiple channels.
• I have ideas I haven't shared publicly.	• I create new content regularly without burnout.	• My calendar is packed with speaking and writing.
• I only share in paid engagements.	• I could continue this pace indefinitely.	• I'm approaching burnout from the pace.
• I wait until ideas feel complete before sharing.	• My sharing pace balances with other priorities.	• I struggle to maintain quality.
• I share when asked but don't initiate.	• I publish, even when it's imperfect.	• If I stopped, my impact would drop immediately.

Interpret Your Results

PATTERN	DIAGNOSIS	NEXT STEP
LOW VELOCITY	Sporadic sharing. No momentum. Ideas don't spread unless you push them.	Commit to one format for ninety days at a sustainable cadence. Match format to your comfort and audience interest.
UNSUSTAINABLE VELOCITY	Constant effort. High vulnerability. Impact drops if you stop.	Slow down before burnout forces the decision. Build systems to reduce personal dependence.
SUSTAINABLE VELOCITY	Consistent sharing without burnout. Balanced pace that preserves energy.	Maintain current schedule. To expand reach, build system velocity instead of increasing personal effort. See "What Are Sources of System Velocity?"

Tips

Personal velocity creates the foundation for system velocity. You need consistent personal sharing before others will share your ideas.

Ask yourself, "Do my ideas spread through others' efforts?"

- If no, focus on establishing a consistent pattern before worrying about frequency.
- If yes, your low personal velocity is strategic.

If you're starting your practice, low personal velocity is normal.

Reassess every ninety days. Life circumstances change, and your sustainable pace will shift accordingly.

V→ "What Are Sources of System Velocity?"

Your ideas can't reach everyone through your personal effort alone. System velocity multiplies your impact—others spread your ideas without requiring your ongoing involvement.

The key identifier is "not you." If each encounter requires your direct effort, that's personal velocity.

Instructions

The activity lists different ways to create system velocity for your ideas.

Mark each source below with one symbol:

- ⋆ = Working well (generates encounters without your repeated involvement)
- ↑ = Building now (developing but not yet reliable)
- ○ = Want to build (planned for future)
- ☒ = Not for me (doesn't fit your model or capacity)
- — = Discontinue (phasing out)

Ways to Create System Velocity

Owned Media

- ☐ Podcast episodes
- ☐ Newsletter issues
- ☐ Blog posts
- ☐ Articles
- ☐ Social media content (posts, videos, threads)

Products and Tools

- ☐ Books
- ☐ Individual assessments

- ☐ Organizational diagnostics
- ☐ Online courses
- ☐ Enterprise licenses

People Who Teach Your Work

- ☐ Your team members delivering programs
- ☐ Third-party licensed facilitators or trainers
- ☐ Internal trainers inside your client organizations
- ☐ Channel partners or franchisees

People Who Amplify Your Work

- ☐ Content creators (writers, ghostwriters, social media managers)
- ☐ Sales and marketing specialists
- ☐ Agents (speaking, literary, management)

Others' Platforms (Guest Appearances)

- ☐ Media coverage
- ☐ Podcast guest appearances
- ☐ Guest articles
- ☐ Anthologies and compilations
- ☐ Cross-promotion with complementary thought leaders

Institutional Adoption (Formal Structures)

- ☐ University courses or textbook inclusions
- ☐ Research citations
- ☐ Foundations, think tanks, and institutes
- ☐ Executive education programs
- ☐ Community networks (organic spread)

- ☐ Self-sustaining fan communities
- ☐ Peer learning groups (facilitated by others)
- ☐ Designated successors or protégés

Your Next Steps

After marking all sources, check for these patterns and determine your next step:

- **No * symbols?:** You rely on personal effort to create velocity.
- **No ↑ symbols?** You may have system velocity, but you're not growing it. Pick one ○ source. Start implementing it.
- **Three or more ↑ symbols?** You're potentially overextended. Develop one to * level before starting another.
- **Many ○ symbols?** Build one ○ source where you have audience access.
- **Heavy concentration in one category?** Single-source dependence creates vulnerability.

% "What's My Audience Share?"

Imagine someone asks, "Who is your target audience?" How would you reply? Many thought leaders say, "Virtually anyone could use this at home, at work, or in your community." That sounds great until you do the math. Here's the formula for audience share:

$$\frac{\text{Your current audience}}{\text{Your total potential audience}} = \text{Your current audience share}$$

Let's say you have five thousand people following your work. And your audience is anyone. There are currently 8.2 billion people in the world.

$$\frac{5{,}000}{8{,}200{,}000{,}000} = 0.00006\% \text{ audience share}$$

This is the denominator problem. When your audience share approaches zero, your impact drops to zero.

Step 1: Reduce Your Denominator

Most people claiming to serve "anyone" actually mean something much smaller. Be honest about who you're really trying to reach. Instead of "anyone," consider how to narrow your target audience and make a 1 percent audience share achievable. The table below shows what 1 percent audience share requires for different target audiences:

POSSIBLE AUDIENCE	ESTIMATED NUMBER	DESIRED SHARE %	REACH REQUIRED
Everyone	8.2 billion people	1%	82,000,000
Healthcare workers in the United States	18 million	1%	180,000

Physicians in the United States	1.1 million	1%	11,000
Chief medical officers in the United States	12,500	1%	125

Use search and AI to query reliable sources about people in a profession, organizations in an industry, etc.

If your target audience is too large (and impractical), you need to reduce it.

Your refined target audience: ______________________________

Size of this audience: ______________________________

Primary source: ______________________________

Your actual target audience size is likely smaller than the raw demographic count. Psychographic factors and organizational context will further narrow your realistic audience. For now, use the demographic count as your denominator. As you gain experience with your audience, refine your estimate based on actual conversion rates.

Step 2: Estimate Your Current Share

How many people in your target audience currently know about your core ideas? Look at the list of potential ways you engage with your target audience:

- Social media followers who fit your target audience
- Newsletter subscribers who fit your target audience
- People who've heard you speak from your target group
- Past clients within your target audience

Now make an imperfect estimate of how many in your current target audience you reach. It doesn't have to be an exact count. Refine this number, if needed, later.

The current number of people you reach in this audience: ______________

Starting practitioners will have low numbers here, and that's acceptable.

Step 3: Calculate Your Share

Current Share ÷ Target Audience Size × 100 = Your Audience Share %

For example:

500 Current Share ÷ 12,500 CMOs × 100 = 4% Audience Share

Your share: ________ percent

What This Tells You

The larger your claimed target audience, the smaller your actual audience share.

In the Impact Equation, all factors multiply together. When your audience share approaches zero, impact approaches zero—regardless of idea quality or effort.

These calculations measure awareness only. Not everyone you reach will use your ideas, and fewer still become buyers or advocates. Here are some questions to consider:

- What would it take to reach 0.1 percent of your target audience? What about 1 percent? Or 10 percent?
- For the people in your target audience who know your work, how many use your ideas?
- In your current reach, how many are buyers or potential buyers?

Your Next Step

Smaller, focused audiences amplify your other Impact Equation factors.

When you narrow from "healthcare leaders" to "chief medical officers in the United States," audience relevance becomes easier to demonstrate. You shift from hypotheticals to real examples and relevant case studies.

Tight professional networks also generate velocity. Chief medical officers know each other, attend the same conferences, and reference the same thought leaders. Your ideas travel faster in concentrated networks than diffuse ones. Focus on increasing your share of a precisely defined group.

% "How Do I Reach a Target Audience?"

Reaching the right people is never easy. The landscape shifts constantly. What can you do? It's easy to blame the algorithm or chase the latest technologies.

There's a better way: Focus on your distribution strategy using this evergreen framework.

How you share ideas determines your audience share.

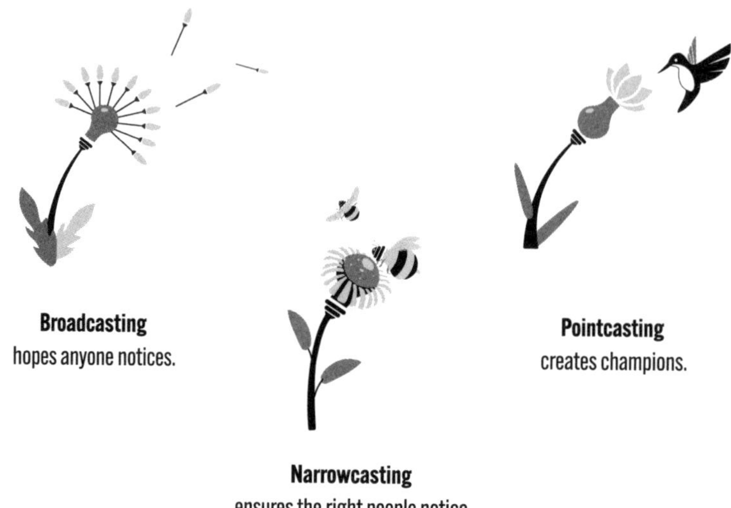

What These Look Like

- **Broadcasting:** Sharing ideas widely without targeting any audiences. A LinkedIn post on "leadership lessons" reaches whomever happens to see it.
- **Narrowcasting:** Targeting audience segments who need your ideas. An article titled "Leadership Transitions in Health Systems" in *Healthcare Executive* magazine reaches decision makers facing that challenge.
- **Pointcasting:** Communicating directly with individuals, such as an invitation to three executives for a private dinner discussing a challenge they all face.

Step 1: What's Your Recent Distribution Pattern?

Review your last year's distribution activities (posts, articles, presentations, etc.). List each significant activity, and categorize it as broadcasting, narrowcasting, or pointcasting. A careful review will reveal deeper patterns than quick percentage estimates.

Broadcasting:	Narrowcasting:	Pointcasting:
_____ percent	_____ percent	_____ percent

Interpret Your Results

Review each of the three percentages above. Are you getting the ROI you want from each strategy?

Broadcasting

We've seen many practitioners invest 70 to 90 percent of their effort in broadcasting. However, they see little impact. Never make broadcasting your default approach. It's OK to occasionally broadcast, but each time you use it, make sure it's a conscious choice. Track ROI relentlessly.

Narrowcasting

Make narrowcasting the heart of your outreach effort. It may take time to shift from broadcasting to narrowcasting.

- Identify where your target audience gathers (publications, conferences, professional associations, online communities).
- Pick one channel, and apply effort there over the next quarter.
- Track your results.
- Already narrowcasting? Audit whether your channel selection still aligns with where your audience gathers now versus where they gathered when you started.

Narrowcasting doesn't require more money or effort. You need to refocus.

Pointcasting

You cannot pointcast to everyone.

- If you're building credibility, wait until narrowcasting establishes it.
- If you're established, identify which of your relationships matter most.

Pointcasting demands greater preparation per interaction—sustainable only in small, strategic doses—but delivers highest value per interaction. What makes pointcasting work? You don't shout into the void. You don't speak to a crowd. You serve an individual.

- Be brief: Make it worth their time.
- Be provocative: Reframe their perspective.
- Be generous: Point toward a path forward.
- Be distinctive: Create personalized value.

This pointcasting list intentionally echoes our criteria for a core idea. Pointcasting personalizes your core idea for someone's current situation and needs. Your core idea doesn't change. You deliver it with white-glove service. Show others the path ahead. Encourage them. Give them the tools they need to act. They will create impact for themselves and for others. Because you do all that, they will create impact for you.

- Thought leadership is a learnable skill.
- *Why* you practice matters more than *how*.
- You have a duty to speak imperfect truths.
- Ideas can serve the commons and build your business.

DO THE WORK. FIND THE JOY.

References

Note: All *Leveraging Thought Leadership* episodes are produced by Thought Leadership Leverage. The episodes can all be found at thoughtleadershipleverage.com or wherever you get your podcasts.

CHAPTER 1: ILLUMINATING THE DARKNESS

***Leveraging Thought Leadership* Podcast Episodes**

Briceño, Eduardo. "Episode 685," December 18, 2025. 38:17.

Bodell, Lisa. "Episode 331," August 5, 2021. 20:21.

Wiseman, Liz. "Episode 560," April 18, 2024. 20:20.

CHAPTER 2: THE UNCOMFORTABLE MIRROR

***Leveraging Thought Leadership* Podcast Episodes**

Ferrazzi, Keith. "Episode 661," August 10, 2025. 29:51.

Morgan, Nick. "Episode 131," June 30, 2019. 26:11.

Morgan, Nick. "Episode 375," February 20, 2022. 45:26.

Morgan, Nick, and Joseph Michelli. "Episode 429," September 22, 2022. 33:39.

Stanier, Michael Bungay. "Episode 209," April 2, 2020. 26:50.

Stanier, Michael Bungay. "Episode 512," August 23, 2020. 33:03.

CHAPTER 3: HOBBY, PRACTICE, OR BUSINESS?

Leveraging Thought Leadership Podcast Episodes

Conant, Doug. "Episode 323," July 1, 2021. 21:46.

Hutchens, David. "Episode 489," May 7, 2023. 30:56.

Le, Bryan Quoc. "Episode 594," September 15, 2024. 23:37.

Le Gentil, Hortense. "Episode 622," January 30, 2025. 20:55.

Li, Charlene. "Episode 113," April 28, 2019. 21:01.

Pontefract, Dan. "Episode 380," March 17, 2022. 22:45.

Pontefract, Dan. "Episode 528," November 2, 2023. 31:33.

Rueff, Rusty. "Episode 606," November 14, 2024. 18:44.

Scott, Kim. "Episode 608," November 21, 2024. 21:02.

CHAPTER 4: THE FOUR ELEMENTS OF THOUGHT LEADERSHIP

Leveraging Thought Leadership Podcast Episodes

Benjamin, David. "Episode 101," March 17, 2019. 19:23.

Bodell, Lisa. "Episode 331," August 5, 2021. 20:21.

Hyun, Jane. "Episode 653," June 29, 2025. 39:10.

Komlos, David. "Episode 107," April 7, 2019. 19:42.

Sanders, Tim. "Episode 45," August 21, 2018. 27:21.

CHAPTER 5: THE IMPACT EQUATION

Leveraging Thought Leadership Podcast Episodes

Clark, Dorie. "Episode 279," December 6, 2020. 23:48.

Clark, Dorie. "Episode 455," December 29, 2022. 28:33.

Covey, Stephen M. R. "Episode 33," July 10, 2018. 25:47.

Covey, Stephen M. R. "Episode 385," April 7, 2022. 19:59.

Covey, Stephen M. R. "Episode 454," December 22, 2022. 31:31.

Books and Other Media

Bingham, Millicent Todd. *Ancestors' Brocades: The Literary Debut of Emily Dickinson.* Harper & Brothers, 1945.

Chernow, Ron. *Mark Twain.* Penguin Press, 2025.

Gordon, Lyndall. *Lives Like Loaded Guns: Emily Dickinson and Her Family's Feuds.* Viking, 2010.

Robinson, Andrew. *Einstein: A Hundred Years of Relativity.* Princeton University Press, 2015.

CHAPTER 7: THE GROWTH-MINDED CEO

Leveraging Thought Leadership Podcast Episodes

Foutty, Janet. "Episode 556," March 14, 2024. 20:00.

Goldin, Kara. "Episode 90," February 7, 2019. 21:46.

Goldin, Kara. "Episode 274," November 15, 2020. 22:57.

Misner, Ivan. "Episode 140," August 1, 2019. 24:26.

Stimpson, Kerry-Ann. "Episode 397," May 29, 2022. 33:48.

Wright, Kelly Breslin. "Episode 376," February 27, 2022. 37:32.

Books and Other Media

Goldin, Kara. *Undaunted: Overcoming Doubts and Doubters.* HarperCollins Leadership, 2020.

CHAPTER 8: THE IMPACT AND LEGACY EXECUTIVE

Leveraging Thought Leadership Podcast Episodes

Amram, Yosi. "Episode 589," August 18, 2024. 40:14.

Davis, Joe. "Episode 651," June 12, 2025. 17:42.

Fass, Rose. "Episode 32," July 5, 2018. 24:38.

Kolditz, Tom. "Episode 318," June 6, 2021. 39:56.

Kraemer, Harry. "Episode 281," December 20, 2017. 19:05.

Massie, Noel. "Episode 647," May 25, 2025. 41:47.

Radin, Amy. "Episode 67," June 11, 2018. 17:40.

CHAPTER 9: THE THOUGHT LEADER ON THE RUN

Leveraging Thought Leadership Podcast Episodes

Barrett, Morag. "Episode 378," March 10, 2022. 28:16.

Barrett, Morag. "Episode 478," March 23, 2023. 29:24.

Huffman Polson, Shannon. "Episode 17," May 15, 2018. 22:02.

Huffman Polson, Shannon, and Jan Rutherford. "Episode 396," October 6, 2021. 30:59.

James, Dravon. "Episode 564," April 21, 2024. 41:27.

Michelli, Joseph. "Episode 195," February 13, 2020. 23:58.

Michelli, Joseph, and Nick Morgan. "Episode 429," September 22, 2022. 33:39.

Shapiro, Stephen. "Episode 5," April 3, 2018. 25:22.

Shapiro, Stephen, and David Burkus. "Episode 409," July 10, 2022. 31:21.

Waldman, Waldo. "Episode 18," May 18, 2017. 20:11.

Waldman, Waldo, and Freddie Ravel. "Episode 404," June 22, 2023. 32:44.

Books and Other Media

Benjamin, Walter. *The Work of Art in the Age of Its Technological Reproducibility, and Other Writings on Media.* Edited by Michael W. Jennings, Brigid Doherty, and Thomas Y. Levin. Belknap Press of Harvard University Press, 2008.

Csikszentmihalyi, Mihaly. *Flow: The Psychology of Optimal Experience.* HarperPerennial, 1991.

Kotler, Steven. *The Rise of Superman: Decoding the Science of Ultimate Human Performance.* New Harvest, 2014.

CHAPTER 10: THE IN-HOUSE EXPERT

Leveraging Thought Leadership Podcast Episodes

Accius, Jean. "Episode 226," May 31, 2020. 26:51.

Faus, Ashley. "Episode 358," December 5, 2021. 36:28.

Faus, Ashley. "Episode 646," May 18, 2025. 55:07.

Joseph, Craig, and Jerome Pagani. "Episode 442," November 6, 2022. 36:06.

Seth, Jayshree. "Episode 327," July 18, 2021. 42:55.

Seth, Jayshree, and Amanda Diekman. "Episode 565," April 28, 2024. 46:12.

Woerner, Stephanie. "Episode 613," December 15, 2024. 43:18.

Books and Other Media

Anderson, Cindy, and Anthony Marshall. *The ROI of Thought Leadership: Calculating the Value That Sets Organizations Apart.* Wiley, 2025.

CHAPTER 11: THE HALL OF FAME THINKER

Leveraging Thought Leadership Podcast Episodes

Clark, Dorie. "Episode 279," December 6, 2020. 23:48.

Clark, Dorie. "Episode 455," December 29, 2022. 28:33.

Covey, Stephen M. R. "Episode 33," July 10, 2018. 25:47.

Covey, Stephen M. R. "Episode 385," April 7, 2022. 19:59.

Covey, Stephen M. R. "Episode 454," December 22, 2022. 31:31.

Goldsmith, Marshall. "Episode 170," November 14, 2019. 20:07.

Gonzalez, Martin. "Episode 576," June 16, 2024. 41:24.

Goulston, Mark. "Episode 3," March 20, 2018. 21:28.

Goulston, Mark, and Ryan McCarty. "Episode 426," September 11, 2022. 31:00.

Goulston, Mark. "Episode 524," October 12, 2023. 30:46.

Wiseman, Liz. "Episode 560," April 18, 2024. 20:20.

Books and Other Media

Goulston, Mark. "I'm Dying to Tell You." YouTube video series. Accessed November 12, 2025. https://www.youtube.com/@Imdyingtotellyoudrmark/videos.

Plato. *Republic.* Translated by C. D. C. Reeve. Hackett Publishing Company, 2004.

CHAPTER 12: THE DUTY TO SPEAK

Leveraging Thought Leadership Podcast Episodes

Elton, Chester. "Episode 1," March 6, 2018. 21:52.

Goldsmith, Marshall. "Episode 170," November 14, 2019. 20:07.

Books and Other Media

Drezner, Daniel W. *The Ideas Industry: How Pessimists, Partisans, and Plutocrats Are Transforming the Marketplace of Ideas.* Oxford University Press, 2017.

Hess, Charlotte, and Elinor Ostrom, eds. *Understanding Knowledge as Commons: From Theory to Practice.* MIT Press, 2007.

Ostrom, Elinor. *Governing the Commons: The Evolution of Institutions for Collective Action.* Cambridge University Press, 1990.

Plato. *Republic.* Translated by C. D. C. Reeve. Hackett Publishing Company, 2004.

CHAPTER 13: THE THOUGHT LEADER AND THE POWER OF PUBLISHING

Books and Other Media

Hoge, Merril. *Brainwashed: The Bad Science Behind CTE and the Plot to Destroy Football.* Amplify Publishing, 2018.

Linkner, Josh. *Big Little Breakthroughs: How Small, Everyday Innovations Drive Oversized Results.* Post Hill Press, 2021.

Linkner, Josh. *Hacking Innovation: The New Growth Model from the Sinister World of Hackers.* Fastpencil Publishing, 2017.

Linkner, Josh. *The Road to Reinvention: How to Drive Disruption and Accelerate Transformation.* Jossey-Bass, 2014.

Shapiro, Stephen M. *Invisible Solutions: 25 Lenses That Reframe and Help Solve Difficult Business Problems.*

Shapiro, Stephen M. *Pivotal: Creating Stability in an Uncertain World.* Amplify Publishing, 2024.

Thompson, Kelli. *Closing the Confidence Gap: Boost Your Peace, Your Potential, and Your Paycheck.* Amplify Publishing, 2022.

Wardle, Duncan. *The Imagination Emporium: Creative Recipes for Innovation.* Amplify Publishing, 2024.

CHAPTER 14: THE PATH TO PUBLISHING

Books and Other Media

Bernoff, Josh. *Build a Better Business Book: How to Plan, Write, and Promote a Book That Matters.* Amplify Publishing, 2023.

Crawford, Jonathan. *Surviving Jonathan: The 360 Degrees of Resilience.* Amplify Publishing, 2025.

Estis, Ryan, and Chad Estis. *Prepare for Impact: Driving Growth and Serving*

Others Through the Principles of Human-Centered Leadership. Amplify Publishing, 2024.

Jaggard, Jason. *Beyond High Performance: What Great Coaches Know About How the Best Get Better*. Amplify Publishing, 2023.

Koenig, Urs. *The Hybrid Publishing Handbook: Everything I Wish I'd Known Before Writing, Producing, and Marketing My First Book*, self-published, 2025.

Koenig, Urs. *Radical Humility: Be a Badass Leader and a Good Human*. Amplify Publishing, 2024.

Scheinman, Greg. *The Midlife Male: A No Bullshit Guide to Living Better, Longer, Happier, Healthier, and Wealthier and Having More Fun in Your 40s and 50s (Which Includes More Sex . . . and What Guy Doesn't Want That?)*. Amplify Publishing, 2022.

Yamamoto, Britt. *The Soil of Leadership: Cultivating the Conditions for Transformation*. Amplify Publishing, 2024.

Acknowledgments

Bill Sherman

I, and this book, have been shaped by others' ideas and effort. My father, Bud, slyly planted books around our house for me to find and read. My mother, Marilyn, showed me how a warm, provocative question creates space for vulnerable answers. Lonnie Harmon gambled on a young, pony-tailed academic dropout and added me to his team. Tim Sanders invited me into his intellectual attic and sparked my career in books and ideas. Peter Winick said, "We've got a lot of podcasts. Let's write a book." He always has my back, even when I glibly say, "Sure, that sounds easy." Hilary Lewis, my spouse, carried my share of caregiving duties for over a year; she still found time to review this manuscript.

Our clients entrusted us with their goals, struggles, and successes. The *Leveraging Thought Leadership* podcast guests went "on record" and shared their vulnerability. Their stories make the patterns visible. Chris Duffield, our rock-solid producer, has listened to all our interviews and guided me to be a better host.

The TLL client team—Jessica Duffield, Ree Soesbee, AJ Marsden, and Andy Scheurer—collaborated on client work and helped find the larger patterns: the Four Elements and the Impact Equation. We drafted, sharpened, tested, and tried again. Renée Hawthorne has reshaped my scribbles into clear visuals for decades, including the art in this book.

Naren Aryal, our friend, coauthor, and publisher, embraced the book's big idea and delivered two chapters on publishing rather than just one.

Amplify's production editor Myles Schrag shapes raw ideas and says, "Here's how we can do that." Editor Sylvia McCluskey guided us from overcapitalization to compound nouns. Josh Taggert designed the cover, and Shannon Sullivan designed the interior.

Peter Winick

I'd like to thank all the thought leaders who have inspired me along the way (the list is far too long for me to attempt to personally thank them individually and luckily continues to grow daily). I'd like to thank those who have impacted my thinking and those who've given me the privilege to help and support them along the way.

I'd like to thank the team at TLL. I'm blessed to work with people far smarter than me every day!

I'd like to thank my friends and colleagues in the thought leadership industry. The publishers, advisors, publicists, ghostwriters, etc., who do the hard and sometimes thankless work every day to get top-quality work out into the world. A special thanks to my dear friend and coauthor Bill Sherman. This is one of the biggest ideas we have worked on together, and I'm proud of what we've created.

Naren Aryal

I am energized by working with people who have big ideas, and fortunately I get to live in that space every day. Collaborating with Bill and Peter is as good a testament to that as I can think of. We had fun, we challenged ourselves, and we produced something we're all proud of. What could be better than that?

I want to thank the entire Amplify Publishing Group team for their consistent dedication and hard work—the results speak for themselves. I specifically want to thank Myles Schrag, whose efforts were instrumental in this book's development.

Above all, I express my gratitude to the hundreds of authors who trust us to help them bring their ideas to the world. I'm blessed to be surrounded by talented, motivated, intelligent people from all over the globe.

About the Authors

Bill Sherman

As the COO of Thought Leadership Leverage, Bill Sherman helps people make impact with good ideas.

He has spent over twenty years bridging the worlds of thought leaders and Fortune 500 organizations through idea codification, productization, and consultative sales. Cohost of the *Leveraging Thought Leadership* podcast's 700-plus episodes, Bill is recognized as a leading voice in thought leadership. He stumbled into the field in 2004 when a C-level executive asked him, "How can I take the ideas in this book to scale?" That question launched his career helping everyone from *New York Times* bestselling authors to Thinkers50 recipients develop strategies that generate attention, create impact, and drive revenue.

Bill's graduate studies in high-modernist literature and theater dramaturgy uniquely prepared him to simplify complex ideas and put them "on stage" for business audiences.

He lives in Las Vegas, Nevada, where he went from complete heart failure (2014) to marathon finisher (2024).

bill-sherman-aha-moments

Peter Winick

Peter Winick has deep expertise in helping those with deep expertise. For over two decades, he's transformed brilliant ideas into profitable businesses.

As founder and CEO of Thought Leadership Leverage, Peter knows what it takes to scale beyond the individual expert. He knows how to build systems that multiply impact. Today, he cohosts the *Leveraging Thought Leadership* podcast. True to form, he practices what he preaches through weekly LinkedIn videos on thought leadership strategy and guest appearances and presentations on thought leadership at conferences, podcasts, and webinars. He's interviewed the likes of Tom Peters, Daniel Pink, Dorie Clark, Stephen M. R. Covey, and hundreds of others.

His clients range from *New York Times* bestselling authors to Fortune 50 CEOs. He's worked with Speakers' Hall of Fame members, Thinkers50 award winners, and world-renowned academics from the London School of Business, Yale, Wharton, and Harvard. Each engagement focuses on building platforms that create lasting business impact.

He lives in the New York metropolitan area.

in peterwinick

Naren Aryal

As the CEO of Amplify Publishing Group (APG), Naren Aryal advises industry experts and thought leaders on the opportunities and challenges that exist in the ever-evolving world of publishing. He launched the company with a single title in 2003 and guided it to what it is today—one of the fastest-growing and most respected hybrid publishing companies in the world.

APG is home to seven genre-focused imprints: Amplify Publishing, an imprint for business and thought leadership titles; 100 Coaches, in partnership with *New York Times* bestselling author and the world's #1 leadership coach, Marshall Goldsmith; Thinkers50; RealClear Publishing, a joint venture with RealClearPolitics; Subplot Publishing, a home for excellent fiction; Mascot Kids, a space for children's literature; and the flagship, multigenre imprint, Mascot Books.

Prior to entering the world of books, Naren worked as a lawyer, advising technology companies in the Washington, DC, area. He is a frequent speaker on all things publishing, including content development, book production, retail distribution, marketing, and author branding.

in narenaryal